Música
Brasileira

Acknowledgements

The author wishes to thank the copyright holders for permission to quote from the following songs:

Editora Moleque ('Má-gica', 'Sangrado', 'O Sabia Contou ...'), Editora Cooperativa ('Pelo Telefone', 'Já Te Digo', 'A Voz de Morro'), Mangione and Filhos ('Fita Amarela'), Editora Vitale ('Aquarela do Brazil', 'They Say I Came Back Americanized'), Editora Euterpe ('Samba da Minha Terra'), Editora Rio Musical ('Asa Branca'), Editora Arapua ('Desafinado'), Geraldo Vandré ('Pra Não Dizer Não Falei De Flores'), Editora Cava Nova/Arlequin ('Cinco Crianças', 'Corrente', 'Tanto Mar', 'Homage to a Swindler', 'O Que Será', 'In Spite of You', 'Meu Caro Amigo'), Editora Gapa ('Domingo no Parque', 'Alegria, Alegria', 'Tropicalia', 'Deixe Eu Dançar', 'Menino do Rio', 'Refavela', 'Alteza'), Editora Mangione ('Cicade Maravilhosa'), H Martins/Gotela ('Praça Onze'), Candeia ('Testanento de Partideiro'), Editoras Tres Pontas/EMI ('San Vincente', 'Coraçao de Estudante', 'Canção da América', 'Em Nome de Deus'), Cartola ('As Rosas Não Falam'), Dom Helder Camara ('Oração a Marianna'), Alceu Valença ('Rima Com Rima'), Belchior ('Rapaz Latino Americano'), H. Alvarenga/UBC ('Salario Minimo'), Ivan Lins ('Novo Tempo').

The author wishes to point out that all song lyrics quoted in this book are protected by international copyright laws. No reprint and no duplication should be made without having first obtained permission to do so from the song publishers and/or writers.

Claus Schreiner

Música
Brasileira

A History of Popular
Music and the People of Brazil

Translated from the German
by Mark Weinstein

Marion Boyars
New York • London

First published in the United States and Great Britain in 1993
by Marion Boyars Publishers
237 East 39th Street, New York, NY 10016
24 Lacy Road, London SW15 1NL

Published originally in German under the title
Música Popular Brasileira
by Verlag Tropical Music GmbH, Darmstadt, 1977, 1985
© Claus Schreiner 1993
© this updated and translated version Marion Boyars Publishers 1993

British Library Cataloguing in Publication Data

Schreiner, Claus
  Música Brasileira
  I. Title   II. Weinstein, Mark
  780.981

Library of Congress Cataloging in Publication Data

Schreiner, Claus.
  [Música popular brasileira. English]
  Música brasileira / Claus Schreiner : translated from the German
by Mark Weinstein.
    Includes indexes.
    1. Folk music—Brazil—History and criticism. 2. Popular music–
–Brazil—History and criticism. 3. Jazz—Brazil—History and
criticism. 4. Samba (Dance)   I. Title.
ML3575.B7S313   1992
781.64'0981—dc20   92–19894

ISBN 0–7145–2946–X Cloth

Printed and bound in Great Britain by
Biddles Ltd, Guildford and King's Lynn

Contents

Preface to the 1993 edition

As my postwar generation first became acquainted with Brazilian music at the beginning of the sixties through the bossa nova, my interest in it as a jazz fan lay, at most, only in its fringe areas. It was not until several years later that I took special note of a young Brazilian guitarist whom I heard in a recording made at the 1967 Berlin Jazz Festival. Then I did everything I could to engage Baden Powell for a European concert tour. Two years passed before the tour could begin. Our partnership went on for another seven years after that. It was Baden who first said to me: 'You have to go to Brazil to get to know the country, its people and its music!'

This learning process still remains incomplete today, even after numerous visits to many different parts of the country. It would be presumptuous to regard this book, therefore, as all-encompassing. I am not a musicologist. I describe here what I saw and heard, or what I discovered through other sources. Personal contacts always provided more than the multitude of very learned studies on the Brazilians. So over the years during which this book was published in German in 1977 and in an updated version in 1985, the number of portraits of the contemporary representatives of Música Popular Brasileira (MPB) was specifically increased. Similarly many of them, Luiz Gonzaga, Luiz Gonzaga Jr., Vinicius de Moraes, Cartola, Clara Nunes, Elis Regina, Waldir Azevedo, Vitor Assis Brasil, Nara Leão and others, are no longer with us today.

In devoting more space in this further updated edition to certain artists and composers, I have certainly neglected others equally important to MPB. For this I ask forgiveness. In my opinion, this method of depiction, 'living history,' provides a better understanding in the end.

Scarcely had the first edition of this book appeared in Germany when I became curious about the folklore and popular music of other Latin American countries. I wanted to see whether I could apply to Argentina and Chile what I had learned from my work in Brazil. The result of this research was the book published in 1982, *Música Latina — Musikfolklore zwischen Kuba und Feuerland*. I mention this to encourage anyone to use Brazil as a gateway to Latin American culture. Certain principles by which Brazilian music developed can be applied to other Latin American areas of culture. Not only do related forms of musical and dance expression exist in Argentina or Colombia; Brazil and its Latin American neighbors share a similar past, from colonial times until today.

This book only explores to a small extent what goes by the label *Rock Brasil* in MPB. This is not because I am not a lover of rock music, but because Brazilian rock music of the eighties and the early nineties is not very different musically from international rock music and does not justify a specific place in the history of MPB, despite its important commercial role within the Brazilian music industry.

I have observed the discovery of Brazilian popular music in the United States and Canada since 1987. Brazilian artists, backed by United States record companies, have been featured throughout the world in increasing numbers. This would be impossible without a growing consumer interest. This English edition should provide a better understanding of MPB's personalities and musical sources. It is my wish that the broad term 'Latin music' should be replaced by more specific ones like *Música Popular Brasileira* in English-speaking countries. With this book I hope to help English-speaking music lovers approach Latin American music in a new way. No longer should this music be regarded as 'something the Latins have imported from our popular music.' Listen instead to the powerful music they have created for themselves over the centuries.

Claus Schreiner, Marburg, Germany

Introduction

Brazil is a nation
Of thrushes and canaries
Making music without knowing
For whom and why they sing.

Julio Medaglia

Only a tiny fraction of one per cent of all the possible forms and variations within *Música Popular Brasileira* (MPB) — to be specific, the samba, baião, and bossa nova — have gained renown outside the borders of this South American country, the continent's largest in both area and population. On top of that, the ignorance of the Western music industry has managed to present even these three popular forms as nothing more than exotic rhythms, thereby distorting their real value.

Brazil is so rich in forms of musical expression that it could offer the world a new dance, a new song form or a new rhythm each year for centuries to come without ever having to repeat itself. The ethnic conditions for the growth of such a rich folkloric tradition were established at the beginning of the sixteenth century, as a result of the meeting of European, African, and Amerindian cultures. Although North America was settled under similar conditions, this folkloric interaction between musical cultures was largely absent there. Furthermore, where it did occur, it was swallowed up by the music industry and returned to the people in an industrially processed form. Brazil is a different case altogether. Ninety-nine per cent of Brazil's musical folklore never ran the risk of becoming commercialized, and has therefore been preserved in an almost pure, unadulterated form right up to today.

While comparable conditions exist in other areas of Latin America, Brazil still occupies a special position among the world's countries in this respect. The meeting and intermixing of three races of different continental origin, the climatic and geographic differences in the various parts of the country, their political, economic and social history all acted as preconditions, forming both a breeding ground, and a catalyst, for the development of the folkloric variety still present today. At the same time, the country's history is weighted down by negative aspects: the extermination of Indian tribes, a trade in African slaves that lasted about three hundred years, cultural repression under Portugal's colonial rule, wars and plunder, and economic and political crises. The development of MPB could quite possibly have followed a different route under different conditions.

In the seventies I was constantly confronted by two slogans that attempted to characterize the situation in the country during the twenty-year dictatorship: the official governmental aphorism: UM PAÍS QUE VAI PRA FRENIE (A country striving forward) and the unofficial observation of various intellectuals: UM PAÍS DE ABSURDO (Land of the Absurd). For a Brazilian, however, the two were not mutually exclusive. Despite political repression and the country's immense economic problems, and the resulting social and economic injustice, and in view of the expectation of the long heralded 'democratic opening' (*abertura*), Brazilians all stood with their hearts behind their country. As Milton Nascimento, the Brazilian composer and singer, once said to me: 'The people are good. It's the conditions that are bad.' Despite increasing democratic development, these conditions did not really change until the nineties. However, people inside and outside Brazil have noticed a focussing upon additional problems like drugs, AIDS, pollution, the destruction of the rain forests and violence.

The Brazilian sociologist Gilberto Freyre characterized Brazil as a land of 'Portuguese tropicalism' — a cultural synthesis of European thinking and indigenous elements that arose under tropical living conditions. Our usual image of Brazilians is that of the '*morenidade*', with their pale brown skin and their deep sense of *tristeza, alegria* and *saudade* (sadness, joy and longing). A natural affinity with music and dance also belongs in the picture. An elderly lady makes her way to the dance floor in Rio, spontaneously and unasked, and executes the most unbelievable samba steps. A cowboy from the dry, dusty Sertão region in the Northeast gives voice to his melancholy *aboio*. Everywhere and at all times, music is a part of the Brazilian awareness of life — spontaneous, unplanned and arising from real needs. An outsider might find it hard to enter the Brazilian mentality, even if the Brazilian's generosity encourages him to do exactly that. One has to shed the caution one has learned and forget all prejudices and clichés about exotic lifestyles.

A clarification of terms is necessary at this point. What is the difference between folkloric music and popular music? In 1954, the International Congress for Music Folklore in São Paulo developed the following definition:

Folkloric music is the product of a musical tradition that develops by way of oral transmission. The following factors determine, or have determined, this oral tradition:

1. continuity, uniting the present with the past;
2. variety, arising from the creative impulses of the individual as well as the collective;
3. selection by the community, which determines the concrete forms in which folkloric music is passed on.

The musicologist Vasco Mariz, in his book *A Canção Brasileira*, commented on this definition:

> This concept of folkloric music is valid for all types of music exhibiting a rudimentary musical praxis and stemming from a community which, without a doubt, has no contact with popular and classical forms. This conception applies as well to music recognized and incorporated into the living oral traditions of the community, but which was created by a single composer. On the other hand, this conception can never include the popular music which may be recognized by the community, but which has not been influenced by the above-mentioned factors.

Renato Almeida, the director of the Congress, regards folkloric music as, 'a music used anonymously and collectively by the uneducated classes of a civilized nation. It is created anonymously and collectively by these classes themselves, or it adapts popular and classical works which have lost their original vitality within the milieu in which they were created.... It is born and lives intimately connected to the social interests and activities of the people.... Popular music is music composed by known composers, or is more or less widely heard and used by all strata of the population.'

For many years participants at such congresses have been engaged in a continual struggle to arrive at some sort of generally valid definition of the concept 'folklore'. For Brazil, the differentiation from popular and even pop music has proven to be particularly difficult. On the one hand,

Brazilian pop (ular) music, which is practically all we know of Brazilian music, is based predominantly upon folkloric primary, 'raw' material (*materia prima*). On the other hand, since the middle of the last century it has profited from an amalgamation of fashionable European dance forms (polka, mazurka, waltz) and Anglo-American (jazz, rock) and Caribbean (habanera) rhythms. Here we must ask ourselves to what degree Brazilian music in general can be considered national music. Wouldn't it be more logical to regard the original Amerindian music of the land's native inhabitants as the only true Brazilian music? Mario de Andrade, one of the first musicologists to deal intensively with Brazilian music in his analyses and essays about forty years ago, says in his book *Aspectos da Música Brasileira*: 'If "national" is only what comes from the Indios, then the Italians shouldn't have played the organ, which as we all know, originated with the Egyptians; or the violin, which is Arabic; or the church hymn, which is Greco-Hebraic; polyphony, which is Nordic, Anglo-Saxon, Flemish, and the devil knows what else.' Andrade concludes that, 'each and every national musical creation is Brazilian music, whether it has an ethnic character or not.'

Música Popular Brasileira (MPB) is therefore a generic term including folkloric and popular forms of expression. The following schema helps to illustrate the genre:

Folkloric Music

Occurrence: Mainly rural areas and cities with strong traditional character.

Character: Anonymous origins or authors from among the people.

Dissemination directly among the people. Passed on from generation to generation, or spontaneously created and forgotten. Local unity of occurrence, character, performer, and consumer.

Intent: Not intent on success outside the immediate, authentic milieu.

Examples: aboios in the Sertão, cururús in the south, rural sambas.

Popular Music

Occurrence: Mainly city centers with internationally influenced musical scenes.

Character: Authors or adapters from various strata of the population.

Dissemination predominantly by media (records, TV, radio); that is, the means of distribution are not usually owned by the author or artist. Mainly short-term success. Engagements, occurrence, etc., are not controlled.

Intent: Success with target groups, commercial use.

Examples: sambas at carnival, city *baiãos*, tropicalism, bossa nova.

Historically, popular music first arose at the turn of this century and in the years following, and was aided by the emergence of phonograph records and radio, as well as by the institution of the samba school. In terms of chronology:

Folkloric Music

From the beginning of colonization until the present we can observe a steady process of development. However, no two songs or dances carrying the same name but performed at different locations are necessarily identical. The performer alone decides upon the form and content of his song or dance, according to his traditions. And these can be interpreted very differently from one day to the next, from one occasion to the next.

Popular Music

A **primitive phase** lasted until the middle of the nineteenth century (*maxixe, lundu*, and others). The Belle Epoque with polka and waltz influences led into a **transitional phase** lasting until the beginning of the twentieth century (*choro, frevo, marchas*); a **stabilization phase** until around 1927 (urban samba); a **golden phase** until around 1946 (further development of samba); **premodern phase** until around 1956 (*baião*, etc.) and a **modern phase** reaching into the present (bossa nova, tropicalism, *Rock Brasil* and mixed forms with African and Caribbean music).

The various stages of popular music's development have also seen musicians time and again establish standards that introduced folkloric raw material into the musical metropolis of Rio de Janeiro (Luiz Gonzaga, Dorival Caymmi, João Gilberto, the Baianos).

For all that has been said above, the boundary between popular and folkloric music still remains fluid. Even composers of so-called serious music (*música erúdita*) are sometimes considered popular, whereas Ernesto Nazareth's *choros* are assigned to the category of classical music.

Heitor Villa-Lobos, Guerra Peixe, Radamés Gnatalli, and Marlos Nobre for their part have employed original folkloric material in their works.

Today, even after four hundred years of musical evolution, this raw material is still so strongly present that other nations and cultural areas can make use of it, much more so than in the past. And this is possible without having to enter totally on foreign terrain, since the similarities with Asian, European, and African music can still be strongly felt. For some years now, the international music business has introduced a new category, so called 'world music'. The term covers mainly pop music with traditional/folkloristic elements from Third World countries. Pop singers and musicians are now often filed under the title of world music — even though it might be pure pop or rock music. This is, however, just another way of the music industry keeping the 'South' outside its traditional marketing and business strategies.

The further development of MPB does not depend, however, on the interest of the rest of the world. In addition to certain important economic, political and social factors, it is in need of conscious cultivation and care from the Brazilian people themselves, from the myriad anonymous authors and artists among the people, as well as from those professional artists and composers who create for the commercial music industry in absolute artistic freedom.

> The task of each and every artist
> Is to speak his truth clearly.
> What heights he may reach
> God alone knows.
>
> *Milton Nascimento*

Chapter I

The Beginnings

What is this person?
It was a snake, not a person

From an Amerindian song

Brazil was colonized twice after its discovery by Pedro Alvares Cabral in 1500. The first colonizers were the Portuguese. They came by chance, even if driven by the necessity of opening up new markets. The second 'colonizers' were African slaves. They came in chains, against their will. The Catholic Church sensed the existence of a new world, and so sent its representatives aboard the first ship expeditions to the land of *Pau-Brasil*. Its missionaries looked after the Indians and African slaves, and in both cases attempted to Christianize them, primarily through the medium of music (but with violence as well). European interest in exercising secular and religious power in Brazil was reflected in a century-long conflict in cultural, economic, religious and political spheres. The big losers, however, were the Indians, once the sole owners of the land. The process by which three races merged to form a single nation of 'Portuguese tropicalism' proved the Portuguese and Africans to be the stronger. They were, in a certain sense, capable of forming coalitions and thus were able to assimilate the 'weak' Amerindians into their Afro-Iberian mixed culture.

Amerindians

The Afro-Iberian encounter had already begun during the fifteenth century in Portugal, which had lived under Moorish rule, for eight

hundred years. In 1436, the first twelve slaves were transported from
Africa to Lisbon. By 1466, there were over a thousand, and by 1535,
nearly ten thousand. Since the slaves were forbidden to do their tribal
dances and were allowed to dance only the saraband and fandango, a
Portuguese-African interaction had already begun to develop in the
mother country prior to the colonization of Brazil as the slaves added
attributes of their own culture to the Iberian songs and dances.

For the Portuguese the encounter with Amerindians, Latin America's
native inhabitants, was new. And it was by no means a peaceful
encounter, since the Portuguese were intent on sending home booty
taken from them. The Amerindians' different mentality also provided
the seeds for conflict, allowing them little sympathy for the Portuguese
in this respect. The Frenchman Jean de Léry tells us of a discussion he
had with an Indian during his expedition to Brazil in 1578. The native
asked Léry whether his people really needed such an excess of wood,
and whether the person who would receive the wood was immortal.
Léry: 'He'll die, just like all other humans.' The native countered: 'But if
he's going to die, who are all these riches for?' Léry: 'For his sons, if he
has any.' The Amerindian: 'Well, you French are really crazy! Why do
you bring all these hardships upon yourselves? We have sons too, but we
have confidence that the earth will give them after our death what she
gives us today.' This exchange has a disturbing significance when
considered in relation to the wholesale destruction of the Amazonian
rainforests.

Compared to the French, the Portuguese were not very popular with
the cannibalistic savages. Hans Staden in 1557 tells us that, when he
announced he was a Frenchman to keep himself from being eaten, chief
Quoniam Bebê responded, 'I've already devoured five Portuguese who
claimed they were French. But they weren't telling the truth.'

In 1549, the Portuguese set up fifteen administrative districts in
Brazil, with a capital in Salvador da Bahia de Todos os Santos. They
hoped in this way to keep out the Spanish, who also had colonial designs
on Brazil after the French were expelled. In the south, at the site of
today's city of São Paulo with its more than nine million inhabitants, the
Jesuit priest José de Anchieta established a missionary outpost.

Jean de Léry had already reported on the great musicality exhibited
by the native Amerindians:

> Standing side by side, hands joined together, they form a circle.
> They sing so harmoniously that no one could claim they don't
> know music. Their choral singing contains multiple chords.
> Cadence and refrain are repeated after each stanza.

He, he aye, heyra, heyayre
Heyrá, heyré, ueh

At the end they stamp their feet on the ground and sing:

He, hyá, hyá, hyá ...

The Jesuits quickly saw an opportunity to fulfill their Christian missionary duty — on the one hand by offering the Amerindians protection from the colonists within their missions, and on the other hand by spreading their Christian belief by means of musical collaboration. They heard the Amerindian chants, which were sung in unison, shrouded in magic and mystery, accompanied by dance to the beat of stamping feet, the sound of flutes and the rattle of maracás. These they confronted with Gregorian chants from their own religious order. The natives were attracted to these European hymns because they were similar to their own chants. The music historian José Ramos Tinhorão studied the source material from this period and came to this conclusion in his volume *Peguenha Historia da Música Popular*: 'The Indians took over the rigorous logic and construction of the Gregorian church music for themselves. Under the direction of the Jesuit baton they continued to sing in unison, to be sure, but a main melody carried by all the voices had now replaced the continual repetition of incantations with expressions of Christian piety.'

Father Anchieta and fellow friar Manuel da Nobrega began from this point on to compose many songs in the native tongue (Tupí-Guaraní), as well as to gradually replace the primitive Amerindian instruments with European ones. In the place of bone flutes and rattles made from human skulls they introduced the organ, harpsichord and bassoon and instructed the mission Indians in their use. Tinhorão states: 'Learning these instruments meant that Indian music lost its function.' The Jesuits were very strict in allowing only the use of those Amerindian instruments of which they approved, in addition to the European instruments that they themselves supplied. This meant that music was uprooted from its natural socio-cultural context. Like the Africans, the Amerindians had always experienced music and dance as part of definite social and religious events in which certain instruments had a function only insofar as they were linked to the ritual life of the community.

Father Anchieta went even further. He wrote a play exclusively for the Amerindians treating the *mysterium Jesu*. 'It was an immense success,' Gustav Faber wrote. 'Indians wearing the robes of Saint Sebastian, the Holy Mother, Lucifer, and old Indian forest spirits happily converted to the beliefs of the white newcomers. Drums resounded from the deep forest, wild singing echoed through the air, feathered Indians performed a dance of joy, until, in the end, devil and demons alike lay defeated underfoot.' These Jesuit plays can be regarded as forerunners of the folkloristic performances, the *autos* (of Portuguese tradition) and the *folguedos*, which appeared later and in greater number, usually with African participation. They are, moreover, the first dramatic compositions written and performed in Brazil. The first of these *autos sacramentales* are recorded in chronicles dating from 1555 and 1567.

The Jesuits' missionary zeal most certainly saved several tribes from slaughter, slavery and extermination. At the same time, however, the Jesuits almost completely suppressed the authentic music of these tribes, thus committing, in fact, cultural genocide. They forced their own European culture upon the Amerindians, thereby hindering a far-reaching interaction from taking place between the two cultures.

The Jesuits were expelled from Brazil in 1759. The Amerindians who had been in their settlements were left defenseless against the brutalities committed by all sorts of adventurers, settlers and conquerors (among them the *Bandeirantes*). In a cultural sense, even those who could save their necks by hiding in the surrounding woods remained uprooted. Two hundred years of 'Jesuit care' were enough to make a return to their traditional Amerindian music and its accompanying rituals impossible. An integration with the Afro-Iberian forms that had arisen in the meantime was equally impossible.

Since the beginning of colonization, Amerindian tribes (Tupí, Guaraní, Temiminos and others) had increasingly withdrawn from coastal areas into the country's interior. Many tribes were exterminated after the expulsion of the Jesuits. Others fled to the forests of neighboring states. Those Indios who had been 'pacified' and domesticated by the Jesuits were better able to adapt. As the economic exploitation of Brazil's south began (1730), Indios supplied the largest reservoir of labor there, making the transport of African slaves into the area for the most part unnecessary. As a result, traces of Amerindian music can still be felt today in Rio Grande do Sul and in parts of the state of São Paulo, even though they have not yet been authoritatively proven. On the other hand, there is evidence of a Father Sepp from the Tyrol (Austria), who taught his Amerindian charges in southern Brazil to yodel. Relics of this technique are still heard in the area today.

Since it was mostly African slaves who were forced to work on the sugar, coffee and fruit plantations of the coast, 'pacified' Indios found work (if at all) as cattle herders in the vast steppe region of the Sertão in the Northeast. This activity was not foreign to them, since it ap-

proximated their earlier nomadic lifestyle. Since then, *caboclos**
mamelucos and *cafusos* — the offspring of Amerindians who intermarried
with whites and Africans — have dominated the ethnic composition of
the Northeast, especially in the country's interior. Traces of Amerindian music are still recognizable today in their musical folklore (non-
modulated, monotonic).

The romantic era saw renewed interest in the lot of Brazil's native
inhabitants. Carlos Gomes in his musical work *O Guaraní* described the
fate of this tribe and earned success with it even in Europe. Renato
Almeida in his *Historia da Música Brasileira* rates *O Guaraní* as the first
work of national Brazilian music.

From São Paulo in the 1920s the brothers Mario and Oswald de
Andrade brought the plight of Brazil's Indios once again to the forefront
of public concern. Oswald propagated his 'anthropophagism', and
Mario laid the foundations for a new understanding of Brazilian
language and poetry in his novel *Macunaima*. One of the sources for this
novel was a study done by the German researcher Theodor Koch-
Grünberg (from Grünberg near Giessen) on the customs and rituals of
several Amazon tribes. Mario de Andrade became known in his day not
only as a modern author but also as a musicologist and ethnologist. In
one of his standard works on Brazilian culture, *Ensaio sobre a Música
Brasileira*, he wrote:

> Today's Brazilian has more in common with a Japanese or
> Hungarian than with an Indian. The Indian element has been
> psychologically assimilated into the nation, practically to the
> point of nonexistence.... The Indian has ceased to be a par-
> ticipant — he may still live in our country, but he is not Brazilian.

An autonomous, *música indígena*, was doomed. Having been taken up
and incorporated into the many folkloric musical forms produced by the
Afro-Iberian encounter, it exists today in its original form solely within
the cultures of the 'savage', Amazonian tribes, totally isolated from
mainstream Brazilian music and scorned by it as some sort of foreign
creature. The contemporary composer-musician Egberto Gismonti and
his Academia de Dança attempted to work together with Indios from
the Xingu National Park on a music and dance performance. It merely
earned him this comment by a so-called savage: 'The white man's music
sounds like the music of werewolves.' Reactions might have been

---

* *Caboclo* has several meanings: a person of mixed Indian and European blood; a
Brazilian peasant; a *caboclinho*, in Sergipe and Alagoas, is someone who is black
and mestizo and who imitates the *Indios* and their customs.

different in 1989 when Milton Nascimento came to visit them and later on mixed authentic recordings of their chants with his music on the album *Txai*.

The number of Amerindians on Brazilian territory has suffered a steady decline. A report prepared in 1964–65 by the Conselho Nacional de Proteção aos Indios counted only 250,000. And even these few have fled from civilization into the inaccessible regions of the Amazon. To this day we still hear regular reports of massacres of the Amerindian community by settlers and of retaliatory attacks on the persecuted natives. The destruction of the tropical rainforest in the Amazon basin has affected those who live far from Brazil, due to the worldwide climatic catastrophe that is expected to result from it. However, many have also realized for the first time the fate of the Amerindians living in the forest. The British pop musician Sting became an advocate in the late eighties for the legitimate claims of Amazon tribes. Increasingly within Brazil itself attention is being called to the problem. Luiz Gonzaga Jr. wrote the following on the death of Amazonia in his song *'Ma-gica'* ('Evil Magic'):

And as the flowers wilted
The river's water died
The sun shone no more
And the sky had only one color
Day was like night
Everything the same
Quiet, loneliness
And the fruits of this earth grow no longer

The death of Amazonia
The death of Pantanal
Beauty that exists no longer
And these weeping children
Lost in the garbage
The contract for the death of the Indio
For the life that doesn't return.

The presence of Amerindian blood has been established for a high percentage of the Brazilian population. Amerindian culture has been passed on in painting and sculpture over generations and is still evident today. In music we are more dependent on vague suppositions, but we are convinced that *música indígena* had a formative influence upon the rich panorama of folkloric music and popular music in Brazil.

Carvalho, a musical ethnologist, thought that 'Portuguese songs were intermixed with Indian expressions and African onomatopoeia.'

In other Latin American countries where there were no African populations, Amerindian musical forms have been preserved. I assume that in Brazil the interrelationship of African polyrhythms with European melody and harmony did not allow Amerindian music, which was so often characterized by monotonous chants and simple rhythmic figures, the chance to be integrated. The synthesized African-European music that arose out of the constraints of acculturation overtook the populace too powerfully and too rapidly. On top of that, Amerindians had been exiled in the forests and steppes of the country's interior, while the musical development leading to *música popular* occurred in the urban centers of Salvador, Rio, and São Paulo.

The African Slaves

'The sociological truth of the matter,' writes Gilberto Freyre in his essay 'Aspectos da Influenca africana no Brasil,' 'is that African Negroes arriving in Brazil as slaves came mostly from areas and cultures at a higher stage of development than the Amerindians.' Alfons M. Dauer, chairman of the Afro-American Department at the Institute for Jazz Research in Graz, Austria, has substantiated this statement. According to Dauer, North American blues, as a precursor to jazz, did not develop in the South, but arose at a much earlier date in the savannas of West Africa. He found textual and melodic elements in Sudanese music that were very similar to North American blues and, moreover, unique in all of Africa. Dauer's mentioning, in connection with Brazilian music, of a type of fiddle that developed from the Arabic *rebab* is intriguing, since a kind of rustic fiddle called *rabeca* or *rebeca* is widely used in the music of northeastern Brazil.

The music which the slaves brought with them from Africa (chiefly from the west coast) exhibited the following characteristics: multiple percussive lines or parts, polyrhythms, polymetric vocal polyphony, choreographic features, mystical-religious references, the use of a stanza-refrain form, and specific instrumentation.

African song, dance and instrumentation will be discussed later in the relevant passages of this book. For the moment it is worth mentioning some of the music's most general characteristics. African music is, in principle, rich in rhythmic form, while poor in melodic variation. It is instinctive and sensitive. With the exception of griot chants and other traditional songs performed on special occasions, the lyrics are not extremely poetic. Verse rhyme is practically unknown. The lyrics refer to events and things in the natural surroundings as well as to super-natural occurrences. As was the case with the Amerindians, music and dance were social activities that almost always occurred together.

The Africans had a knack for continually coming up with new rhythms that they liked to play in ensembles of different percussion instruments. The presence of syncopation in Brazilian music has often been ascribed to African influence. But syncopation seldom occurs in African music, even if the tendency is present among the drummers. Tonyan Khallyhabby's essay, 'A Influencia africana na música brasileira', has advanced a very interesting theory to account for the presence of syncopation in Afro-Brazilian music. In it, he postulates that, earlier, when blacks accompanied syncopated European melodies such as the Iberian fandango, they simply played along with the syncopated melodic parts instead of maintaining a constrant rhythm. They may later have carried this over into other musical forms.

African music, accustomed at first to modal scales and pentatonic and hexachordal systems, adapted itself in Brazil to the European seven-tone scale. 'Blue notes', which arose in North America as a result of this adaptive process, are hardly present in Brazilian music at this time. Still, Africans did introduce many characteristic features of their vocal techniques into Brazilian music, including melismas, glissandos, falsetto techniques, and much more.

While the Amerindians had already begun to participate in Christian mystery plays just 18 years after the Jesuits' arrival in Brazil, it was another 160 years before the interaction of African and European music began to produce results. This occurred at a time when Amerindian music had long since been either assimilated, or isolated in the distant forests of the 'unpacified' Amerindian cultures.

The development of African music in Brazil went through various stages. Until around 1600, the slaves were able to preserve their own culture, brought from Africa. They did this in secret, as African culture was forbidden by the slavemasters. A process of unification based on the slaves' common cultural values was necessary, since those working on the Brazilian plantations came from many different African regions and cultures. The next stage saw the adaptation of the ruling culture (an acculturation of the values offered by the Church and plantation aristocracy). Here they used the opportunity to develop organizational forms that contributed to strengthening African culture. Finally, after the freeing of the slaves, there came a period in which African musicality could flourish unfettered. This period marks the actual beginning of MPB.

For many decades after the beginning of colonization, African slaves were left little room to foster their own musical heritage. Church and plantation aristocracy forbade the practice of supposedly obscene dances. One could only hear their songs during the workdays on the plantations, farms, and sugar mills, sometimes as solo chants (*boiado*), at other times as an interchange between singer and choir (*dobrado*). Furthermore, both Church and colonizers allowed music and dance only on certain recognized holidays. The slaves were housed on the *fazendas* and plantations in simple huts (*senzalas*) in which they secretly worshiped carved images of their African gods by night. During the day they were forced to cross themselves in front of the crucifix and images of the Virgin Mary. Each large *fazenda* had its own chapel. Smaller ones had at least one site where Catholic services were held for Europeans and slaves.

In contrast to the way the Jesuits brought Christianity to the Amerindians, where it was not uncommon for priests to offer the natives a measure of protection from their colonial masters, the Catholic Church worked together with plantation and *fazenda* owners to convert the Africans. In doing so, a separation between whites and blacks was implemented within the Church from an early date. The result, however — Brazilian syncretism which will be dealt with at the end of Chapter Two — can hardly have been satisfactory for the Church even today. Tinhorão comments in his book *Música Popular*: 'Priests and colonial masters had no problem in finding agreement on one important point: the channeling of the surplus energy of the slave masses into the Church's domain served to control their feelings and instincts, and guaranteed a path of cultural development along Church lines.' The slaves maintained their respective tribal rituals and dances under Church jurisdiction (and in secret as well), while at the same time allowing religious and secular masters to use them for their musical purposes. Priests trained talented slaves in European instruments for liturgy and processions. The plantation aristocracy occasionally developed slave orchestras, which they had play at their festivals, or which they even hired out to other *fazendas*.

Slave Resistance

In the seventeenth century, escaped slaves began to construct small defensive villages beyond the reach of the Portuguese soldiers, called *mocambos* (today the name of the Recife slums). These communities of runaway slaves were later united into the federation of *quilombos*. The best-known among them, Palmares, was destroyed in 1694 after having existed for over two generations and having almost achieved the status of an independent kingdom. (The *Missa dos Quilombos*, with music by Milton Nascimento, was premiered in 1982 in a church in Minas Gerais.)

In addition, slaves on the *fazendas* and in the cities organized themselves into brotherhoods (*irmandades*) under the patronage of the Church and the patron saint 'Nossa Senhora do Rosario' (Our Lady of the Rosary). This occurred in 1639 in Rio, and in 1680 and 1682 in Salvador, Recife and other cities. These organizational forms, for the first time, lent the blacks a semblance of belonging within the social fabric of the still-young Brazilian people and can be regarded as the beginning of what later would become their complete integration into society. Furthermore, blacks within the brotherhoods were better able to work together to raise money among themselves to buy slaves their freedom. Pressures to assimilate led the brotherhoods to coordinate their cultural activities within the ruling culture. They preserved, on the one hand, their traditional African culture in their annual festivals, such as the *congadas* while on the other hand, they integrated into these festivals cultural norms borrowed from the Europeans and parodied them at times as well. By electing their King of the Congo or Queen of Maracatú each year (although they may have been choosing a potentate without power or property), they were creating an important manifestation of their resistance within the *quilombos* — here the tolerated kings of the brotherhoods, there the illegal free kings of escaped slaves.

The Jesuit Father Antonio Pires had observed organized African groups in processions in Recife as early as 1552. But it was not until the creation of the *irmandades* in the seventeenth century under the auspices of the Catholic Church that blacks and mulattos began to participate officially in the development of Brazilian folkloric music. Initially, Church and colonial masters had either prohibited African music or utilized it as a means to furthering their own colonizing ends. Now, however, through their music, slaves were on the verge of becoming a part of the Brazilian populace. Through it they fought for status as a recognized social class (even if a lower one), without which the individual's climb up the social ladder would not have been possible. This phenomenon in turn made possible the preservation of significant forms of African music, a fusion with European and, to some extent, Amerindian traditions. The concentration of Africans in the cities of the east coast and their numerical superiority over the white immigrants accelerated this process. In a similar manner African cuisine had previously been able to establish itself outside the *senzalas* and *quilombos* in the cities.

Nevertheless, large-scale musical activities by blacks continued to be restricted to holidays. It seems there was no shortage of them. According to reports, there were thirty-five Church holidays alone. Add Sundays and it came to over eighty. On these days the *irmandades* marched in their processions through the streets of Recife, Salvador, and Rio. In addition to the already formed *congos* and *reinados* — syncretic pageants put on by the different African nations, ending with a symbolic crowning of king and queen — they invented a host of other festivals having the character of folkloristic performances, such as *bumba-meu-boi, marujada, chegança* and others. Chapter Two discusses in detail how these *folguedos* often arose, modeled after early Portuguese forms, with the participation of mixed-race groups such as mulattos, mestizos, and caboclos. A large number of popular songs and dances of Brazilian origin arose in just such street festivals. The development from the Portuguese *entrudo* (carnival) to the Brazilian *carnaval* is hard to imagine without organized African participation at the *Penha* (Rio) and *Bonfim* (Salvador) festivals and other such occasions.

The Austrian botanist Johann Emanuel Pohl reported on his trip to Brazil (1817–21) in his essay 'Vom Rio Grande zum La Plata':

> The Negroes celebrate a festival in honor of the black saint Eufigenia. According to custom, fourteen days beforehand a Negro delegation went to the Padre vicar with a request to celebrate the festival. The request was granted. On the evening of the same day several Negroes dressed in Portuguese uniforms mounted their horses.... At first they galloped up and down the alleyways a while, and then finally rode up to the church. There they got hold of a flag with a likeness of their saint portrayed upon it and set it on top of a tall pole in front of the church entrance.... Accompanied by continual drumming and the sound of instruments from the Congo, the night was then spent in the house of the emperor (for an emperor is chosen during this festival). A Negro cried 'Bambi' throughout, answered by the full choir's '*domina*,' which means roughly, 'The King governs all.'

A lengthy description of the three-day event (in the church and on the streets) follows. Pohl comments:

> The entire performance was presented in rather poor Portuguese verse with lots of African words thrown in. The Negroes are extraordinarily keen about this festival. They have the oppor-

tunity to turn out in great pomp, and one could not insult or injure these people more severely than by preventing them from staging this festival, which reminds them in so many ways of their homelands.

In the course of the events described above, one sees a mixture of elements from various ritualistic and syncretic ceremonies with other plot sequences, all of which culminate in the coronation of the next year's King of the Congo (*Rei do Congo*). Pohl also describes the costumes the blacks wore and the sight of powdered hair and wigs, making one think of scenes from today's carnival.

Brazilian blacks also remained in contact with their home continent. It has been reported that several tribes in Africa regularly sent news to their relatives in Brazil. Return migration to Africa occurred even at the beginning of the nineteenth century, when the Moslem Haussa and the Yoruba people in Bahia (nine-tenths of the slave population in Bahia came from some region in Nigeria) sparked off a religious war against converted blacks, and its leaders were eventually banished to Africa.

Black Participation in MPB

The eighteenth century witnessed the first results arising from the acculturation between African and European music. Tinhorão's *Música Popular* summarizes: 'One could observe the initial results stemming not only from the conflict between primitive Negro and European culture, but also between the different African tribal cultures themselves.' This was the period of the baroque in Europe. The beginnings of Brazilian classical music, or *música erúdita*, occurred here, based chiefly upon the Gregorian chants of the Jesuits and upon the musical training and education they conducted among the Amerindians, Africans, and half-castes. Haydn and Boccherini were soon being played on Brazilian-made instruments. They also served as an inspiration for musicians and composers outside those exclusive circles that chose to cultivate European chamber music within the confines of their fashionable salons. Rio's first theater was opened in 1748, the Opera House in 1767. Literati and poets formed circles and founded academies. However, the state — the colonial power, Portugal — declared the theater to be immoral and prohibited women from appearing on stage. Printing presses were outlawed, and bookstores were viewed with suspicion. Lisbon mistrusted the creative and intellectual energies that might emerge from the independence of their colony. In 1792 there were 216 bars in Rio, 52 hairdressers, and a single bookstore. Music from the preclassical period was of a particularly high quality in Minas Gerais (where gold was discovered at the beginning of the century), a fact which Francisco Kurt Lange was the first to document in the fifties when he discovered scores dating back to that period.

At that time, according to travelers' reports, there already existed among the common people large quantities of *cantigas* and *modas* (song forms). Folksingers performed them either in troubadour style or in a verse-choir interchange during folk festivals, alongside traditional worksongs and ritualistic festival songs. The *lundu* appeared at the end of the eighteenth century as the first documented synthesis of African and European folklore. The Englishman Lindsey described the *lundu* at the time (without recognizing it as such) as 'a mixture of an African dance and Spanish and Portuguese fandangos.'

After the declaration of independence from Portugal (on July 9, 1822) and the proclamation of the Brazilian empire, the new regents (Dom Pedro I and his successors) proved to be far more open and tolerant of the arts than their predecessors. Pedro I is even said to have had bohemian tendencies. His special love was for troubadour serenades and *lundus* from the lower classes. Pictorial art, literature, painting, and theater were all noticeably revitalized, receiving impetus from, among other sources, French neoclassicism. Under Dom Pedro II's patronage, musicians and composers were also able to develop more freely. Finally, three hundred years after the beginning of colonization, the first tender buds of a *Música Popular Brasileira* could begin to blossom.

Under black, mulatto, and mestizo influence, African-European mixed forms, such as the *modinha* (song) and *maxixe* (couple dance), as well as precursors of the urban samba, began to develop. Singer Caldas Barbosa popularized Brazilian modinhas in the nineteenth century even in Lisbon. Songs and dances with African color found their way for the first time into the salons of high society and into the theaters and opera houses. A kind of musical two-way street formed: songs and dances of the lower classes appeared in high society in milder, watered-down form, while the nobility's preferred minuets, polkas, and, later, waltzes were taken up by folk musicians and infused with new life. As was also the case in other Latin American countries, it was almost always these musicians from the lower social classes who, by first undertaking such syntheses, created new national music and dance forms.

The abolition of slavery in 1888 brought about, to be sure, new sociological conditions and problems. Musically speaking, however, emancipation encouraged the full deployment of the black man's talent, which had been restricted under slavery. From now on, Rio de Janeiro stood alone as the center of a new period of creativity and development, leaving its earlier partner, Salvador, by the wayside. Musicians from the poor and underprivileged quarters of the city (*cidade nova*) with their performing groups — *ranchos* (Bahian processions in Rio) and *ternos de pau e corda* (small instrumental groups composed of flute, cavaquinho, and guitar), *choro-conjuntos*, and military orchestras — all combined with bohemian café scenes to fill the streets and squares of Rio with rhythm and melody. Again and again, black musicians and mulattos stood out in this initial phase of MPB to lend decisive impulses to the musical development: Callado for the choro; Donga and his colleagues for the urban samba; Pixinguinha for modern arrangements and harmonies. The African heritage has remained alive today, both in the songs, dances, texts and instrumentation of MPB as well as in Brazilian syncretism, with its maze of regional forms and variations. One senses this in the smells of a city like Salvador, where the *muquequas* of Bahian street cuisine mingle with the odor of incense.

One century after the freeing of the slaves, many of Rio's samba schools took stock; for example, the distinguished Mangueira, the Estação Primeira da Mangueira, one of the oldest in Rio, whose song was titled 'One Hundred Years of Freedom, Reality or Illusion':

> Can it be that freedom shone
> Or was it all an illusion?
> Slavery's end is not yet come.

The samba school Unidos de Vila Isabel invoked the black abolitionist Zumbi and the black leaders of the past once again. The magic, power and art of the black culture were praised — and at the end came the demand: apartheid must disappear.

The samba school São Clemente was even more pointed in its samba for Carnaval 1988. The destruction of flora, fauna and the Indios of the Amazon were decried. 'Women, fight for your rights. The children sing of he-men and overlook the evils of our earth ... freedom — I want to live in another world, where freedom governs and there is no war.'

Africa in Brazil. That's also the Mercado Modelo in Salvador's harbor, where industrially produced consumer goods are put up for sale side by side with colored powders meant to cure impotence and lovesickness. Where batuques and samba de roda compete against the berimbau, agogo and pandeiro-playing vendors for tourists and Baianos, but later combine in a changing, concerted fashion.

Africa in Rio. For me, that was Clementina de Jesus. This eighty-year-old lady lived like a queen in her shanty at the foot of the morro quarter in Mangueira. She grew up nurtured by the *jongos* and *corimas* her mother sang to her. As a young girl she experienced the birth of the urban samba with her friends Pixinguinha and Donga. Clementina never gave up her predilection for songs from her African heritage: *cantos de trabalho, pontos, linkas de macumba*, and *samba de partido alto*. What Bessie Smith was to North American blues, Clementina de Jesus was to Afro-Brazilian music. Her deep, powerful voice cracked now and then, and she stressed the syllables with a guttural tone at the end of a line of verse in a way typical of African music.

I was there to extend to Clementina an invitation to the Horizonte Festival in Berlin. 'Then there's no war going on in Europe now, huh?' was her first question. Clementina was a simple, modest woman who had only become famous in her last years, since young musicians like Milton Nascimento courted her and invited her to do records. Later, in March 1979, when I wanted to make a film with Clementina, she turned me down at first. She was against the the filming taking place at her house, since she knew her neighbors regarded her already as too much of a public figure. She wanted to live with them in friendship and therefore thought it would be better not to make such a big fuss. We did finally end up filming at her place in a narrow alleyway barely one and a half yards wide that connected all the small shanties to each other like a corridor. We invited the neighbors to come along.

Disco music could be heard on a portable radio. That didn't bother Clementina. 'Why not? That's young folks' music. I have to respect that.' She waved majestically to the passing children in the neighborhood as she sat on her stool in the open air, telling them in a motherly way, '*Podes passar, menino*' ('You can pass, kid'). I felt the same. Whenever I visited her, I was so captured by her warmth and vibrancy that I liked to address her as '*rainha*', or queen, and I waited for her instructions: 'Have a seat, my son!'

Chapter 2

Folkloric Compendium

Folksongs and Folksingers

Brazilian music offers a wide range of song styles. Folk songs of Iberian, African, and Amerindian origin belong here, as do mixed forms and further developments from them. The majority of all folk songs are of anonymous origin, having been passed on from one generation to the next. In addition, there are short-lived folk songs created by improvising folksingers and others that can be regarded as semi-classical or artistic.

Folk songs are embedded in a people's manners and customs. Thus Brazil's character as a melting pot of different races and cultures requires us to take the country's large regional differences into consideration when we study its folk songs. A particular song form of Portuguese origin might very well combine with African influences in Bahia, with Amerindian elements in the country's interior, and with an African-Amerindian synthesis in the South, thus appearing each time under a different name and with a different function.

Folk songs always have a function, much like folk poetry (fables, fairy tales, riddles, stories, puzzles), *contos*, or sayings *ditados* — such as '*quem planta e cria, tem alegria*' ('whoever plants his crop and lets it grow will be happy'). Around a hundred years ago, Silvio Romero released a comprehensive collection of Brazilian folk songs in which he attempted to analyze the motivations of the three races present on Brazilian soil: the Portuguese fought, won, and enslaved; the Amerindian defended himself, fled, or was captured; the African was enslaved and worked. All of them sing, Romero continued, because they have a yearning: the Portuguese for his homeland, the Amerindian for the forests, and the African for the straw huts he will never see again.

Logical as this schema might appear, it does not have general validity for a Brazilian folksong tradition, which began to take shape with the beginning of colonization. The strongest group — i.e. the Portuguese conquerors — placed the stamp of their cultural traditions upon the other cultures, and especially upon the developing mixed forms. Most folk songs are sung in Portuguese, with Amerindian or African languages occurring only occasionally in the refrains and verbal tags.

How can we distinguish the many song types from one another? Four possibilities present themselves:

By function: love songs, satirical songs, drinking and eating songs, lullabies, work songs, religious and sports songs, festival songs, etc.

By regional occurrence: songs from the coast, the desert, the forests, the cities, from the north, east, and south.

By character: sentimental, lyrical, narrative, funny, frivolous, erotic, Christian-religious, syncretic, magical, satirical, etc.

By origin or development: African, Afro-Brazilian, Iberian, Mozarabic, Amerindian, caboclo, mulatto, mestizo, Nago, Yoruba, Jesuit, Tupí.

For each of these single categories, we cannot manage without the other three. To employ a fifth category distinguishing form would probably confuse us even more. An example is the *lundu*. Its African origin has yet to be proven, although speculation runs to Angola, where *lundu* dance and song are said to have accompanied religious activities. The *lundu* first turned up in Brazil as part of the *batuque* dance. There exists just as little proof of some sort of relationship with the Iberian *lando* as there does with the Andean *zamacueca* or with formal parallels to the *desafíos* (*picong*) of the calypsonians in Trinidad. Here is Albert Friedenthal's racist characterization of the Brazilian *lundu* in his 1913 essay 'Musik und Dichtung bei den Kreolen Amerikas':

> There is an odd genre among Brazilian songs known as the *lundu*. The *lundu* has always been a Negro song. Their texts present the often confused thoughts of the Negroes, which are sometimes intended to be serious, sometimes funny, but nevertheless always have a comical effect…. Many *lundu* texts are practically impossible to translate, since sentence after sentence contains expressions in dialect spiced up with Negro interjections. The music,

often heard with the simple accompaniment of the Portuguese *fado*, usually fits the theme of the song quite well. The melodies are characteristically played in delayed, syncopated measures with a rhythm that must be precisely observed.

Other sources mention songs and dances called *londum* or *lundum*. Their character varies greatly from region to region, depending on the function and the extent to which they have connections to polka, *modinha*, fandango, etc. The confusion is so great even among Brazilian authors that they apparently mix up the *lundu* and the *modinha*, and sometimes mistake a type of *chula* for a *lundu*.

The following pages therefore will examine the most important types of folk songs more closely in terms of function, regional occurrence, character, origin, development, and form. Folk songs performed mainly in connection with dances and folkloristic performances (*autos, folguedos*) are also treated in later chapters.

A further restriction arises inevitably out of the general character of Brazilian folklore. Songs performed exclusively by choirs, such as those stemming from the Portuguese tradition (e.g., *coretos* in Minas Gerais), where a circle of friends would gather to sing and drink together, are rare. Choirs have an important role, however, during public festivals, competitions, rituals and other occasions, but always in relation to a solo voice. This antiphonal schema is rooted in the traditions of all three ethnic groups located on Brazilian soil.

For these reasons we must distinguish between those songs performed by an individual without listener participation and those where the listeners sing along, either the entire song or only the refrain.

The Importance of the Word

The *cantador* or *cancioneiro* is a type of traveling folksinger, which Luiz da Câmara Cascudo's *Dictionário do Foklore Brasileiro* places in the tradition of bards, minstrels, gleemen, troubadours, mastersingers, minnesingers and skalds: 'He sings to the people what he's improvised or memorized — the life stories of famous and infamous men from the region, the most important happenings, fantastic hunts and rodeos; he meets his opponent for song competitions that go on for hours or even nights; in our cultural tradition he is characterized by a great artistic imagination and originality.'

Such song contests occur during various folk festivals and theater pieces (*bumba-meu-boi* and other *reisados*). They are very popular as *desafios* and *emboladas*.

When I sing, I challenge
I open my vocal chords and interrupt the clamor
I want my breast to feel
The law and rigor of the fado

In the *Desafio*, a poetic contest, one of the singers begins with a challenge, the other answers him employing the theme just introduced. In the *Embolada* one of the *emboladores* continually repeats a certain line of verse while the other improvizes over several verses. Each of them accompanies himself on a percussion instrument (*pandeiro* or *ganzá*); the tempo is steadily increased until it is too fast for one of the *emboladores* and he is forced to give up. The *embolada* is of Portuguese origin and is mainly performed in the Northeast of Brazil. Mario de Andrade even attributes this European influence, in his *Aspectos da Música Brasileira*, to the Greeks and early Christian communities: 'They sing, carefree, with the same rhythmical grace found in their speech. There exists a total unity between music and spoken word. This natural, easy manner of speech determines the melodic flow as well.'

This *desafio* between Neco Martins and Francisco Sales, was recorded by Jouvert de Carvalho about sixty years ago:

Sales: Stop this revelry
Neco, treat me better
For if you don't, maybe
Things will get worse for you
Because Francisco Sales
Has no sympathy with singers

Neco: The occasion is ripe
Attack without regret
I'm not begging you for favors
Today, on such an occasion
I have accustomed myself to troubles
I no longer fear affliction
And least of all a poor blind man
Whom I do not respect

Sales: Colleague, don't say such things
For you could be punished for it
For I will not spare the skin
Of an ill-mannered singer
When I'm in swing
I am the king of the tough boys

Neco: Singers like yourself
Even if you're only a handful

Who've come straight out of hell
Stinking of burnt horn
Have to feel the whip
As I'm used to using it.

In contrast to the *emboladas*, the more melodic *desafios* are accompanied by a *viola* and *rabeca* (in the North) or by a *sanfona* and guitar (in the South).

Desafio with viola

Desafios, spontaneously improvized lyrics characteristic of folk-singers in many parts of Latin America, can be found in all parts of Brazil, especially in the coastal regions. This kind of poetical contest also exists in various forms in Latin America, like calypso in Trinidad and Tobago or trovas in Mexico. The song and verse forms upon which these singing duels are based vary greatly from region to region. While the *emboladas* of the Northeast are performed to humorous or satirical texts at a quick tempo, the singers of the *calango de desafio* in the Minas Gerais and Rio areas improvise their rhymes on animal themes.

The name already suggests that these *desafios* are based on the *calango* in 2/4 time. They are usually divided into different sequences. Sometimes they are preceded by a *martelo*, a twelve-syllable couplet of the Alexandrine variety, named after its inventor, the literature professor, diplomat, and politician Pedro Jaime Martelo (1665–1727). *Martelos agalopados* (presented in forced tempo) occasionally herald the coming of a *desafio*. Mario de Andrade calls the *martelo* a 'historical poem'. The refrain has a short metre and is usually called *carretilha*. The *repente* is also known as a part of the *desafio* in the Alto-Sertão and Zona Matuta regions. A typical feature here is the *viola sertaneja*, which solos particularly between verses during the competition. The *embolada* is also danced to and is called *coco de embolada*. It has been employed of late once again in popular music by the vocal duo Tom & Dito (using a *duplos sertanejos* style) and by Alceu Valença. *Música caipira* draws heavily on this *duplos* song form.

As the *vaqueiros* (cowboys) pass through the desert wasteland of the Sertão with their herds of cattle, one can hear their songs, the *aboios*, with their long, drawn-out words and vowels. Baptista Siqueira, in his study *Ficção e Música*, has distinguished between the *aboio de curral* and the *aboio de despedida*. In the former the *vaqueiro* calls to cattle that lag too far behind in the pasture: 'E vaca mausa bonita!' (Hey, gentle, pretty cow!), which becomes the long, drawn-out 'E – – – lo ︿– – ô – – –'

E------vacamansabo-----ni-ta ê--ê--ôo

The melody is considerably drawn out, calling to mind the muezzins in Arab mosques as they summon the faithful to prayer.

The other *aboio* signals the departure from relatives and farm. It is sad and despairing, suggesting the *vaqueiro* might never return:

> Adieu ... Lita, Adieu ... Lita
> See you in two weeks
> Adieu ... Lita, Adieu ... Lita
> I'll bring you a dress
> Made out of the finest cotton
> Lita

Gilberto Gil, Caetano Veloso, and Luiz Gonzaga Jr. have utilized these characteristics in several of their own songs.

One of the most frequent forms of folk poetry is the *ABC*, which is also performed in song form in 3/4 time by folksingers throughout the country:

> I'm sending you here, my dear
> An ABC of love
> So that you can see in it
> My sighs and sorrows

Utilizing a form of differing verse lengths, and with each beginning assigned a different letter of the alphabet, the ABCs offer advice and practical tips for all of life's situations: for unrequited love, for bachelors, for the turmoil of modern times, etc. In Portugal, such ABCs were being performed as far back as the fourteenth century.

Another song form imported from the colonizers' homeland is the *romance* and its multiple variations. Over time it was assimilated to become an independent Brazilian product. It, too, reflects the life and mentality of the inhabitants of the Sertão and the forests of the interior.

The first romances passed on to us stem from the second half of the eighteenth century and deal with animal themes (see under the heading Modinha).

Even more widespread are the romance-related *xácaras*. Transmitted orally for centuries, xácaras are today the oldest documents available treating historical happenings, primarily from Portuguese history, which they narrate and comment upon. As a song genre in Portugal they are usually performed separately from dance and festivals. In Brazil the xácara is part of the folkloristic performance during reisados, fandangos, and marujadas. For example the xácara, *A Nau Catarineta*, is very famous, narrating in epic scope the fate of the Portuguese warship *Catarineta*. Luiz da Câmara Cascudo observed in the *xácaras de Cego* parallels between the Scottish ballads from the time of King James V in the sixteenth century and his ballad 'The Gaberlunzie Man'.

> Woman of the house,
> Take a look at this poor fellow
> Even if I come a beggin'
> I still remain a nobleman
>
> It can't be a nobleman
> Who comes begging
> I have nothing to give you
> You can be on your way

Another form of romance is the *toada*, a melancholy sentimental air consisting usually of four lines with stanza and refrain. An example from the Amazon:

> You say that love doesn't hurt
> In the depth of the heart
> Get yourself a love and live far from her
> O, beautiful Cabocla —
> See whether it hurts or not
>
> Woman of the house
> I have a request of you
> A half an hour
> O beautiful Cabocla
> So that your sweetheart can enjoy himself

Toadas are executed antiphonally in the *folguedos* of the *folia de reis*. In modern *música popular* Milton Nascimento turned his attention especially to the toadas of his home region, Minas Gerais.

Toada by a violeiro (after M. de Andrade)

Finally, the *modas de viola* belong to this class of lyrical, narrative songs. *Violeiros* play them in the Northeast in improvisatory style to the strains of the *viola sertaneja*. Finished texts and compositions are used as a basis for this style in the country's eastern regions, where the form developed from the Portuguese *moda*. Thematic material consists chiefly of legends about ox-herders, anecdotes and tragic stories about love and death.

In a broader sense, then, modas also belong to *poesia repentista*, the poetic art of the improvising folksinger. They and the above-mentioned cocos and emboladas are exemplary of the wide-ranging repertoire mastered by this species of singer: the *partido alto* in Rio, the *cururús* in São Paulo state, the *trovas* with their toadas and *milongas* in Rio Grande do Sul, or the *quadras* in northern Minas Gerais. Brazilians call the practicing of this art form '*tirar versos*' (to pull a verse) or '*jogar versos*' (to play a verse). The Northeasterners call the event itself their *cantoria*.

Câmara Cascudo's book *Vaqueiros e Cantadores* describes these popular singers:

> Oddly enough, hardly any of these singers has a good voice. When one listens to them during rapid, lively passages of alternate singing, one hears only *des sons glapissants nasillards*. No melodiousness. No delicateness. No nuance. Completely lacking in deep tones. The *cantador* sings rhapsodically in a higher key than the one in which his instrument is tuned. He exaggerates with shrill tones. His voice is hard, stiff, without flexibility; his blood vessels are swollen from exertion, his face is flushed, eyes fixed in order not to lose the beat. He pays hardly any attention to the beat. The verse cadence is all that matters, and rhythm is everything. He does not care about melody either, for beautiful music is not his goal. The result is uniformity, monotony, simplicity, primitiveness. The melodies of the various verse forms, such as *colcheias*, *martelos*, or *ligeiras*, are unimportant. The verse rhythm alone is what counts. If it fits the music, everything is all right. The singer does not hear a wrong note; a wrong rhythm he hears immediately.

Moreover, the lyrics of the toada, romance, trova, and moda usually have a greater significance for the *romanceiros*, *repentistas*, and *cancioneiros* than the accompanying melody, which is often simply repeated from one verse to the next. The song's rendition is, in accordance with its character, more esthetic and full of feeling.

Itinerant folksingers were at one time closely connected to *literatura de cordel* (chapbooks, 'stories on a string'). In the past it was just a small step for the folksinger to make the transition from simply singing sage proverbs and ballads aloud to actually creating them himself. He would sell his artistic products in the form of small ten-page booklets, strung up on a cord in the marketplace kiosks of Brazil's Northeast. Many of the (anonymous) authors came from the people and treated in simple language themes taken from everyday life, thereby highlighting extraordinary heroes, deeds, events and passions. Of course, advice for solving the myriad problems of everyday life had to be included, too. Topics ranged from how to win over a stubborn spouse to concocting remedies for impotence. Folksingers often had to sing the contents of their booklets aloud, since only a small percentage of the rural population could read and write.

The same is basically true today. These small pamphlets can still be found today at the *feiras* (markets) between Rio and Belém, their covers decorated with woodcuts having more or less folkloristic motifs. More recently, it is even possible to see spaceships depicted. An edition can run as high as 100,000 copies per booklet. There are already over 10,000 different titles available. Only the nonstop flow of 'entertainment' from *radio-pilhas* (portable radios) with their soap operas (*novelas*) has become their serious rival. As the modern mass media made headway, folksingers saw their ranks greatly reduced in number. At the beginning of the eighties they held a congress in Rio where they tried to make the public, and therewith the Brazilian government, aware of their importance as an occupational group.

Two musical movements of the seventies took the cantadores and literatura de cordel as their reference point: the *movimento armorial*, which combined music of the Northeast with classical techniques, and the group Cearense, which combined these same roots with jazz and rock.

Chula Paraná (after Siguera)

Humorous texts and a lively rhythm characterize the *chula*. Here, for example, is one from the Amazon:

Turn to the portside, starboard
To the bow and to the keel
Turn rearwards
Turn there
I don't know exactly if it's right

But if not
Just turn back there!

Chulas are similar to the modinhas of Brazil's colonial period. They are also danced to in Bahia. Their origin goes back to the interaction between the Portuguese and the slaves imported into Portugal. It could be that the lundu arose here, too. The relevant text passages on dance will discuss this later.

Brazilian religious song evinces a high degree of influence from the liturgical repertoire of the Catholic Church. Examples are the *benditos* (petitional hymns), *orações* (prayers), and *ladainhas* (litanies). In addition, there exists a great number of songs sung at popular Church festivals, processions, and folkloric performances. They are usually identical to folk songs, both with and without dance accompaniment. Several of their particular forms include the *Canto de São Gonçalo* (from the festival of São Gonçalo), *folias* (especially the *folias de divino* and *folias de reis*, both performed at Christmas), the *cantos de peregrino* (pilgrims) and *rezas* (with which one prays for rain and prosperity).

The borderline between such songs originating within the domain of the Catholic Church and those springing from syncretic religious impulses became more fluid with time. On occasion, liturgy and religious hymns intermixed with songs of invocation and glorification from *macumba*, *umbanda*, and *candomblé*.

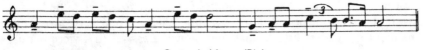

Canto de Xango (Rio)

Folk songs and folksingers as I have described them here were not part of the Indio's world. Music and singing were for him collective activities performed for particular ceremonies and rituals. Solo singing was a privilege chiefly reserved for the tribal shaman. Nevertheless, that part of today's Brazilian musical folklore performed by the solo singer received important stimuli from the musical and poetic creations of the country's native inhabitants.

Drinking song of the Indios

As mentioned before, European melody and poetry and African poly-rhythms and vocal techniques complemented each other in important ways. The Amerindian component is noticeable both in the pre-dominantly Portuguese-influenced song forms (solo and song contests), as well as in chiefly African forms (antiphony and dance), even if this presence has yet to be authoritatively documented.

The monotonous recitatives and the nasal tones in both voice and instrument could serve as proof of Amerindian influence in the *repentistas* and *emboladores*. Amerindian poetry, with its picturesque features, its closeness to nature and sense of the mystical, is surely present in other song forms as well. The musicologist Baptista Siqueira, of Amerindian descent himself, made a comparative study of the rhythms and har-monies found among various Northeastern melodies of the same Amer-indian type, and showed how difficult it is to neatly categorize folkloric music from the Northeast within any of the existing modal systems. It must be seen instead as an end-product of a popular, faulty, refined adaptation of the Gregorian chants, which had been introduced much earlier by the Jesuit priests. And since, according to Siqueira, the Jesuits introduced these hymns solely among 'pacified' Amerindians, and as Amerindians and half-castes (caboclos, mestizos) comprise the largest part of the Northeastern Sertão population, one would have to conclude that Amerindian musical folklore would be reflected, at least mar-ginally, in the music of the Northeast.

Mario de Andrade in *Aspectos da Música Brasileira* asserts: 'We have no traditional folk melodies.... Melodies come and go, never to be heard again. It's true: the people don't remember them.' If one disregards for a moment the widely known melodies of *música popular* that were popu-larized with the help of the mass media, one could conclude that the scarcity of traditional folk music is chiefly due to the improvisatory character of Brazilian folk music. The improvised texts used by itinerant folksingers and song-contest participants always employ a similar melodic frame (corresponding to the particular occasion), whereby the melody is automatically adapted to the improvisation.

In other cases, the situation determines the rhythm and tonality of the melody. Songs sung during work are often improvised, with varying texts and melodies, based on traditional song forms. In the *engenhos* (sugarmills) or on the *fazendas* we hear again how the rhythm of the work, whether performed by an individual or in communal, neigh-borly harvests (the *potirão*), determines the choice of the song to accompany the task.

Working song (Ronda) — after M. de Andrade

This helps explain how the song-and-dance form *coco* arose from the rhythm of the workers as they broke open coconuts. Plantation workers, fishermen and workers in the sugar mills and in other manufacturing branches all have their own specific songs.

Together with fairy tales and proverbs, song texts have been trans-mitted among the people for centuries. At the turn of the century Silvio Romero's *Cantos Populares do Brasil* collected together 556 so-called *quadrinhas*, or *quadras*. These are four-line verses that in various forms precede a repeated refrain. Here is quadra from Rio Grande do Sul.

> My father is an old fogey
> He plays the marimba
> My mother is an owl
> She lives in a knothole

A samba, for example, has virtually no chance of becoming successful in Brazilian popular music if it is played purely instrumentally. The lyrics, no matter how trivial, help people retain the melody.

The folk song in Brazil is still a song of the people. Despite de Andrade's assertions to the contrary, the people possess such a rich abundance of authentic, unadulterated melodies and rhythms, repre-senting such an integral part of each individual's thoughts and feelings that they can get by remembering only the texts. Everything else follows naturally.

The Modinha

Both Brazil's popular and serious music speak in a like manner of the *modinha* as their first independent point of development during the colonial period. While other song forms (lundus, chulas, aboios) are categorized generally as folklore, having exerted their influence on popular music only up until the beginning of this century, the modinha can claim for itself, in Brazil at least, a semi-classical status.

Little is known about how the modinha began. For lack of better sources, most musicologists cite the seventeenth century as the period in which it grew out of the Portuguese *moda*. Afro-Brazilians of the colonial era gave the once-lyrical Iberian song somewhat lascivious lyrics in which they treated predominantly erotic themes, either unaccompanied or accompanied by guitar. According to contemporary chronicles, the Rio mulatto Domingos Caldas Barbosa shocked Lisbon's high society in 1775 with such modinhas. The shock must have been rather pleasant, however, since Caldas Barbosa was soon famous all over Portugal. Tinhorão reported that the discovery of gold in Minas Gerais at the time led to a great increase in the number of prosperous families in Portugal. The families of the *nouveaux riches* especially turned away from absolutist morals to enjoy these free, unrestrained song lyrics. Like this one from Caldas Barbosa:

> Tam, tam, tam, tam, big drum
> Wonderful military life
> To defend king and country
> And afterwards to laugh and laze

Caldas Barbosa was performer, guitarist, composer and lyricist all in one. The authors of most modinhas, however, remained anonymous. Their melodies and texts have been passed on from generation to generation. The modinhas of Caldas Barbosa became, so to speak, the property of the people. After their initial popularity in Portugal they soon were in vogue in the Brazilian centres of metropolitan life, something that might well have been expected in a society that enthusiastically absorbed every new trend from Europe. By the beginning of the nineteenth century, then, modinhas had found great favor chiefly in the salons of the city (*modinha de salão*). Just as Caldas Barbosa's songs had already influenced composers of Italian opera in Europe (such as Bellini), name composers and performers in Brazil now began likewise to turn their attention to this song form. The Italian opera singer Augusta Candiani is said to have opened a concert in Rio with modinhas in 1845. Her success was so great that many other singers imitated the practice soon after.

With the arrival of the waltz at the outset of the romantic era, the modinha began to lose much of its earlier aristocratic luster. Its earlier fresh, frivolous lyrics fell victim to increasing sentimentality. Its 2/4 beat changed to conform to the general 3/4 fashion of the day. According to Câmara Cascudo, who has also undertaken very intensive research on the modinha, it eventually disappeared completely from the salons, only to reappear in the streets and bars of the city in the 4/4 time of the schottische. A whole new generation of romantic poets and composers had rediscovered the modinha for themselves. They met regularly in the bohemian café of the mulatto Francisco de Paula Brito (1809–91) to exchange ideas on literary and musical topics. These new troubadours of the *modinhas da rua* were accompanied in those days for the first time by an instrumental trio, which later became the original ensemble of *choro* music: the flute, *cavaquinho* and guitar.

In those days, artistic centers for the new romantic modinhas with literary ambitions were Salvador in Bahia and Rio de Janeiro. In 1860 the Salvadoran singer and guitarist Xisto Bahia appeared in Rio. He is lauded to this day as the leading modinha singer of the past century:

> Did you not know
> That I love you and adore you
> That I live to suffer?
> You knew nothing of these tears
> Which I shed
> For my sad life?

Xisto Bahia was a *seresteiro*, a serenading minstrel from the Iberian tradition. These troubadours from the second half of the nineteenth century (*seresteiros, modinheiros* and *cancioneiros*) stood in competition with each other, to be sure, but at the same time shared the common problem of being unable to tune into the tastes of the lower social strata with their sentimental, melancholy airs.

Modinha from Rio Grande do Norte

Catulo da Paixão Cearense attempted to approach the musical needs of wider segments of the common people. He came to Rio in 1880 from the north of Brazil and immediately set about bringing the modinha back to the level of the first romantics. He demanded simpler, more understandable language and topical material related to regional themes. Together with his partner, João Penambuco, the self-proclaimed 'troubadour of the poor,' he composed long verses in the style used by folksingers from Brazil's Northeast.

> Don't you see the lake
> There in the valley, there
> When you look

It always looks back at you
But when you leave
Good-bye, never to meet again
What it does with you
It does with every other who comes
So take a good look at the lake
It is like the female heart

Tinhorão explains how Catulo passed the test of his initial recitals in evening attire before Rio's aristocratic families. This picture of the folksinger in full evening dress could be observed at the same time in Buenos Aires, where *milonga* singers (a popular form influenced by the Cuban habanera) came to the capital from the country's hinterland to present their art in theaters and circuses.

While the musical foundations for the creation of the *tango porteño* were being laid in Buenos Aires during this period, *choro-conjuntos* in Rio de Janeiro were enjoying a growing popularity among the lower classes with their new instrumental manner of playing polkas, *valsas*, Brazilian tangos (habaneras) and choros. By playing purely instrumental music, they were able to attain the popularity that Catulo had aspired to, with his reformation of the modinha, but had never achieved.

In 1905 Eduardo das Neves published a collection of Brazilian modinhas under the title *Mistérios do violão* ('Mysteries of the guitar'). Neves had already been regarded as a bard of the people, even if a high-carat one (his nickname was *O Diamante Negro*, 'The Black Diamond'). He was often compared with the chansonniers of French vaudeville, with whom the *cariocas* (the people of Rio) were somewhat familiar on account of the popularity of a French restaurant on the Morro da Urca. His first disc recording was completed three years earlier; Casa Edison recorded him singing modinhas and lundus in 1902. It numbers among the first phonograph recordings in Brazil. Das Neves's texts, a blend of realistic and patriotic themes, signaled a change in the character of the traditional modinha, so much so that in this century it ceased to be known under the name modinha. Today it is known primarily under the appellation *canção*. The similarity of this name to the French *chanson* certainly corresponds to a similar function played in Brazilian music. In addition, it is thoroughly legitimate to compare the canção with the Latin American *canción*, especially in light of the fact that the Cuban habanera left its stamp upon both. Still, composers of *música erúdita*, such as Villa Lobos and Marlos Nobre, continued to regard and utilize this form as a modinha.

Eduardo das Neves's son, Candido, carried on composing in the new genre of the modern modinha (or canção) along with other artists of his generation: Joubert de Carvalho (1900–?), Freire Junior (1881–1956), Domingo Publico, Jaymme Ovalle (1894–1935), and Hekel Tavares (1896–1969). The appearance of radio and record players on the scene, the birth of the samba, choro and Brazilian tangos, as well as an invasion of new musical genres from abroad, all set favorable conditions for the birth of new mixed forms — samba (*samba-canção*), choro (*choro-canção*), valsa, tango etc.

Serenata a moda antiga (Dorival Caymmi)

The presence of lyrical, songlike melodies with solemn tempi in MPB still serves to remind us today of the earlier modinha tradition. Chico Buarque, Antonio Carlos Jobim, and many other contemporary composers have written modinhas. Caldas Barbosa, Xisto Bahia, Catulo and Eduardo das Neves all undoubtedly played a role in influencing the twentieth-century troubadour's interpretive styles — until João Gilberto came along in the fifties — and set the tone for Brazilian artists for at least three generations to come.

The modinha's significance and quality have always been subject to controversy. When Silvio Romero released a two-volume work of Brazilian folk songs in 1897, he refused to include modinhas, since he regarded them as totally unimportant. Mario de Andrade saw the modinha as a watered-down version of a European melody from the latter half of the eighteenth century: 'The melody always sounds forced.'

In 1971 the modinha moved somewhat unexpectedly to the forefront of public interest once again, when people believed they had detected in the film *Love Story* a plagiarized modinha, '*Dores de Coração*' (Pangs of the Heart), written by Pedro de Alcantara in 1907.

Dances

Ethnologists generally differentiate between solo dances, couple dances, and group dances. Another classification, which I made use of in a more analytical context in my book *Música Latina*, is by function and content and by origin. It would actually be necessary then to distinguish between *bailes*, dances with an informal party character, and the *danças*, with their religious, ritualistic themes. What follows, however, does not attempt such an analytic approach, but rather presents several important Brazilian dances as illustrative case studies.

Without a doubt, dance is after lyrics and music, the third fundamental element in musical folklore. What was said about the folk song is equally true for the multitude of dance forms coming from an Iberian, Amerindian, or African heritage. It applies as well to the many mixed forms, their ordering and place in their cultural context, and the general difficulty in distinguishing so many forms having both similar and contradictory names.

Amerindian Influences

From Jesuit accounts, and from other early visitors to Brazil during the colonial period, we know today that the native inhabitants accompanied all their rites and rituals with dance music. That applied even to the communal devouring of a dead foe. The Homburg mercenary Hans Staden gave us the following account from 1557 in his *Zwei Reisen nach Brasilien*:

> After shearing off my eyebrows, the women led me to a hut where their idols, the *maracás* rattles, are kept. They formed a circle around me. Two women next to me tied various gadgets to my leg and to the back of my neck with a string, so that a four-cornered fan made out of birds' tail-feathers stood high atop my head. They call this an *araçoia*. Thereupon all the women began singing. I had to stamp my leg, to which all the rattles were tied, to their beat so that it rattled and matched their song.

Four hundred years later, Claude Lévi-Strauss described the dances of the Brazilian aborigines in his work *Tristes Tropiques*:

> During the first few evenings we attended the dances of various Tugaré clans: the *ewoddo*, the dance of the palm tree tribe, and the *paiwe*, the dance of the hedgehog tribe. In both cases the dancers had covered themselves with leaves from head to foot. Since one could not see their faces, it seemed as if they were at the height of the feathered diadem. This so completely dominated their appearance that one thought them to be much taller than they really were. In their hands they carried palm stalks or leaved branches. There were two different types of dances. The dancers first

appeared individually, separating themselves into two quadrilles so that they stood opposing each other at each end of the square. They then began to run toward one another, yelling loudly as they went spinning around and around, until the original arrangement had been reversed. The women joined the scene later, forming an inextricably tangled knot of human bodies moving back and forth, led by naked dancers advancing backward and shaking their rattles, while other men squatted on the ground singing.

According to the sources available to me, there are a number of features present in Amerindian dance that can also be found in the dances of present-day primitive tribes in Brazil. Choreography and organizational form, for instance, are subject to rigid, traditional rules that are determined by the ritualistic character of the dance. Important here are both the scenic representation of certain events, as well as the transmission of a spiritual message through a choreographic symbol system. Other components of this communal, ceremonial way of life are sports competitions, song contests, and individually performed satirical verses, stories, and puzzles. These latter features have their parallels in certain folkloric forms — such as *desafios*, *autos*, and *folguedos* — in regions with a high percentage of caboclos in the population.

Brazilian folklorists are quite sure of the Amerindian influence in the dances *catira*, *cateretê*, and *cururú*. The catira is danced in São Paulo, Minas, and the greater Rio area. It is a group dance. Men and women form two rows; they clap their hands to the sound of the guitar and stamp their feet in rhythm. In some regions only men take part, in other regions only women. The guitarists sing *modas* in moderate rhythms to the sound of their guitars.

The *cateretê*, a variation of the catira, has a more pronounced Iberian flavor. There are researchers who ascribe its origins to the old Portuguese *carretera* dance. The degree of Iberian influence, nevertheless, differs greatly from region to region, so that a Portuguese origin is difficult to maintain, all the more so since many cateretês are also sung in the Tupi language.

> O virgin Mary
> Mother of the true Lord
> The people of this world
> Are so good to you

The best-known song and dance form arising under Jesuit influence is the *cururú*. Making use of a very simple choreography, the dancers form a circle around a musician and two singers — the *violeiro* and the *canturiões*. The beauty of the cururú depends primarily upon the quality of the improvised rhymes and texts. A kind of master of ceremonies, whose presence indicates earlier influences from the European quadrille, guides and directs the course and flow of the dance with his commands.

The cururú is a caboclo dance in Goiás, Mato Grosso, and in old settlements of São Paulo state. It is danced at the semiofficial church festivals of *Dança de São Gonçalo* and *Dança de Santa Cruz* after certain sections of the ceremony. It has been conjectured that Amerindian influences are also present in the following caboclo dances: *caboclos de pena, caboclinhos, pagelança* (with shamanistic elements), *puçanga, curupira, folgazão, boitatá, caiapós*, and *tribos*. In several of these dances the caboclos don masks as the Amerindians once did, and imitate the dances of the Indios living in nearby Amazonian areas.

African Influences

The oldest reference that I know to African dances in Brazil is from the Frenchman Pyard de Laval. On August 8, 1610, he reported how on Sundays and Christian holidays the slaves danced in the streets and squares of Salvador with the permission of their owners.

The word *batuque* is a synonym for a large number of African dances in Brazil. Tinhorão, in *Música Popular*, comments: 'The colonialists labeled every loud noise the blacks made a batuque.' Batuques came out of Africa as collective, ritualistic ring dances. Men and women join a lead singer and musicians, arranging themselves in circular or row form. What especially characterizes the batuque in addition to its collective movements and steps, is the solo dance of an individual performer who is then supported by the other dancers with a choral chant and rhythmic hand-clapping. The lead singer improvises verses to the repeated refrain of the chorus. The ritual by which the solo dancer exits from the circle can vary. The most common form is one in which the dancer touches one of those standing nearby on the belt or the hip, and thereby takes his place in the circle. Acrobatic-like leaps and contortions to accelerating rhythms announce the change of soloists in advance.

Vamos quebrar jirau
O ... lê....

This phrase is sung over and over again by the chorus until the exchange has been completed. The dancers do have room to improvise (*a vontade*) within the *roda*, either individually or in pairs, yet certain steps and choreographic figures must nevertheless be repeated.

Batuque rhythm

Batuques such as this can be found in all regions of the country having a black population. Batuque is often used as a general term for communal singing, dancing and music-making. The *calenda* and *chica* dances in other Latin American regions may very well represent a parallel development to the batuque. Variants of the batuque are *bambelô, carimbó, caxambú, coco, semba, samba* and *umbigada* (named after the touch to the dancer's belt, which also characterizes the samba forms *tambordecrioulil, bate-pau* and *jongo*). Further variations of the batuque were the *baiano* and *lundu*. Both have largely disappeared from today's folklore scene, however. The *baião* and the *xaxado* developed from the baiano. Both are mixed forms from the earlier batuque, combined with European dances like the quadrille, contredanse and polka. The number of documented batuque derivations, which are known generally as *samba*, runs into the hundreds.

Edison Carneiro has put together a *samba* topography for Brazil in his *Folgue dos Tradicionais*:

Coco region, in the North and Northeast. The *bambelô, virado, coco de roda, mineiro-pau, milindó* and others are found here. In the coco, Andrade noticed similarities to Portuguese round dances. In actuality, though, the coco and its variants are a combination of batuques and Amerindian dances, especially the *tupi*. Coco verses (without dance, it corresponds to an *embolada*) are improvised by the *tirador* and answered by a repeated choral refrain. Only percussion instruments (*cuica, ingonos, ganzá* and *pandeiros*) accompany the dance. Variations on the coco acquired their names from the feature of the instrument used (*coco de ganzá*), the poetic texts (*coco de décima*), the locality (*coco de usina*), or the nature of the contest (*coco de embolada*).

Samba region, in the North and between Rio and São Paulo. *Tambor, samba-rural, samba lenço, batuques* and *bate-pau* belong to this group. Characteristic of the tambor-de-crioula dances in the North (Maranhão, Piaui) are the large log drums, which are played together with triangle and *cabaça*. Samba forms often exhibit regional differences only in their instrumental accompaniment. In Rio and Minas Gerais, for example, we find atabaque drums quite regularly, while in other localities string instruments, such as *cavaquinhos* and *viola sertanejas*, as well as *pandeiros* and other percussion instruments, come into the picture.

Congo region, also in Rio, São Paulo, and Goias, with couples dancing in circular form (*roda*). Foot-stamping and daring acrobatics follow a complex step pattern. The customary division into stanza and refrain for lead singer and chorus are reminiscent of the *pontos* of Afro-Brazilian cults.

Bantu slaves from Angola brought *capoeira* to Brazil. Among friends it is a game and a duel; between enemies, a form of combat. It was not unusual to see capoeira used in street fights in Rio, Salvador, and Recife right into this century. Capoeira combatants were officially engaged in Brazil's war against Paraguay. Today fighting capoeira are forbidden. Still, they occur.

There is a clearing in a forest outside Salvador where small waterfalls tumble down the rocky cliffs. Here, on weekends, *candomblés* are held. As I arrived I observed a small wooden house surrounded by a slatted fence so that one could look in but not enter. There were two capoeira fighters in the house, and nothing else. Berimbau players and percussionists were also outside the house. As I had missed the beginning, I caught only the last part of the match. Choreographically, it differed only in one respect from capoeira one can see at the Mercado Modelo in Salvador: the dancers feet did not stop short of the opponent's body, as if halted by an invisible hand, as they do in non-combative capoeira. The head of one of the combatants was already bleeding. His strength was visibly diminishing, until finally he let the other fighter know that he wanted to quit. It took some time before the superior fighter acknowledged this, drink and the goading of the spectators had thrown him into a blind rage. Somewhat later I saw him in front of the house, engaged this time in friendly struggle with other capoeirists. It is a well-known fact that capoeira* dancers are able to deliver deadly blows with their feet. There are many types of capoeira, differing according to region — *capoeira de Angola, angolinha, são bento grande, jogo de dentro, santa maria, conçeição da praia*, etc. These designations are applied at the same time to the individual *toques*, that is, the rhythm, the basic musical figures, from *ligeiro* to *samba da capoeira*. If a visitor approaches, a signal is given, and

---

* In many regions capoeiro used to be identified with 'derelicts' or 'underworld figures.'

the dancers change into a special rhythm called a *calvaria*. Common to all capoeiras is their character — a harmony of strength and rhythm, poetry and movement. Force is translated into rhythm, power into melody. The capoeira dancer is, at one and the same time, artist and athlete, performer and poet.

The capoeira de Angola, the most frequently danced of this form, looks like this: a semicircle forms made up of berimbau players, percussionists, spectators and, later on, participants. The chanting begins to the sound of berimbaus, *chocalhos* and pandeiros. The dancers squat in front of the semicircle in deep concentration, attempting to achieve contact with the saint. The concluding strophe is a signal:

Hey, come back to the world, comrade!

The dancers advance to the middle of the circle in a handstand and there they begin the dance, at first slowly and then in an accelerated tempo. Berimbau, percussion and chorus determine which figures are to be executed next, for example:

AU = somersault into a handstand.

RASTEIRA = scythe-shaped swinging of the leg to the foot of the next dancer, in order to trip him up.

The *camarado* attacked in this manner counters with a defensive figure (known as 'golpe', a Brazilian term for a beat). One can often hear the spectators shout their appreciation from the circle. They voice their wish to see a particularly figure executed, which the musicians then introduce. Capoeira dances are also governed by a code of honor, in existence since the last century, that defines proper and improper clothing and behavior. Capoeira is still very popular. It attracts many young people in other cities where capoeira schools have been opened. The most famous capoeira teacher was Mestre Bimba, who opened his academy in 1932 in Salvador.

In Recifer, capoeira* owes its persistence to the *frevo*, a very popular carnival dance form. Since the middle of the nineteenth century, capoeira dancers and musicians have taken part in the carnival processions in Recife. Their groups would march out between two military orchestras that often competed with each other for the favor of the parade viewers. By the end of the century it had become unavoidable that march orchestras should show the effects of capoeira. The product of this encounter between polka marches and *maxixes* with capoeira

---

*In the eighties one could observe dance figures similar to capoeira in breakdancing and other dances accompanying rap music.

rhythms, supported by their choruses, was a *polca-marcha do fervor* (*ferver* = to boil) — a lively march polka with the syncopation typical of capoeira *toques*. Individual dance was known even in those days. It was characterized by an accentuated, swaying, almost syncopated waddling step originating in the hips. The dancers executed their steps to orchestral backgrounds, accompanied by acrobatic movements of the arms and upper body. Later, they took hold of colorful parasols that they moved up and down during the dance. The frevo dance is an extremely difficult art form, demanding a high degree of body control. Split leaps high into the air are among the easier exercises.

As a consequence of linguistic adaptation the general feeling of *ferver* changed into a *frever*, until at last one spoke of the *frevo*. The name appeared for the first time in a Recife newspaper in 1908. Aluizio Falção offers the following poetic description of the frevo: 'It is like a river, full of bends and turns; it follows an undulatory course and is rough, frequently cascading into a waterfall.' The *frevo-canção*, a salon piece heavily influenced by the modinha, and the *frevo-de-bloco* were two variations that soon joined the *frevo-da-rua* (the original carnival version) in the opening decades of the century. It arose out of a situation in which Recife's suburban youth were denied access to the existing carnival-like *cordões* in clubs of craftsmen and sailor. So they formed their own *blocos*. They marched along in the procession with their small family orchestras composed of *pau e corda* (woodwinds and string) — that is guitar, cavaquinho, flute, percussion and their own version of the frevo.

Closely related to the frevo is the *maracatú*. It should actually be considered among the folkloristic performances, but as its choreography is so similar to the frevo, it will be described only briefly. Maracatús are processions put on by blacks and mulattos who have joined together to form 'nations' (*nação*). Through them they wish to remember and commemorate the African groups to which their ancestors once belonged during the slave period. The queen of the respective nation (and sometimes the king, too) dances in the middle of the procession under a canopy, in the form of a large parasol. The strains of the maracatús, so similar to the frevo, accompany the whole procession.

Frevo and *samba da carnaval* are not only rivals. They also exhibit common elements in the organizational form of their groups at carnival, as well as in their derivation from polka and *marchinha*. It would be possible, in fact, to confuse certain marchinhas at the Rio carnival with frevos. For a while, the big hit songs at the cariocas' carnival were able to steal the show from their northern 'brother', even at the Recife carnival itself. The frevo, on the other hand, could never gain a foothold in Rio. After a school for capoeira, the Centro Cultural Fisica e Capoeira Regional, was opened in 1932 under the direction of the excellent capoeira masters in Bahia, a new school for frevo dance was set up a number of years ago in Recife. And there are certainly more than a few cariocas who are sick and tired of their own carnival and who would like to experience three days of uncorrupted, uncommercialized carnival in Recife, the center of the frevo, or, better yet, in Olinda.

The *baião*, known earlier as *baiano*, is not to be confused with the *balaio*, a dance characterized by a stamping of the foot (*sapateo*) in Rio Grande du Sul. The baião was a popular dance form in the Northeast during the nineteenth century. Vasco Mariz's *A Canção Brasileira* traces it back to the instrumental interlude played by the *viola sertaneja* that folksingers used as a bridge between verses during the desafios. Little is known about the etymology of the word *baião*. One guess would be that it derives from *rojão*, that is, the interlude itself. Siqueira postulates a linguistic shift from *bailão* (*bailar* = to dance) to *baião*, due to the caboclos' inability to pronounce 'll' and 'ss' correctly.

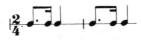

Baião rhythm

Variation

It seems almost inevitable that the baião would occasionally be identified as a samba, and that the word *samba* would be used as a synonym for 'party' in the Northeast. In contrast, the baiano is actually defined as a *samba rasgado* (quick samba) and as a further development of the lundu.

The sanfona, a diatonic accordion typical of the Sertão region, is the most important instrument for the baiões. In the forties Luiz Gonzaga, together with Humberto Teixeira, presented his urbanized version of the baião. Themes present in his famous baião 'Mulher Rendeira' (from the film *O Cangaçeiro*) can be found in the texts of rural baiões.

The *xiba*, considered to belong to the batuque genre, is primarily danced in rural districts. The tunes are sung to the accompaniment of guitars, *viola de arame* and cavaquinho.

European Influences

The *ciranda*, a traditional Portuguese round dance, was occasionally subject to batuque influence in Brazil. Regional variations abound. In Pernambuco, it is associated with São João, Midsummer Day, celebrations. A *cirandeiro* guides the dance from the middle of the circle with improvised four-liners; in Rio the ciranda belongs to the rich treasure of *samba-rural* dances from the batuque family; in the South it is part of the local *fandango*. Children also dance the *candeeiro* — singing in a circle, with foot-stamping, and only under a full moon.

> Candeeiro ô
> Is in the hand of Ioiô
> Candeeiro á
> Is in the hand of Iáiâ

The general difficulty of classifying Brazilian dances with sufficient accuracy is especially apparent with the *fandango*. As with contredanses, quadrilles, polkas and habaneras, the Iberian fandango lent significant features to many European, Amerindian and African mixed forms in almost all regions of Latin America during the colonial period. Curiously, these features have yet to be defined exactly. It is debatable whether or not the fandango could be a Latinized form of Iberian dance, or at least of Mozarabic origin. In my research I have come across countless examples of colonial chronicles carelessly employing the term 'fandango' to indicate Iberian dances of the fandango-flamenco family and related species. Consequently, there is no useful information to be had about the actual influence in Latin America. This may provide an explanation for the confusion currently present on Brazil's folk music map. In the North it is known as a couple dance of the *marujada* genre, with a quick rhythm in three different time signatures. Only in the South does the fandango still exhibit features reminiscent of its Iberian past (sapateos).

Vincente Salles associates several fandangos with a series of dances that may originate in the Azores, and that are still known there today under the same name. Fandangos characterized by a succession of different dances, with which the caboclos and fishermen in southern Brazil celebrated their festivals, belong here, too. The *chamaritta de louvação* starts it all off; the *violeiros* welcome the festival patron and comment upon regional happenings. The various *marcas* (sections) follow — the *marcas batidas* (played with a ponderous rhythm in unison) and the *marcas valseadas* (a light rhythm). *Marcas bailadas* and *rodas passadas*, which benefit from a wide variety of different rhythms and choreographies (*dom-dom, meia-canja*, etc.), then follow. The dancers, or *folgadores*, are accompanied by a *rebeca* [fiddle], *adufo* and two *violas*, all of which have primarily a rhythmic function. The violas are played *rasgueo* (scraped) and *ponteio* (strummed). The fiddles do short, improvised solos.

In the São Paulo area the fandango (like the *malambo* in Argentina) is danced only by men:

Que moca bonita, Fandango from São Paulo

In the East, on the other hand, individual rhythms and variations were given other names: *cana verde, fandango-rufado (bailado)*. These names, indicating particular choreographic features — such as with or without foot stamping, solo or in couples around the circle — have been replaced regionally by the following — *serra baile, dança de São Gonçalo, tatu, tirana, galinha morta, balaio, bambaquerê, quero-mana, anu, andorinha, xará, sapo, porca* (from 'polka').

Mario de Andrade accurately accounts for the existence of such a multitude of fandango versions: 'In general, "fandango" is a synonym for dance. Mainly regional dance figures are performed in it.' In other words, *batuque* and *samba* are generic terms for predominantly African-influenced dances in the north and east. Fandangos are representative of a large number of predominantly Iberian-influenced dances in the south and parts of the east.

The *galpão* is a gaucho dance in the south of Brazil. The word refers alike to the gaucho way of life, living space, meeting places and even a particular dance step of these inhabitants of the pampa. The main instruments are the *sanfona* and *gaita* (harmonica). One can encounter folkloric forms in the south that are very similar to those in the La Plata states.

The *lundu* has already been discussed as a member of the batuque family. It deserves special attention here because of the decisive influence it has had upon the development of urban song and dance. The Brazil researcher Von Martius described the lundu as a dance normally performed after meals in Bahia: 'The ladies danced very gracefully.' This is an unmistakable clue that Von Martius was not observing the African lundu-batuque. Full stomachs and graceful movements do not fit the picture of a batuque which is characterized by pelvic thrusts and lascivious gestures. Apparently there were two kinds of lundus. The general term lundu has been in use since the latter half of the eighteenth century. Before this time the Portuguese fandango underwent rhythmic modifications as a result of cultural interaction with Negro slaves in Portugal. The frivolous *chula* song form may have been born here, ending up finally alongside the fandango in Brazil. The fandango advanced quickly in Brazil, becoming the most fashionable dance for Europeans there at a time when Spain ruled over Portugal (1581–1640). Tinhorão documented the rhythmic shift from the slow 6/8 time, customary in Spain, to an African influenced 3/4 time in Portugal, over to a lively, syncopated 2/4 time in Brazil. The Iberian-oriented fandango found a new home in the south of Brazil. It was acculturated by blacks and mulattos into new mixed forms in the regions of the African slave plantations. This new mixed form, known as the lundu, was born of the marriage between fandango choreography and batuque rhythm; it was quickly taken up by whites, becoming in short time even more popular than the Portuguese *fofa*.

Folkloric Performances

Another type of popular cultural event can be found in great abundance in all parts of Brazil. Mario de Andrade was the first to characterize them as *dramatic dances*. More recent ethnological studies (for example, those of Edson Carneiro) refer to them as *traditional plays*. The so-called *folguedos* or *autos* are meant here. We can generally speak of folguedos to describe scenic elements with musical and choreographic accompaniment in the following forms:

— Street processions
— Scenic representations of particular historical events or symbolic stories; religious cults
— Popular musicals
— Sport, poetic and musical contests

These *danças dramaticas* in Brazil find their parallels in the *danzas* that occur in Latin American cultural spheres under Spanish influence.

Danzas are in fact ritualistic dances, even if the actual ritualistic or religious moment has been covered up or lost in many localities. Danzas nearly always arose as a combination of Amerindian or Afro-Latin ritualistic traditions and Catholic church ceremonies. In contrast, the *bailes* were based largely on European dance patterns that evolved over time as a result of interaction between Afro-Latins and Amerindians.

The principle of scenic-dramatic action within a ritualistic story was well known to all three ethnic groups during Brazil's colonial period. The contribution of the European Catholics was the most attractive of the three. The pomp and splendor of their productions, together with a wide array of previously unknown instruments, made it very exciting to participate in their stagings. The Catholic priests for their part often incorporated large parts of Amerindian staging into their productions. They only changed the texts in order to document their Christian beliefs and, most important, to use the whole spectacle as a propaganda vehicle for their Church.

The life and passion of Jesus Christ has appeared in dramatized form in Europe since the Middle Ages. It was no rarity to see, for example, choreographic representations with popular appeal in the Spanish Church. Spain's oldest religious drama (*autos sacramentales*), entitled *Los Reyes Magos*, or the Three Magi, dates back to the twelfth century. Secular themes were also frequent in the late Middle Ages.

The Amerindians who had been resettled in the missions were the first under the direction of the Catholic priests to 'slip into' the various roles of the apostles, Judas and devils. At a later date, slaves shipped over from Africa followed the priestly summons into the costume room. Catholic priests were not unfamiliar with enthronement ceremonies of black potentates in front of the church. They had seen such enactments in the Festivals of Irmandades do Rosario. By letting the African slaves generally have their way, the priests undoubtedly moved closer to their goal of Christianizing them. Moreover, having already forbidden the blacks all other music and dance except on Church holidays, the priests were able to steer slave activities — by means of such Church co-productions — into spheres that they controlled or influenced. This intended indirect acculturation was, over the centuries, only half successful. It set off a reaction among the blacks that ultimately gave birth to such syncretistic religions as Candomblé, voodoo and Santeria.

Only in recent decades have Brazilian folklorists begun to examine the rich context of these folk plays more closely, and a series of detailed field studies initiated by FUNARTE (Fundação Nacional de Arte) has appeared on the topic.

In regard to the bailes — it is important to note that there really is no such thing as a *dança* without a baile to go with it. A Brazilian folk festival in most cases embraces all the customary forms of folkloric expression in a particular region. A separation between religious and secular song and dance is, with few exceptions, unheard of.

Bumba-meu-boi

The most popular and frequently performed folkloristic drama in Brazil is undoubtedly the *bumba-meu-boi* (ox play), a popular burlesque of mystical character. The main role in all these plays is that of the ox, whose function is to parody representatives of the local community. These plays exhibit great variation in their manner of presentation, depending on the region. The following is one example:

Cast of Characters

Mateus, the Negro, capadocio
Gregorio, the caboclo
Caipora, mythical beast of the Indios
Doctor
Aunt Catarina
Surjão
Priest
Vaqueiro
Master, the owner
Cavalo Marinho, symbolic figure
Others

The performance often begins with the actors arriving at a farm or house and requesting entrance. The dramatic development varies according to region. Sometimes the ox becomes ill and is revived with an enema. Other times the pregnant wife of the Negro has a craving for ox tongue, which she is prevented from taking just in time. The roles are divided up between actors who present the scenes in a mixture of song, dance and drama. Bumba-meu-boi is a lower-class satirical creation. It exposes the bad attitudes of the local upper-class representatives. The play finally ends on a general note of exuberance, dance, singing and copious consumption of alcohol.

Silvio Romero's notes prepared near the beginning of this century for his *Cantos Populares do Brasil* in Pernambuco will help us understand the play's content.

Reisado de Cavalo Marinho and Bumba-meu-boi.

Scene 1

(*Cavalo Marinho dances, chorus*)

Chorus:

Cavalo Marinho
Comes making advances
Asking permission
To dance.
Cavalo Marinho
If you want to be noticed
Take a bow
Before your capitão
Cavalo Marinho
Dance well;
He can call himself
A coward, meu bem
Cavalo Marinho
Dance a good baiano;
You could be good
A Pernambucano
Cavalo Marinho
Go to school
Learn to read
And to play guitar.
Cavalo Marinho
Dance your balanco
Which I wish to see

Cavalo Marinho
Dance your balanco
Which I wish to see
Cavalo Marinho
Dance on the square;
For the master of the house
Has lots of money.
Cavalo Marinho
Dance up on your heels
Since the master of the house
Has boiled chicken.
Cavalo Marinho
You have already danced
But go there
And take what I give you.
Cavalo Marinho
Let's be on our way
Make a bow
To (the ladies)
Cavalo Marinho
Have an ox sent
For your wages
And be sure the people
See it.

Scene II

(*Amo, harlequin, Mateus, ox, chorus, Sebastião, Fidelis*)

Amo:

O, harlequin
O, my sins
Go and call Fidelis
O, my harlequin
Go and call Mateus
Come with the ox
And his companions

Harlequin:

O, Mateus, come here
The lord is calling
Bring your ox

And come to dance.
I only thought Mateus
I didn't think Fidelis.
It's good to say the Negro feels
No pain in his skin.

Amo:

O, Mateus, where is the ox?

Mateus:

Óla, óla, óla
The ox is already here
The ox is already here

When my ox arrives
I'm here....

Chorus:
Play the guitar well
For the Baiano
So that Mateus and Fidelis,
These characters, may dance
In time to the Juriti,
Tico, Tico, Rouxino,
Fidelis dances well,
Mateus dances better.
The guitar player has very
   fine ears,
The sound of your guitar
Strikes me like the open sky
I want a good guitar
To play the whole festival
   long,
The good pandeiro plays
The samba in the forest.
I am one of those born
Under the sign of Cancer.
The more love I give
The more I am disdained.
Since I am a son of the people,
I have the gift of simplicity
I am not happy,
But I survive

Chorus:
Come, my ornamented ox.
Come, do it with elegance.
Come and dance beautifully.
Come, take a bow.
Come, perform a mystery
Come, do it well
Come show us what you know
From nature.
Come, dance my ox,

Have fun at the square;
For the master of the house
Has lots of money.
This beautiful ox
Must not die;
For he was only born
To live here.

Mateus:
Dance beautifully
In the middle of the square
Play this guitar
It is rather small
My ox, you know
You should dance with style.
With all my poverty.
Dance, my ox. Dance,
   Mateus.
Dance, all you vaqueiros;
Dance, for today we celebrate
A great festival on the square.

Mateus:
Wait, Wait, Wait!
I have to announce some
   thing:
The ox danced and danced
But now he's lying
Flat on his back!

Sebastião:
Oh, my friend,
The lord's ox is dead.

Mateus:
Oh, come on you fool,
The ox has spent himself.
Now he is tired;
Use the tip of the goad
And you'll see how he rises
And throws you to the
   ground.

Scene III

(The same, the doctor, captain of the forest [capitão do mato], Sra. Frigideira the landlord's lady, Caterina and the priest. The ox lies on the ground, Fidelis flees, the captain of the fields is summoned to hold the ox still, while the doctor heals it. The priest comes to marry off Caterina.)

Mateus:
My ox is dead.
What will become of me?
Send for another
There is Piaui.

Amo:
Oh, Mateus, where is the ox?

Mateus:
Lord, the ox is dead.
(Mateus distances himself from Amo)

Amo:
Oh, Mateus, go and call
The doctor so that he might
Cure my precious ox:
I would love to know from Fidelis
Where he has gone.
Oh, Sebastião, go quickly
Call the captain of the fields
See to it that Fidelis
Puts up with my presence.
(Doctor arrives and prepares to treat the ox with Amo.
Appearance of Sra. Frigideira, Caterina, and Sebastião, whom she wants to marry.
The priest enters.)

Priest:
Whoever sees me dancing
Does not think I'm crazy;
I'm not a priest, I'm a nothing;
I am unique, like the others.

Chorus:
Oh, people, is that
The function of a priest?
It is time for a wedding
Or maybe a confession.

Priest:
Strike the strings.
Beat the baton.
The function is now getting started
And will not stop again.

Doctor to Mateus:
Oh, Negro,
Your insolence
I knew it already.
When you had me called
It was for the people
And not for an ox.

Mateus:
Ah, uê, ah, uöê!
You'll be suitably paid.
(Capitão arrives with Fidelis and goes to seize him.)

Capitão:
I'll arrest you, black man.
I'll bind you in chains, you scoundrel.
You're finished, bastard.
(Fidelis is enchained)

Chorus:
Capitão of the fields,
See how the world turns.
He was in the forest in order
To capture the Negro
But the Negro clings to him.

Capitão:
I'm known far and wide
For a bravery which doesn't
    exist;
Just give me a scare
And I'm off in the other direc-
    tion.
(*End of the scene. Everyone sings.*
At the end of the play — after the

ox has been healed — the following
song is often performed:)

Rise up, ox.
Let's be on our way.
The day is breaking
And the rosy dawn glimmers.
ox has been healed —

Luiz da Câmara Cascudo remembered: 'On the entire Iberian penin-sula there is no comparable performance having this dramatic force, satirical expression, spontaneity in regard to social life, and improvisa-tion of dialogue.' Still, it is evident that the roots of the ox drama are to be sought on the Iberian peninsula, where the bull is not only the center of interest at bullfights, but is also present at a range of other festivals. A quick glance at other Latin American countries shows us the presence of the bull-cow-ox motif in the *toritos-danzas*. The sequence of the 'miracu-lous healing' of the ox has its parallel in the healing of a wounded sparrow (*pajaro guarandol*) in a Venezuelan danza. There are also indications of a possible African connection to the *kagba* ritual of the Senufo on the Ivory Coast. The focus of this initiation rite is the *nasolo*, a huge ox made out of wooden slats and spotted mats. But this ceremony symbolizes intellectual and physical perfection, and thus can hardly be compared to the bumba-meu-boi.

All actors in the ox play are masked and dressed up in costume. The ox is colorfully decorated, and his head is painted. Two men are concealed beneath the ox to direct its movements.

Toadas, chulas, xácaras, and *romances* are sung, accompanied by the rebeca, viola sertaneja, páfanos, zabumba and many different percus-sion instruments.

The bumba-meu-boi is generally performed in all parts of the country from the pro-yule period right up until carnival. Several regional variants are: the *boi de mamão* (Santa Catarina with fantastic ap-pearances), *boizinho* (abbreviated version without episodes), *boi bumba, reis de boi* (Espirito Santo), *adjunto e boi* (Bahia), *bumba à mulinha* (Minas), *mulinha de ouro/drome-dário* (Bahia), *cavalo marinho, boi de matraca, boi de zabumba* (Marahão), *boi de orquestra,* etc. The bumba-meu-boi often goes on for eight hours; plenty of cachaça is drunk, and several scenes may even have to be repeated due to their great popularity. Afterward the actors pass around the hat for their performance. Female roles, such as Dona Frigideira (ironically, *Mrs. Frying Pan*), are taken by men as well.

Kings, Warriors and Sailors

Several folklorists regard these caboclo and mestizo ox plays as belonging to the genre *reisado*. Reisado actually refers to the Festival of the Epiphany. In northern Brazil, however, it is no longer celebrated in this European form. The ox plays have taken its place or have become part of the reisado. In other localities Portuguese Christmas cantatas (*cantatas reis*) have combined with Afro-brazilian *congada* plays, thus adding a new reisado to the wealth of Christmas festivals in Brazil. The encounter between reisados and Amerindian-Portuguese cabo-clinho cults gave birth to the *guerreros folguedos*.

Whoever visits Brazil at Christmas will best be able to enjoy an extensive offering of popular festivities away from the big cities: *folias de reis* and *ternos e ranchos de reis* (representations of the three magi), or *pastorinhas* and *lapinhas* and such songs as *folias de divino* and *folias de reis*. The groups are called *ranchos* and *foliões*; their musicians are *ternos* and play guitar, sanfona, cavaquinho, pandeiro, *pistão* (trumpet) and marching drum.

Lapinha, *presépio* and *pastoris* are pastoral plays at the Christ Child's crib.

Bailes pastoris have scenic content: *bailes da tentação* (Satan abducts a gypsy woman who has bewitched a priest), *quatro partes do mundo* (conversation between continents) and *bailes de liberdade* (themes concerning freedom, despotism, peace, war and unity).

Many of these *ciclo natalino* (Christmas cycle) festivals end with a farewell:

> Oh, lords, masters of this house,
> So God would have it
> Until next year
> If I am still alive.

Brazilians have a special liking for sailors' epics and dramas of chivalry. In many reisados a sailor, Moorish king, or mounted knight celebrates his resurrection. The oldest historical theme from such dramatical festivals is known from Mexico and features the Emperor Charlemagne and the twelve peers. Camara Cascudo discovered that the first written version of this story appeared in Portuguese in 1615. The three Moorish princesses mentioned there (Floripes, Galiana and Angelica) still turn up today in the cast of characters in the *folguedos* of *chegança dos mouros* from Laranjeiras. There are even passages of the text of the romance of Charlemagne contained in it. The early directors of these originally Portuguese Moorish plays most certainly borrowed different episodes from other dramatic sources over the years and used them in their own productions, although disregarding the historical facts.

'Atraca, atraca, all clear to go ashore!' With this cry the chorus (called *Mar e Guerra*, Sea and War) announces the Moors' arrival in Sergipe. The Moors visit many other Brazilian cities each year in the *chegança dos mouros*, the *cavalhada*, in the *reis dos mouros*, in the sailor epic *Nau Catarineta*, in the *mouros* and *marujadas*. These *autos, folguedos* and *folganças* are often identical in detail. Sailors' epics and Moorish wars in the cheganças of northeastern Brazil are also related to one another. Participants are mariners of every rank and the Moorish king and his royal court. The sailors wear white uniforms with blue-and-gold braid. Dressed in a red robe and wearing a crown and other symbols of authority, the Moorish king enters onto a stage that has been erected either within the church or in front of it, or even on the beach.

The conspicuous master of ceremonies is the helmsman. As in the *batucada* of the samba school, he uses a small whistle to mark the beginning and end of the various scenes and musical parts. Spoken dialogue is interchanged with instrumental interludes and songs in responsory chant-form. Beatriz Dantas's research shows the *cheganças* to have been influenced both by the repertoire of Church song, as well as secular European melody and rhythm. In addition, there is evidence of songs that most definitely arose out of a tradition of Brazilian folklore, and those which were composed within the genre of *música erúdita*.

Marches, identified by the *toques* (number of main beats, or tempo), play an extensive role in the musical arrangement of the *cheganças*. Some examples are *marcha ligeira, marcha batida, marcha bailada* and *marcha lenta*. Instrumentation is scanty. Usually, only pandeiros are used. There is hardly a choreography to speak of, and the story line is very stiff and schematic. Everything takes place on board a Portuguese ship: all of a sudden, the enemy ship of the Moorish sultan comes into view. The sultan then comes on board, but refuses to allow himself to be baptized. A scuffle takes place, and the sultan loses. Sometimes he is baptized, sometimes decapitated. Other episodes dealing with smugglers, bad weather or mutiny are occasionally added.

When battles with the Moors are lacking and there are no heathens to be baptized, the play is then called *nau caterineta* or *marujada*. In many localities the mariners drag little ships behind them in the procession; it saves them from having to erect big sets. Moors and Christians also attack each other in the *cavalhadas*, based on the Portuguese plays of chivalry from the seventeenth century. Horses and harness, however, are made of cardboard. On the whole, the Christian-Moorish dramas are neither identical with their Iberian ancestors nor with any other later creations in Latin America. It is impossible to miss the irony that shimmers through the elaborate costumes and sets. The very same caboclos, mulattos and mestizos whose forefathers were once converted to Christianity now appear in the role of evangelizing disciples. Such irony was surely understood during colonial times, even if it emerged only between the lines or in gestures and hints.

We also cannot seriously assume that the principle actors and supernumeraries simply accepted without thinking all these scenes put on by the Catholic priests and their charges (although initially they were more effective), glorifying and exalting the superiority of their colonial masters. One could look at it in this way: by documenting the values and symbols of the oppressor through play, text, costumes and props, they could well have felt that they were robbing their rulers of their exclusive claim to these values, in addition to making fun of them through the nuances of the presentation.

This might help to explain the fact that the Christian king of the *congadas* and *congos* is ostensibly an African potentate — even if this role is seldom played by a black man. Such congadas are a kind of street theater performed both inside and outside the church on the holiday honoring the black patron saint, São Benedito. The plot comprises the selection and enthronement of the Congo kings, processions, liturgical stories and battle scenes as a result of the enemy's refusal to be baptized. African traditions are included using Iberian dramatic models.

The Rei do Congo, his princes, dukes, secretaries and the rest of the royal court now enter, dressed in splendid robes copied from the haute couture of the Portuguese royal house during the colonial period. Along with them is Queen Ginga and her tribal chieftains and warriors, the *conguinhos*. African names are no rarity here. The Rei do Congo is sometimes called *zambi*. After entering, the actors line up in two facing rows to the left and right of the Rei. He delivers an opening address in honor of the patron saint. Drum rhythms then summon the nobility to the dance floor. The strains of accordion and fiddle are sometimes heard as well. Envoys sent by the Queen of Angola are then announced. They inform the Rei in no uncertain terms that he must withdraw from his Congo kingdom. The king is not pleased with this demand and thereupon declares war upon the Angolan Queen. The royal court quickly gathers in military ceremony to prepare for battle. The ensuing war is presented in dance, with single combatants fighting it out. The Angolan envoys lose, of course, but the Rei do Congo bestows his royal pardon and requests the head ambassador to finally get down to the real business of his visit. The ambassador surprises everyone with the announcement that they had actually heard about this festival and would very much like to take part in it. Musicians and dancers appear and dance in honor of Saõ Benedito. The ambassador and other envoys take part and then depart. A grand procession, in which dance and song express the notion of brotherhood, brings the whole presentation to a close. The individual sections of the story are divided into strict choreographic sequences.

Song and dialogue are also in part recited in African languages of ancient times:

> O' gingana, O' gingana, O' ginganoé
> Ginganoé, gilanguelo, O' gibbagaloé

A variant of this Congo spectacle (but without the crowning ceremony) is the *ticumbí* the festival of Espirito Santo in the North. All actors are dressed in white. Colorful ribbons lie across their long white shirts, and upon their heads the participants wear white kerchiefs laced with bright flowers and paper ribbons. Church dramaturgy prescribes a competition between the two kings for the right to stage the festival of São Benedito. The Rei Bamba loses out in the end to the Rei Congo. The ticumbí dance is performed to the accompaniment of *chocalhos* (rattles) *pandeiros* (tambourines) and viola. Everyday themes from the people's lives are inserted into the texts. This helps keep the performance from getting lost somewhere in an indefinite past.

Ticumbís and *bailes do congos* are, according to Guilherme Santos Neves' *Espirito Santo* a 'sung or narrated inventory of local Brazilian or world happenings. The ticumbí is like a narrated newspaper, full of fate, destiny and events' (G. Santos Neves).

Once again we encounter here the master of ceremonies with his *apito* (whistle). An extra large, star-shaped *maracás* (rattle) belongs to his insignia during *cambinda* festivals.

Danças and bailes de congos take place primarily in July (Festa de Santana) and October (Festa de N. S. do Rosario). Desafios — the folksinger's song contests — warm up the festivities. In 1954 an association of Congados de N. S. do Rosario was founded in Minas Gerais, made up of representatives from over three-hundred local congada groups.

Closely related to the congos but more African-like in appearance are the *maracatú* festivals. *Porta-bandeiras* (standard bearers), *dama-de-paço* (carriers of the *calunga* puppets), *Baianas* (Bahian women), caboclos, *reis* and *reinhas* (kings and queens), all take part in this Afro-European co-production. The song form heard most often is the toada. *Bombo* drums, *zabumba, ganzá, chocalhos* and *agôgô* follow the beat of the *atabaque* drums.

The afoxé groups in Bahia refer back to their African roots with their displays, especially to African gods like Oxúm.

The *moçambique* (in Goias, Minas, São Paulo, Rio Grande do Sul) is reminiscent of a certain African dance having a combat-like character (the choreography includes mock fencing with sticks). This variant of African-influenced dramatic dance provides for a snake-like choreography by the gorgeously attired participants, as well as the simulation of traditional funeral processions as they were once practiced by slaves shipped to Brazil from Mozambique. Such processions remained confined, however, to the closed family circle. Later on, descendants within the same nation were allowed to participate. The moçambique was, according to Camara Cascudo, a collective dance during the years of slavery, but has lost all traces of its African heritage today. Furthermore, the Brazilian moçambique is entirely unknown in Africa. According to Cascudo, only at festivals honoring N. S. do Rosario in northern Portugal can one encounter something comparable.

The *dança de São Gonçalo*, found in the south and southeast of Brazil, is of pure Portuguese origin as well. Gonçalo is a Portuguese saint who died on January 10, 1259, in Amarante, and became the patron saint of women ready for marriage. Since popular art always depicted him as a dancer and lutist, guitarists also made him their patron saint.

> Fun or curiosity are never reason enough to dance. A vow is the only real reason. It is a holy dance. Only he who is able to pay for his vow may request the singers and dancers of São Gonçalo to come, oblige them to perform, and afterward distribute small gifts. The poor fellow who cannot afford such a do shows up at the next man's festival. There he receives a *jornada* 'salary' to fulfill his vow, whether he is sharing the costs or not. Saturday is chosen. The festival usually begins during the day and ends at sunset. Hardly any masters would have dared reject their slaves' request to attend a São Gonçalo dance when it concerned the fulfillment of a vow (Câmara Cascudo, *Dicionário do Folclore Brasileira*).

The *dança de São Gonçalo* corresponds to the *fandango rufado* (with which it is occasionally confused). Foot-stamping and hand-clapping provide the rhythmic accompaniment to the toada and moda melodies. In between, one can hear the particular songs of this festival day (*terços de São Gonçalo*).

Many other folk performances fill the Brazilian folkloric atlas. Based on their particular features, almost all of them can be assigned to one of the above-mentioned groups. For example, the *quilombos* (primarily found in Alagoas, historical representation of the battles of Palmares) and various other *autos* of Amerindian and half-caste tradition (*caiapós, caboclinhos, caboclos de itaparica, tauias, cordões de bichos de pássaros*) belong to the *reisado* genre.

The dates and times of the folk plays have evolved historically in such a way that they orient themselves largely around the Church's calendar. Most festivals occur between Christmas and Easter, and their frequency increases steadily after Christmas until a hiatus arrives on Ash Wednesday. In addition to the official holidays of the Church year there are numerous festivals dedicated to local saints and local happenings. The same brotherhoods or groups organize the folkloristic performances in their locality each year. Respectable town citizens often have to spend large sums of money for the festival to take place. In many areas the Church is hardly involved anymore. A marked religiosity in many of Brazil's rural regions has given rise in places to strange forms of religious fanaticism. Thus the hinterland, which colonial priests used to avoid as the devil's domain, has given birth to its own independent sphere of culture. The folkloristic performances represent the high point of the year.

Musical Instruments

In the initial period of Brazil's colonization the musical instruments belonging to the three ethnic groups there stood at very different stages of development. Sixteenth-century Portugal was already familiar with the organ, clavichord, lute, viola, gamba, trombone, shawn, harp, etc. The Africans brought with them a number of percussion instruments and simple melodic instruments, such as the fiddle. Amerindian instrumentation, on the other hand, knew nothing of string instruments. It was limited to various drums, rattles, musical bows and simple flutes, all similar in kind.

As instrumental accompaniment to song and dance most easily enabled communication to take place between different peoples in the colonial period — despite the still existing language barriers — a very lively interchange soon developed. The Jesuits improved the instruments of the Amerindians and taught many of them to take part in liturgical ceremonies on the organ, harpsichord and bassoon. African slaves began to play brass and string instruments (given to them by their colonial masters) in their own small music and percussion groups and occasionally even played the colonizers' music in order to ease their

Calendar Excerpt from Pernambuco

January
1 New Year's Bumba-meu-boi (B-M-B) and pastoril
6 Dia de Reis (Epiphany)
8 Feast of São Gonçalo in Itapissuma
8 Feast of São Sebastião (B-M-B, pastoril and mamulengo (Puppet Show)

February
2 Feast of N.S. do Desterro (Agrestina) with quadrilhas, xaxados and maracatú

March
   Quaresma (Lent) with performances of *Malhação de Judas* and *Serra Velho*
19 Feast of S. João (B-M-B, pastoril)

April
3 Feast of N.S. dos Prazeres in Jaboatão (F. da Pitomba)
23 Feast of São Jorge, syncretized with Ogum, war god of the Pernambuco Xangô cult

May
   Month of festivals honoring the Virgin Mary

June
3 Feast of São Felix in Recife
23 Feast of São João and syncretic cults (Xangô)
24 Feast of João with folguedos, cocos, forró, xaxado
29 Feast of S. Pedro with traditional fire games

July
15 Feast for the Northeastern cowboys (vagueiras) in Serrita. Violeiros, cantadores, aboios, desafios and *Missa do Vaqueiro*

August
6 Feast of Senhor do Bom Jesu in Araripina

24 Dia de São Bartolomeu (Exú in the syncretic cults). Noite das Garrafadas (bottle night). The Fulniôs Indian's *Walk to Ouricuri* with totemistic customs also begins in this month.

September
7 Feast of Santa Quitéria in Flexeiras, with thousands of pilgrims, bands, fireworks and festivities
7 Feast of Santa Teresinha in Sitio dos Moreiras, with novenas, processions, zabumbas, violeiros, etc.
27 Feast of Santos Cosme e Damião in Igaraçu. Syncretized with Ibeji, tutelary goddess of children

October
   Feast of Inhame, commemorates African harvest rituals.

November
2 Feast of Iansã of syncretic cults (corresponds to Santa Barbara)
3 Feast of Santo Antonio, with cirandas, cocos, violeiros, etc.
17 Feast of São Benedito in Goiana
17 Feast of in homage of Nossa Senhora de Escada, with coco-de-roda
19 Feast of Santana

December
7 Large festival at the *terreiros* of the syncretic cults for Iemanjá (N.S. da Conceição). Ritual dances and more.
13 Feast of Santa Luzia in Caruaru, bandas de pifanos
24 Christmas Eve Natal with Pastoril, B-M-B, lapinhas, presépios, missa do Galo at midnight
31 Big end-of-year syncretic festival honoring Oxalás (Senhor de Bonfim)

lot as slaves. But from the very beginning, musicality was also an opportunity for the oppressed to improve their own social standing within their community.

In any case, musically talented slaves were in great demand. A newspaper ad of 1819 asks, 'Who wants to buy a slave who plays piano and marimba?' On the other hand, Tinhorão's *Pequenha Historia da Música Popular* tells us that slaves made themselves more easily identifiable this way. Escaped slaves were described in newspaper lists like this: 'Plays rabeca with his left hand, likes to drink ...,' or 'Plays fiddle, can read ...' Many plantation owners exploited their slaves' delight in music by supporting the creation of orchestras that they could then rent out for money. From the travelogues of Spix and Martius at the beginning of the nineteenth century we gain detailed information about musicians and instruments. For example, 'A private orchestra for vocal and instrumental music put together by the successor to the throne (D. Pedro II) out of Indian mestizos and Negroes is sufficient to prove the musical talent of Brazilians.'

Another travel account from colonial times (1583) mentions that a particular Catholic monk had been a first-rate berimbau player (the Portuguese Jew's harp is most certainly meant here, and not the African musical bow). Musicians playing pandeiros, pifanos and tambores are also mentioned. In 1610 mention was even made of bands with thirty musicians, and in 1697 the Church opened the first music school in Olinda. Finally, we know from the year 1752 that the governor of Marinhão state offered the Amerindians 500 Jew's harps in a barter transaction. At the same time restaurants in Rio were posting fiddle players at the entrance — usually blind slaves, say the reports.

The most important of these instruments are described below.

String Instruments

The most widely used string instruments are the *rabeca* and *viola* in popular folk music, the *bandolim* and cavaquinho in refined folklore and urban instrumental music, and the guitar in popular music.

The rabeca (or *rebeca*: the *rebecão* is a larger model) is a type of fiddle, a rustic violin if you will and is, in fact, the violin's historical precursor. A small bow is guided over four strings tuned in fifths, producing a raw, nasal sound of mideastern character. The rabeca is played as accompaniment to romantic songs and cantigas and at the folkloristic performances of cheganças, cavalo-marinhos, fandangos, etc. Its function is primarily as accompaniment, it is seldom played solo.

The viola is the violeiro's and folksinger's chief instrument. It is similar to the guitar, though in place of a single sound-hole it has several circular openings. It is furnished with ten or twelve strings, and two strings are turned and plucked at a time. There are also violas having five pairs of strings and a middle string (called the *turina*). The viola's sound approximates that of a rustic harpsichord. Those who play it have a wealth of expressive possibilities, ranging from vibrato to portamento to a simultaneous percussive effect. The viola is probably the first stringed instrument to arrive in Brazil from Portugal.

Variations on the viola are the *viola sertaneja* (most common), *viola paulista*, *viola mineira* and the seldom played *viola indígena*, with its three catgut strings. Violeiros usually tune their instrument so that it lies somewhat above its normal tonal range. But the first pair of strings is tuned an octave lower in order to adjust to the pitch of the singer's voice. 'Before the violeiros begin their improvisation, they strum the toada as a melody for their verses,' writes A. J. Madureira. The singer follows with a stanza, his accompanist answers, and after that there is a short instrumental interlude known as the *baião* or *ponteado*. The viola is played both as accompaniment and for improvising solo parts.

Bandolim and *cavaquinho* are the aristocrats of the popular stringed instruments; the guitar is king. The particular significance of these instruments is highlighted by the fact that rabeca and viola virtuosos usually remain unknown to the greater public, while the guitar, cavaquinho and bandolim — all associated with the names of excellent musicians — have gained entry into the fields of popular and even classical music.

The bandolim stems from the family of lute instruments and represents a further development of the Neopolitan mandolin in Portugal (where the name was also assimilated accordingly). By the eighteenth century the bandolim had also found a home in Brazil. The four string pairs of the bandolim are tuned like four violin strings (sol, re, la, mi), and are played with a plectrum. The bandolim, with its predominantly soloistic function, is played in such European-influenced musical forms as the *polca, xotis, valsa, maxixe, modinha, fandango* and *choro*. The most renowned Brazilian virtuoso was Jacob Bittencourt (Jacob de Bandolim, 1918–1969). Some contemporary bandolim players worth mentioning are Joel Nascimento, Deo Rian, Luperce Miranda and Evandro.

The *cavaquinho*, too, made the trip from Portugal to Brazil two hundred years ago. Originally known as the *machete*, it soon changed its name to cavaquinho (a colloquial expression for guitar). It looks like a mini-guitar with four strings that are tuned in fourths (re, sol, si, re). It is also played with a plectrum. But what is important, according to Waldir Azevedo, is *how* one holds the plectrum: the strings (and not the

Origins of some Brazilian Instruments

European*	African	Amerindian
String instruments		
viola, lute, tiorba, bandurrilha, rebeca, rebecão, citara, guitar, bandolim, cavaquinho	berimbau (monochordal); later banjo, fiddle	
Wind instruments		
shawn, trumpet, cornet, flutes, clarinet	flutes	flutes, apitos, trombetas
Percussion		
pandeiro, bass drum, cymbals, tambourine	atabaques (different) sizes) cabeça, güiro, etc.	tambores, guizos, maracás, chocalhos
Diverse		
piano, sanfona, accordion, Jew's harp	cuica, marimba, afoxê	

*to the extent they are used in folkloric and popular music

plectrum) must be made to vibrate. Manuel Antonio de Almeida reports that during Whit-Sunday processions in the nineteenth century small groups of boys would play shepherd's instruments, pandeiros, machetes and *tamboris* in barbershop bands.

The cavaquinho first secured its place within MPB as an instrument to accompany the lundu. Later it could be heard with different songs and dances in urban centers (as with the bandolim), and today it can also be found in various ternos and conjuntos all over the country. At the end of the last century the cavaquinho and bandolim first took on solo parts as well. The best-known cavaquinho virtuoso was Waldir Azevedo, a choro musician who was the first to play entire melodies on only one string ('Brasileirinho', 'Delicado,' etc.). Other important virtuosos are Waldir Silva, Benedito Costa, Jonas, Canhoto, Valmar Gama de Amorim, Zé Meneses and Paulinho da Viola.

The music group Trio Elétrico makes its home in Bahia. Its members — Armadinho, Aroldo, and Osmar — amplify and distort their acoustic cavaquinhos (and other stringed instruments) with the help of a wah-wah pedal and other electric effects common to rock music. They are generally considered to be part of Bahian folklore, while their sons and their sons' friends — A Cor Do Som, Moraes Moreira and Pepeu Gomez — utilize the same principle of sound in rock and pop music (but with the guitar instead).

The *guitar* traveled from North Africa through Portugal to Brazil. Emilio Pujol believes that a Greco-Roman variety had already been extant, which, like its Arabian counterpart later, served as a model for guitar construction during the colonial period. For a long time a rustic version — the *viola* — was the only sort that found wide use in Brazil. With the beginning of the romantic period, when modinhas and lundus were becoming fit for 'proper' society, cançioneiros and sereseiros started singing more frequently to the guitar. Unfortunately, colonial sources can hardly offer us any help on this matter, because their authors were mostly unfamiliar with correct terminologies and had trouble distinguishing *violas, guitarras* (which could also have a mandolin form), *rabecas*, and *violões* from one another.

The first Brazilian guitarist of importance is said to have been the mulatto João Furtado. This seventeenth-century Baiano artist performed his songs with a romantic accent to the accompaniment of his guitar. Since then, MPB has achieved popularity outside Brazil especially because of its guitarists. Instrumental music is not bound by language barriers. Beginning in the fifties, João Gilberto helped awaken the interest of an entire generation of musicians in the guitar. The number of excellent guitarists around today is correspondingly large:

Baden Powell, Sebastião Tapajós, Toquinho, Rosinha de Valença, Paulinho Nogueira, Laurindo Almeida, Luiz Bonfá, Egberto Gismonti and others.

Today the guitar is an instrument played by most composers and performers of MPB. It is, of course, indispensable for the sambistas of both the old and the new schools. It would be difficult to find a *samba-canção* without its guitar or cavaquinho companion. In the *samba-batucada*, on the other hand, it would have no chance of making any headway. The cavaquinho would prevent that: it may be small, but it sure is loud. Since Joaquim Callado's day the guitar has also had an indispensable part in playing the harmonies and bass line in choro music. Some important guitarists who also developed into prominent soloists in this genre are Dilhermando Reis, Cesar Faria, Garoto and Meira. A guitar with seven strings (the *violão-sete-cordas*) was especially developed for choro music. The musicians most in demand recently for this variation are Dino (Horondino Silva) and Rafael Rabello.

Ponteado (plucking), *repinicado* (picking) and *rasgueado* (scraping) are terms used to characterize certain ways of playing the guitar and viola. They refer mainly to the singer's instrumental accompaniment or to the transition between verses. Many guitarists are identifiable by their technique alone. Depending on how an instrument is played (and constructed), we can speak of the *viola* in rural music, the *violão* in popular and classical music, and the *guitarra (elétrica)* exclusively in pop and rock music.

Little is known about the *banjo* in Brazil. The great number of Iberian stringed instruments probably left the lute little room to develop further into a banjo. The only banjoist of any repute, Donga, is still remembered today as composer of the first officially registered samba (1917) and as a musician in Pixinguinha's band Os Oito Batutas.

The Portuguese word *berimbau* denotes both the Jew's harp of European origin as well as the African *uruçungó*, generally referred to as berimbau in Brazil, which the Bantus brought with them from Angola. This instrument from the monochordal, or musical bow, family is made from a bendable stick to whose end a wire is attached. It is stretched in such a way that the whole construction takes the form of a hunting bow. A hollowed-out, half-open gourd is fastened to the lower third of the bow with the opening turned away from the stick and facing the player. The fastening cord is tied around both the stick and wire. The player grasps stick and wire with his left hand, leaving thumb and index finger, which hold a large coin hovering above the string. The right hand, within which is found a small basket rattle (*caxixi*) containing dried seeds and shells, strikes the string with a small, thin stick. While the right hand is striking the string, the left lightly touches it with the coin in a counter movement. This combination of striking the string together with the coin's contact (pressing, lightly touching, or held above) results in the berimbau's typically nasal, whirring sound. The player can influence the sound by varying the distance of the gourd from his body. This is the common berimbau found at the Bahian capoeira.

Berimbau, rhythmic figure

The *marimbau*, or *berimbau de lata*, is better known in the North and in the country's interior. The acoustical principle is the same, the only difference being that it is played in a horizontal position. The string is stretched between one or two tin cans (*latas*) which are fastened to a wooden board. The player touches the strings with a piece of glass. While the Bahian berimbau player is able to modulate the pitch only to a very minimal degree, by applying pressure to the cord, the berimbau de lata player has the option of sliding his glass piece horizontally across the string as he wishes, thereby effecting a change in pitch.

Despite their monochordal character, both types of berimbaus offer the musician an abundance of possible sounds, including different percussive effects.

The marimbau is present at almost all Northeastern folk festivals. Its sound is coarser than that of the Bahian berimbau and, much like the rabeca, has a Mediterranean ring to it.

Some noted berimbau players in MPB are Onias Camardelli, Naná Vasconsellos and Djalma Corrêa.

Wind Instruments

It is not necessary to go into any detail about traditional European wind instruments such as the clarinet, trumpet, saxophone or shawm. Although adopted by the Amerindian and African musicians, they are nevertheless atypical of Brazilian music. On the other hand, flutes and pipes of every sort, introduced both by the Portuguese and by the Africans and Amerindians, deserve our attention. Sometimes it is impossible to discover an aerophone line of descent, however the existence of primitive flutes and pipes among the Amerindians at the time of their conquest has been well documented. Some aerophones still used by primitive tribes living in the Amazon today include:

— Bamboo flutes with curved or straight, thin funnel-shaped ends.

— Ocarinas made of beeswax or clay.

— Small pipes made of birds' bones which are sometimes strung together on a thread to form a *colar-de-apito*, thus serving as a fetish necklace.

Flutes of the same size are also bound together to produce a double-horn effect. One can also find flutes one or two meters long with a deep, almost otherworldly sound. These *uruá*, as they are called by the Kamayurá tribe, are holy tribal instruments, forever kept from the sight of women in a special flute house. These wind instruments are decorated with feathers and other accessories corresponding to a tribe's level of development.

In 1645 Frei Manuel Callado reported that he had heard black musicians with horns, flutes and atabaques making music together harmoniously. The horns he heard were most likely trumpet-like, wooden wind instruments that produced their sound not by being blown into, like a flute, but rather with air forced through the lips.

It is not very difficult to imagine that Amerindians and Africans were quite prepared to give up their own traditional instruments, at least those that were relatively unimportant in a religious context, when the Europeans offered them something better, both in terms of sound and quality of construction. So what remained were chiefly those instruments that could not be replaced by the Europeans in this way, or which were indispensable because of their importance in religious rituals. Some examples are the berimbau, the cuica, atabaque drums and uruá flutes. Africans and Amerindians living in Jesuit missions in coastal areas sometimes tried out different Portuguese flutes and fifes. Other Portuguese instruments, however — the *gaita* (bagpipe) for one — never could take hold in Brazil.

In Brazil today 'gaita' refers to the harmonica. Marcus Perreira told of attending a concert put on by several hundred *gaitistas* in a small city in Rio Grande do Sul. And it is a fact that you can find harmonica players everywhere in the region south of São Paulo. Two gaitistas from Rio de Janeiro are well known in MPB, namely Edu da Gaita (died 1982) and Maurício Einhorn. The latter is also a successful composer, having written several pieces during the bossa nova epoch.

Pifanos occupy a special place among today's flutes and pipes. The characteristic sound of so many orchestras in the North and Northeast is due to them alone. Pifanos are small transverse flutes made from taboco wood, a kind of bamboo. They have seven holes, the embouchure, and six openings for the fingers. They are always played in pairs, by two musicians in parallel form. Guerra Peixe explains: 'When the first flute plays the basic melody, the second follows parallel in thirds or sixths. Sometimes you can also hear harmonic intervals in fourths and fifths, and even once in a while rapid, although not harsh dissonances.'

Dois Pífeiros (Two Flutes) — (after Sigueira)

Only in the *ternos de pifanos* and in other local orchestras do the pifanos take up solo parts. Improvisation is frequent.

Flutist Joaquim Callado enriched urban popular music in the middle of the last century with a new instrumentation consisting of flute (Callado's famous ebony flute), cavaquinho and guitar. This was the beginning of the *choro*, soon to develop into a new musical genre of great artistic sophistication.

Flutes of every kind, and particularly transverse flutes, comprise the third pillar of Brazilian instrumental music, along with the strings and percussion. Since Callado's time MPB's history has been filled with great flutists. Pixinguinha, Altamiro Carrilho, Copinha, Carlos Poyares, Manoel Gomez, Benedito Lacerda and, more recently, Hermeto Pascoal are but a few of them.

Percussion

The percussion instruments played in Brazil today are so numerous that it would be impossible to treat them all here. The 'African connection' has special significance. It is interesting to note, for example, how the pandeiro reached the Iberian Peninsula from North Africa before the discovery of Brazil, quickly becoming a national folk music instrument. Later it was assimilated by African slaves in Lisbon, who then brought it with them to Brazil. As an Afro-Portuguese import, it met up there with slaves newly arrived from Africa. The pandeiro was also integrated into Afro-Brazilian cults. Vinicius de Moraes's 'Canto de Caboclo Pedra Preta' (music by Baden Powell) narrates just such a story. A caboclo observes that the pandeiro does not want him to leave. This is his way of resolving the eternal conflict between love and sex, and its thorny companion, jealousy. The pandeiro — the male element — is dead-set against the caboclo's designs. For in his role as God's helper, he wishes to drag the guitar — the female element — down into the underworld of black magic and mystical sexual rites. Pedra Preta sings about the impossibility of trying to escape one's fate. The pandeiro must drum, and the guitar must play. As the rooster crows, the caboclo's magic hour has come. He disappears, defeated. From now on, the guitar will assume its part in the black mass. Indeed, it will become a priestess of the cult.

The meaning of such a drama will not be completely lost on the foreign visitor to Brazil. He will understand, for instance, those sequences of the performance where the pandeiro player holds his instrument between the outspread legs of the female dancer, as if it were being filled with female secretions.

The pandeiro is played for all types of batuques. It is customarily held in the left hand, with several fingers in contact with the instrument's underside serving to accentuate the rhythm or to modulate the pitch. The right hand beats out the main rhythm, with the thumb accenting the main beat; the fingers syncopate in pearling succession. Like circus jugglers, experienced pandeiro players can bring off the most amazing rhythmic feats. Often the thumb is slightly moistened and drawn over the skin to produce a constant clattering, rolling sound.

We would label the pandeiro a tamborine. But the *tamborim* in Brazil is something else — a kind of small pandeiro about fifteen centimeters in diameter, without jingles. It is struck on its rim and skin with a small stick, while the hand that is holding it can apply varying degrees of pressure from underneath to stretch the skin.

The main drums of African extraction are the *atabaques, tambús* and *candongüeiros*. Tambú and candongüeiro are Bantu drums, while the atabaques stem from the Yoruba people. One can find them in all kinds of African-influenced music (that is, sambas, jongos, corimas). Atabaques are holy instruments within the context of Afro-Brazilian cults. There are even initiation rites for these drums. Their importance results from the fact that the Orixás are summoned by the toques played on the atabaque; the spirits communicate with the cult community through the drums.

Zabumba refers both to a large, commonly used drum in northern Brazil, as well as to a percussion group made up of different instruments (*bombo, surdo*, snare drum and cymbals). Cylindrical drums covered with skin on each side are common throughout Latin America. They most probably borrowed the form from drums found in earlier military bands. The playing principle is nearly always the same. One hand plays a beat with a muffled drumstick, the other hand answers. The second stroke is executed in such a way as to immediately deaden the vibration from the skin after contact. A natural swing arises out of this two-beat combination. In addition to these bass drums which are carried by the drummer around his neck, there are a great number of different-sized marching drums (*caixas*). Often you can see a musician drumming with his left hand and playing the flute with his right. The surdos played in samba music are usually fashioned from metal plates.

The *agôgô, onguê, reco-reco, ganzá, maracá, chocalho* and *afochê* belong to the idiophone family. The agôgô, of West African origin, consists of two metal bells joined on their thin ends by a curved metal rod. It is played with a metal drumstick.

Reco-reco refers to a class of wooden and metal scrapers played by drawing a stick over a row of notches or metal slots. Of Portuguese descent, it would be hard to find even two instruments of this class that are identical in the folkloric domain, as they are so easily made by hand.

An extensive range of instruments produce their sounds with seeds, shells, or pearls. Hollowed-out gourds or coconuts can be filled or enclosed with all kinds of rattling objects. Some instruments from this class are the *ganzá, afochê* or *afoxé, cabaça* and *chocalho* (and variations, such as the *xique-xique* or the *piano-de-cuia*).

The *marimba* and *balafon* belong to the idiophone family as well. They consist of wooden bars of varying size and pitch which are either strung around the player's neck or fastened to an upright stand. This instrument is a rarity in Brazilian music. Its sound is often amplified by placing calabashes under the bars. Another instrument from this family to reach Brazil from Africa is the *sanzá*. It consists of small wooden planks within which metal tongues of differing lengths are fastened. They are struck on one side in a suspended hanging position.

The chief percussion instrument used by Brazil's indigenous tribes is the *maracá*. It consists of a gourd, turtle shell or large nut filled with grain seed or shells. Hans Staden offered the following description regarding the deeper significance of this rattle after returning from his adventurous trip to Brazil in 1557:

> They marched through the countryside ... and claimed that a spirit had visited them and bestowed them with sacred powers, and that every rattle — the maracás — could speak, if they wanted it to. So it should therefore be invested with power, too.... Then each of them proclaims his desire that his rattle be bestowed with

> power.... As soon as they are all together, the shaman takes each
> maracá and fumigates it with an herb they call *pitin*. He then holds
> it up to his mouth, rattles it and says to it, 'Né cora.' 'Speak, and
> allow yourself to be heard if you are in there.' He then says a word
> rapidly in a high voice, so that it is difficult to tell whether he
> speaks it, or the rattle.... Then each person takes his rattle back,
> calls it 'dear son,' and builds a small hut in which to place it....
> These are their gods.

Johann Emanuel Pohl attended the Festival of Saint Eufigenia in
1821. He reports:

> One Negro instrument consists of a bamboo tube one and a half
> yards in length. Another tube is passed back and forth over the
> notches carved along the entire length of the first tube, producing
> a peculiar, unpleasant sound. They also use small tambourines
> and a large four-cornered instrument, two inches thick, which is
> covered with skin on both sides. It is about one square foot in size
> and is hit with a piece of wood. It produces a bright, sonorous
> tone.... They also have another round, drum-like instrument,
> somewhat over a half foot in length and a half foot in diameter.
> The instrument is covered with a cloth, and by rubbing the fingers
> over its surface, it produces deep, melancholy tones.

The last instrument that Pohl describes is probably a *cuica*, known for
a long time not only to the Africans but also in Europe (e. g., the North
German friction drum). A wooden stick is fixed to the middle of the
cuica's skin, which is done when the skin is wet, turned inward within
the metal frame. The player rubs the stick with a moist rag within the
cylinder to produce the sound. He can change the pitch by applying
light pressure to the skin with his other hand. In other parts of Brazil the
cuica is also called *puita, guica, roncador* or *fungador*. These instruments
are used especially to accompany the samba and related forms, seldom
though in syncretic spheres. Inventive cuica players have more recently
added amplifying horns to expand the cuica's sound.

A very important percussion instrument found in many varieties of
music is the *triangle*. One hand hits the metal; the hand holding the
triangle alternatively grasps and releases the metal, thus producing a
tone that varies between bright and clear, and muted.

Like their Latin American brothers, Brazilians are masters of the art
of continually inventing new percussion instruments. There are a
number of Brazilian instruments you will not find in any of the standard
works on folklore. The *sorongo, mangueira, brinquedos das crianças* and *urina*
are but a few of them. They are the creations of the Rio inventor Pedro

Sorongo (born Pedro Mello dos Santos). Packed away in dozens of boxes in his Shanty on the Morro Santa Tereza are all of Pedro's musical inventions from the past decades. Pedro had to learn to control himself, since he can transform almost anything placed in his hands into rhythm and melody. For instance, he once took eight plastic whistles meant for kids, mounted them on a metal plate, tuned them chromatically and attached small bellows to the mouthpieces. He then beat to a rhythm. Another time he soldered together two metal urinals, filled them with oil, closed them up and produced an almost celestial, electronic sound as he hit them with a felt mallet. His most popular invention earned him the name Sorongo. It consisted of eight large metal kettledrums with a special (secret) skin covering. He has even constructed bamboo tubes with sockets for an electro-acoustical sound pickup. Pedro is of course in great demand in Rio. When he enters a studio, he drags along several bags containing hundreds of different objects. He can then choose whatever best suits the title being recorded, depending on sound and arrangement requirements. Often he just leaves his bags outside and does it all with his voice alone. You could swear you were hearing pandeiros, cuicas, parrots and a whole array of Amazonian wildlife.

Among the most important Brazilian percussionists in MPB are Naná Vasconsellos, Airto Moreira, Nenê, Marçal, Jorginho, Djalma Corrêa, Jackson do Pandeiro, Eliseu and Dotor, together with Paulinho da Costa and Dom Um Romão, both living in the United States.

Diverse Instruments

The *sanfona* (from the Portuguese for hurdy-gurdy), an accordion of European tradition, is known everywhere in Brazil. It occurs in folkloric as well as in popular music, from the simplest type with only eight basses to the most technically developed. The sanfona plays solo parts and accompaniment in the Northeast and South. Rhythmically and harmonically it is a suitable companion for the rabeca, viola and pifano. The sanfona's sound is also typical for *forrós, xaxados, quadrilles* and *chamamés* in *música sertaneja*. Its most popular musician was Luiz Gonzaga, whose baiões represented an especially important contribution to MPB in the forties. He also popularized the accordion among young musicians in the years prior to the bossa nova epoch. Gonzaga discovered and promoted the career of the sertão musician, Dominguinhos. Chiquinho da Acordeon (actually, Romeu Seibel) is of German descent. In his hometown, Rio, he developed an electronic accordion that enabled him to reproduce the richly textured sound of the electronic organ, synthesizer and electric piano. Another very popular musician in Brazil is Sivuca, also from the northeast but now living in Rio. Sivuca spent many years outside Brazil including, as he let on to me, time spent playing in a bar in Wiesbaden, West Germany. Most important, however was the time he spent as musical arranger for Harry Belafonte. He returned to Brazil with valuable new experience and know-how as a musician and arranger. It is interesting to note that after years of doing concerts and records in a pop-jazz repertoire Sivuca has been able to make the switch to presenting forrós and xaxados in concert and on disc throughout Brazil. In 1990, a festival in Gonzaga's hometown, Exú, brought together and celebrated for the first time hundreds of sanfoneiros of the Sertão.

The South remains to be mentioned. There the sanfona (also called *acordeón*) is the favorite instrument of the gauchos and their *rancheiras, bugios, galpões* and *chotes*. A folk song from the region, such as the 'Boi Barroso,' would hardly be possible without the accordion. In the latter half of the eighties, an accordionist from the south, Renato Borghetti, became well-known throughout Brazil. Borghetti plays the *gaita ponto*, a type of concertina with a 'keyboard' of buttons like the bandoneon. Borghetti says of his music, which also shows the influence of the Argentine Astor Piazzolla, 'My music is instrumental gaucho music, it is jazz as a philosophy — but I will never lose the characteristics of my country.'

The accordion occupies an important place in Latin American music outside Brazil as well. From Argentina to Mexico it is firmly anchored in the folk music. Colombia's vallenato, the Dominican Republic's merengue, the Tex-Mex polkas; all are unimaginable without the accordion.

Instrumental Groups

The regionally variable dances, folk songs, folguedos, autos and cults were also influenced by the character of the orchestras and soloists accompanying them.

In the initial period of Brazil's history each of the three cultural spheres produced its music in isolation from the others. African slaves played within their settlements (*senzalas* and *mocambos*) and occasionally at church festivals; Amerindians in their villages and in the Jesuit missions; and whites in their salons and parades. Over the course of the acculturation process already discussed, the Amerindians and Africans not only added European imports to their own instruments, but also began to imitate the orchestation use by Iberian bands. The Frenchman Froger complained that at the Ascension Day procession in 1696 'masked bands, dancers, and musicians disrupted the order of the holy ceremony to the utmost with their lewd gestures.'

Black brotherhoods closely associated with the Church played a decisive role in the development of Afro-Brazilian instrumental groups. 'Negroes participated in the life of the Brazilian people in the shadows of the brotherhoods, especially through the Nossa Senhora do Rosario. Since the seventeenth-century traveler's accounts have described how any occasion was opportune for the Negro slaves to take to the streets with their *marimbas, assobios, cangás, atabaques* and *macumbas* and to make music. This music still necessarily had a tribal character to it' (Tinhorão). Blacks, mestizos, and caboclos were not allowed to take part in the colonizers' festivals and celebrations. So they invented their own festivals, theater and ceremonies. And as they had no magnificent palaces or theaters, they performed them in the open air or in the church buildings made available to them. The orchestras would adapt their instrumentation and musicians to the particular character of the occasion and to the local conditions.

Since the latter half of the eighteenth century, barbers have made an important contribution to the development of instrumental music. Tinhorão, in *Os Sons que verm da Rua*, explains that 'free Negroes in the cities often pursued the barber profession. They had free time between customers, which they used to develop their musical activities.' The barbers even learned such difficult European instruments as the trumpet and oboe besides the guitar and cavaquinho.

Tinhorão continues: 'The barbers' music was the music of the people, while the elites were represented musically by military bands, so-called *ternos* (consisting of shawms, pifanos and drums) which were expected to play the national anthem.' Barbershop bands (with similar instrumental arrangement, but with a greater number of musicians) could not compete with the military bands and soon disappeared from the scene. A growing Brazilian national awareness contributed to their downfall, of course. And yet the barbers still helped to give instrumental music great prestige at folk celebrations, thereby laying a foundation for the development of an urban instrumental music in the latter half of the nineteenth century. The maxixe, choro and samba, which came along in the following decades, would not have been possible without them.

Vincente Salles commented upon the barbers' *ternos* and upon the bands, also bearing the name *terno*, which arose from them around the country in the most varied instrumental arrangements. 'Although their musicians originated from the lower social classes, they have been the true representatives of *learned* Brazilian music since colonial days.' (Everything not considered folk or light music in Brazil is referred to as *erúdita*, i.e., learned. *Música clásica* and *Música culta* — i.e., classical and church music — belong to this category.)

One can encounter ternos and *bandas de pífanos* (small rustic orchestras made up of two simple flutes and zabumba percussion instruments) especially at festivals and processions in the North. Similar orchestras accompany the *pastorales* at Christmas time in Spain. Nevertheless, an Amerindian element has become integral to the ternos and their music. Today the best-known group of this type is Banda de Pífanos de Caruarú, founded in 1924 by M. Clarindo Biano with members of his family. Today Sebastião Biano leads it.

Naturally, those folkloric media which relied upon Portuguese models also preserved the original instrumentation or orchestras from the mother country. The particular features of instrumental music and its bands will be treated in the corresponding chapter on MPB.

Instrumental groups bear different names in different regions: *terno, conjunto, orquestra, banda, esquenta-mulher, alvorada*, etc. The instrumental arrangement typical for Brazil is referred to as *banda de pau e corda*, i.e., woodwinds (flutes) and strings (rabeca, cavaquinho, guitar, etc.).

Most instruments are made in Brazil. Patos (in the state of Paraiba), Juazeiro do Norte (Ceará), and Queluz (São Paulo) are, or once were, vital craft centers which supplied the surrounding region with instruments. Much of today's musical instrument industry is settled in the South (in Santa Catarina, for example).

I would like to end this discussion with a quote from Mario de Andrade: 'While most instruments may have been imported, they have a national character today.... The nasal sound of the Brazilian voice and instruments is natural and climatic; it is the *physiological* influence of Indian blood.'

Magical Music — Afro-Brazilian Religions

A knowledge of dates, facts and structures alone will never be enough for a proper appreciation of Brazilian music. One must add to it an understanding of the Brazilian mentality and way of life. The magical-mystical elements found in Brazilian syncretic cults play a fundamental role in the lives of many Brazilians. Afro-Brazilian religions have integrated music and dance in countless manners and forms. Their contribution to MPB has greatly increased since musicians began to interest themselves in Africa. (The fact that the *Movimento Black Rio* in

The Instrumental Groups Most Frequently Used Today

Batuques (samba-rural, candomblé, umbigadas, etc.) atabaques, pandeiro, agôgô, ganzá, chocalhos, occasionally guitar, cavaquinho

Samba-Batucada (samba da cidade) cavaquinho, surdo, pandeiro, chocalhos, cuica, agôgô, apito

Choro flauta, cavaquinho, bandolim, violão, violão-sete-cordas, pandeiro among other percussion (occasionally clarinet, soprano sax)

Baião sanfona, triangle, pandeiro, surdo, caixa, viola, (also 'orquestra de mamulengo' and others)

Terno de Pifanos (Northeast) 2 pifanos, zabumba, caixa, cymbals (also zabumba or banda cabaçal)

Caboclinhos Northeastern procession and Indios-caboclos' auto tambor, maracás, preacas, flauta

Congos/Congadas/ Reisados/Afoxes zabumba, ternos de pifanos, among others

Reisados zabumba orchestra: ganzá, pandeiro, etc., berimbau-de-lata

Desafios viola, rebeca (North), sanfona, guitar (South)

Pastorinhas pandeiros, maracás

Folias violões, sanfona, cavaquinho, pandeiro, pistão, caixa

Lundu Dance atabaques, percussion, guitar or bandolim

Xotes sanfona, percussion

Fandangos (South) rebeca, viola, pandeiro, adufe, machete (cavaquinho)

Coco percussion, ingonos, cuica, pandeiro, ganzá

Frevo trumpet, trombone, clarinet, saxophone, percussion

Capoeira berimbau, pandeiro

Jongo percussion only (tambores do jongo)

Cururú viola, adufe

Dança da Santa Cruz: 2 violas, adufe, reco-reco

Milonga (southern samba) guitar, gaita, percussion

Gaucho Music (bugios, rancheiras among others) sanfona, gaita, viola, percussion the seventies pursued much different goals can only be mentioned here.) Indications of this new awareness of Africa are unmistakable. In 1977 Maria Bethania dedicated her show 'Pássaro de Manhã' to the Candomblé mother Sra. Cleusa Millet (Mãe Maria), declaring that her work had been 'illuminated by bright, hard rays of Ogum.' Gilberto Gil returned from a cultural festival in Nigeria with new insights into the roots of Afro-Brazilian culture. Milton Nascimento even composed a mass, entitled *Missa dos Quilombos*, about the history and fate of runaway African slaves.

My interest is not to portray, as Oswald de Andrade put it, 'Macumba for tourists', but rather to illuminate a serious, fundamental component of Brazilian culture.

Mark Münzel, in *Die Indianer*, described the Latin American hinterland as having a 'fanatic religiosity of hope'. Shamanistic sects in the Sertão have given this sentiment expression for over four hundred years. Even today, a century after the dramatic, and for us incredible, events surrounding Canudos, Antonio Conseilheiro and Padre Cicero, Brazil's Northeast remains fertile ground for the growth of such religious fanatism. One cause lies in the misery that the Sertão natives are forced to endure. Poverty, hunger and death are everyday occurrences. These people are not hoping for an improvement in their conditions; they are hoping for a miracle. The proximity of their settlements to primitive tribal peoples helps us understand how shamanistic sects could mix with African ritual and Catholicism.

The historical and current center of Afro-Brazilian cult forms is the port city of Salvador, in Bahia, where slave ships once unloaded human cargo that had just completed the voyage from West Africa. The blacks brought with them their religious cults — their gods, their music, and their instruments — and have largely kept them alive into the present day. As previously described in this book, there were advantages to be had for a slave who could adapt himself to his master's church. Slave brotherhoods arose under priestly patronage, for example, and obedient slaves were at least allowed to sing and dance on holidays. In the seventeenth and eighteenth centuries blacks accommodated the missionary zeal of the Catholic Church by officially practicing Christianity while clandestinely worshiping their traditional deities. In order to bring some order to this pious chaos — and perhaps thinking that it really could not hurt to invoke both the African god Iemanjá and the Virgin Mary when in need — slaves began to invest each of their African gods simultaneously with a Catholic saint. Such a mixture was also the result of a cultural overlap in ritualistic cycles. Catholic holidays honoring the saints often corresponded to an African ritual calender determined by the natural cycles of planting and harvesting. This form of syncretism enabled the slaves to invoke their traditional gods in the priests' presence.

Many researchers of Afro-Brazilian religion, and, in particular, Roger Bastide in his *As Religiões africanas no Brasil* see syncretism as a form of slave resistance, that is, a calling into question of the white man's religion by depriving the colonists of their sole claim upon their symbols and insignia, and thus de facto lessening their value. Accordingly, a Catholic saint's icon in the terreiro de candomblé does not necessarily have to be interpreted as Christianity's inexorable march forward into this cultural arena.

This form of syncretism took shape in Brazil under various names. To find two cults identical with one another is difficult. The relationship of African, Amerindian and Christian elements within a cult varies according to region. Cults have also been influenced by elements originating from outside Brazil — Cuba and Venezuela, to name but two sources. The centers of Macumba, Umbanda and Kimbanda are located in Rio de Janeiro and São Paulo; of Candomblé in Bahia. In the provinces Pernambuco, Paraiba, and Alagoas one hears of Xangõ, in Pará, of Babassué, and in Maranhão the Tambor-de-Mina or de Nagõ cult is popular. Other forms include the Caboclo cult in Bahia, the Catimbó or Catimbau in the Northeast and Tambor-de-Crioulo in Maranhão. The three basic cults — the Candomblé, Macumba and Umbanda — differ from one another in the following ways:

Candomblé

Yoruba-based cults.
Origin: Nigeria, Benin Republic
Gods: from Africa, nature deities (orixás).

Macumba

Afro-Catholic with spiritistic and occult influences.
Origin: Congo with Yoruba and Amerindian influence.
Gods: African (orixás), *pretos velhos* (Congo-Angolan ancestral spirits).

Umbanda

African-Catholic-Amerindian, modern and focused on this world, elements of spiritism, occult, reincarnation, karma.
Origin: difficult to pinpoint because of its hybrid form.
Gods: African Gods, but also ghosts and dead souls, caboclos, Catholic saints, Pretos Velhos.

Common to all these cults is a belief in supernatural gods and spirits known as *orixás* or *santos*, sometimes also as *mestres*. But their rules and ritualistic sequences are different from one and other. Not only symbols, but even certain foods are prescribed for worshiping orixás. The ceremony is determined by a particular series (*shiré*) of chants and rhythms. Let us take a look for example at *Oxum*, goddess of the springs, Xangó's second wife, Queen of Oyó. Her day is Saturday; she loves *mulucu* (a dish made from beans, onions, and crabs) and *ipeté* (manioc with crabs and onion); her invocation (*saudação*) is 'Ora ieiê ô'; her song, 'Aridebé ôonim — Oniô de bé ô' (Oxum comes, adorned with gold on her hands and feet).

On a Sunday walk through the woods or at the beach you can find traces of nocturnal Macumba ceremonies — dead chickens, bottles with candles, red bandanas, a fire-pit, empty cachaça bottles. But many of the meetings take place in a *terreiro*, usually an out-of-the-way location with a bare floor and a sacred room, or *barracão* located within. A wooden altar (*peji*) for sacrificial offerings is set up in the room. At times there are other rooms located above the different houses. The head of the *casa do terreiro* is the *ialorixá*, the *mãe de santo* (saint's mother) who organizes the Candomblés. Her chief position in the Candomblé hierarchy corresponds to that of the *babalorixá*, or *pai de santo*. Next in order are the *mãe pequenha* (small mother) and the *dagas* (mediums). Even the daughters of the terreiro (*filhas*) are assigned their place in the hierarchy for the length of their membership. The head drummer has to be a consecrated member of the terreiro.

A Candomblé ceremony usually begins in the morning with a sacrificial slaughtering of an animal for the gods. The festival is ushered in during the afternoon by a *roda*. A roda is composed of a series of batuques in praise of the orixás. The gods are informed that their presence in the cult community is desired by playing particular drum rhythms and invocative chants that are dedicated to the particular gods. Singing (by the dagas and filhas), rhythmical clapping and the beating of a drum rhythm with steadily rising intensity all have one goal: to effect the arrival of the orixás among the cult adherents. *Pontos cantados*, *corimas*, *orôs*, *malembes* and other songs of mostly African origin are sung. In Umbanda one can even hear songs from the Catholic liturgy.

The orixás do finally arrive by way of the mediums (the filhas in this case), who have long since fallen into trances produced by the ecstatic drum rhythms and monotonous chanting repetition. When all orixás have appeared, the filhas withdraw, only to appear once again outfitted in the clothes and insignia characteristic of each individual deity. The *mãe de santo* then stands up. The real gods have now arrived. The ceremony culminates with all the orixás dancing in the *barracão*, where the participants can address their individual wishes to them.

In addition to this ceremony, which I have simplified in its presentation, there are others in which the consecration of drums and novices (*yãos*), healing, and other acts are undertaken.

The drummers who accompany these rituals are highly trained musicians. Their instruments are atabaques (elongated African wooden drums with wedgeshaped forms) which come in three sizes. Run (*rum*) are the largest, followed by *Rumpi*, and the smallest are called *lê*. The head drummer is the *alabê*. He plays the *rum* atabaques and is also allowed to sing during the rituals. Other musical instruments played during cult ceremonies are *cabaças*, *agôgô*, *caxixi*, *agüe* and small bells (*adjá*). The latter are used by the cult chieftains to communicate signals within the ceremony.

Hubert Fichte's book *Xangô* records statements from the *pai-de-santo* Pedro concerning the close relationship these instruments have to their African heritage:

> The term 'candomblé', as well as the words 'macumba', 'makulelê', 'umbanda' and 'kimbanda', is most certainly a term from the Congo and refers to a musical instrument. There is a particular drum in Uruguay still known today as candombê.... Time is kept in the Yoruba language with *agôgô*, or more correctly, *akoko*, but is exchanged with the term for 'double-bell' in the Candomblé. There is no god of time for the Yorubans. Even their instruments do not have gods. They have a vague idea of a god of music.

Pedro is wrong on one point, though. In Uruguay, 'candombe' refers to a drum and cult of Afro-Uruguayan origin, in which the parallels and connections to the Afro-Brazilian candomblé are quite negligible.

Hubert Fichte (whose books are worth reading in order to achieve a deeper understanding of Afro-Brazilian cults) reports on the existence of about six-hundred Candomblé centers (terreiros) in Salvador-Bahia, Brazil's 'Black Rome'. The oldest, Casa Branca, was founded 130 years ago.

In all regions of the country Candomblé and its related forms were subject to a variety of influences; to cultural elements from African tribes (Gêge, Congo, Ijexá, Hausá, Cabinda, Ketú, Nagô, etc.); from the Amerindian natives, which can be felt especially in magic and occultism; as well as similar influences introduced from abroad in the form of spiritistic sects (e.g., Kardecism).

Once again several statements from the pai-de-santo Pedro, taken from Fichte's book: 'Three quarters of the population [in Bahia] attend Candomblé festivals. Even those persons who have to pretend not to believe in African syncretism due to their public position have African priests working for them, either in secret or through their servants. All Candomblé disciples are practicing Catholics.... The Catholic beliefs of the Candomblé adherent in Bahia are false. It's a game — a socially conditioned game. As believing Catholic blacks get a share of the better-off white society.'

Umbanda occupies a special position among syncretic cults. It has been around only since the beginning of this century as a hybrid form of Afro-Brazilian religion mixed with magic and Catholicism. It has no dogmas or prohibitions, which is what makes it so attractive for millions of Umbandistas throughout the country. The orixás are *cosmic vibrations*, that is, spirits which never assume form upon the earth. Umbandistas draw their strength from natural forces (of Amerindian influence) that are able to pick up orixás' vibrations. For this reason Umbandistas are against environmental pollution and are frequently vegetarians, too. The cult assumes the existence of one god, in addition to multiple spirits that are identical with the spirits related to other cult gods and their syncretisms. They carry such names as Zambi, Oxalufã and Oxaguiã.

The pontos of the Umbanda were sung in African dialect until 1929. In this year the Umbanda composer J. B. de Carvalho is said to have received an order from orixá to write his songs only in Portuguese from that point on. Since Umbanda was officially banned until 1946, Carvalho declared his songs at first to be batuques, jongos, toadas or baiões. More than a thousand of his songs were recorded on disc. Carvalho once complained that samba composers had copied melodies from his pontos to counter the problem that black religious music had lost something of its topicality among the people.

People of all races and skin color belong to the Umbanda cult. It employs entire sections of the Brazilian economy, functioning like a tightly run business enterprise. Special factories manufacture all types of cult articles, from orixá figures to fetishes to diverse accessories. There are enormous numbers of Umbanda records and literature. Nevertheless Umbanda, as a new addition to the country's cult reservoir, is of much less importance for Brazilian music than are the more traditional Afro-Brazilian religions.

I know musicians who have turned to the terreiros for help in order to get rid of particular ailments. Others have sought out 'miracle healers' from the cult community. Maria Bethania admitted that her long suffering even drove her to attempt suicide. Psychoanlysis had not helped. Then a friend brought her along to a candomblé, which made all the difference. The ethnographer Waldeloso Rego explains, 'What a doctor often diagnoses as an illness is no illness for the candomblé. It is simply evidence that an orixá has acted to fulfill its wish and has occupied the medium.' In answer to the question whether she had had contact with an orixá, Maria Bethania replied: 'No, other than that I'm a medium myself. According to what I've been told, I only have contact when I sing. I only have vibrations.'

Her Bahian collegue Gilberto Gil developed his impressions from a trip to Nigeria in 1977 in a long-playing record entitled *Refavela*. Gil also pays homage to the origins of Afro-Brazilian syncretism:

Spirit elevated to heaven
Astral machete
Of ancestral metal, of natural iron,
Preserved in sacred balsam
Eternal and noble body
Of a Nago* king
Xangô

At the beginning of the sixties, Baden Powell and Vinicius de Moraes composed their famous Afro-sambas with lyrical, melodic and rhythmic material gained from their study of the Bahian Candomblé.

The Candomblé and Macumba are referred to again and again in many songs from MPB. For example, the vocal group Os Tincoas has cultivated the *Canto Coral Liturgico Afro-Católico*, a choral hymn similar in sound to its forerunners in the first candomblé terreiros of the African nations and reminiscent in many ways of the North American spiritual.

Bahia was the scene of a Euro-Brazilian 'happening' in 1972. The Dave Pike Set (with Volker Kriegel, Eberhard Weber, Marc Hellmann) came to Salvador for a few weeks in order to rehearse with the percussion group Baiafro for a recording session and concert tour together. In those days the Grupo Baiafro, under Djalma Corrêa's direction, used to play at candomblés, as well as at concerts arranged by the Goethe Institute in Salvador. The director of the institute, Roland Schaffner, set up the meeting and rented a house for the German musicians just outside Salvador in the picturesque fishing village of Itapoã. The rehearsals were to take place here. I remember well how the jazz musicians night after night discussed the concept this co-production should be based upon. All agreed that it should not be a Dave Pike Set LP with an extended rhythm section. The European musicians

---

*A Yoruban people from southeastern Dahomey, Africa.

were aware that their Brazilian counterparts (Onias Camardelli, Djalma Corrêa, Edson Sant'ana) considered them to be superior musicians in many respects. This made it all the more necessary for them to be careful not to rob the Grupo Baiafro of any of their originality, and not to force prepared arrangements on them. Whereas the Dave Pike Set was accustomed to alternating between fixed structures and free passages, in the Baiafro group one musician would play a rhythmic sequence and a second would respond with a completely different one.

The three atabaque drummers were not used to starting on command, nor to ending their parts within an allotted time. During Candomblé ceremonies they play for hours at a time, first reaching their peak during an evening's drumming.

The problems seemed to become insurmountable when Edinho, a consecrated member of the terreiro Tumba Jussare, refused to perform certain verses of a song that had long since been agreed upon. Apparently the Candomblé would not allow it. The piece, commemorating the capoeira patron saint Salomão, did finally make it onto the record, and Edinho sang the verses in the traditional Yoruba language. I assume, though, that Edinho covered himself against possible punishment in some way (possibly by performing some sort of sacrifice).

During their stay in Itapõa two of the musicians had the opportunity to attend a Candomblé ceremony. Their neighbors, who had earlier viewed them and their instruments with great reservations, had invited them. Marc returned early. He had observed the celebration seated with his legs crossed. This, he was politely informed, indicated a closed heart, thereby disrupting the celebration. Dave came back much later. He was so moved one might think he had felt the orixás' vibrations.

Chapter 3

The Choro

Rio Antigo

The tourist who visited Rio de Janeiro in the middle of the nineteenth century would most likely have been able to visit the Copacabana solely by way of a tiring trek over the hills as part of a Sunday-afternoon outing. There were no tunnels connecting the south zone to Botafogo, Urca and the center in those days. The beaches between Leme and Leblon were practically untouched. Fishermen and opossum were about all there was to see in this undeveloped landscape. Who could have guessed then that a century later millions of tons of concrete would leave free only a tiny strip of sand, a strip that would become famous all over the world?

Rio became Brazil's capital city in 1763, replacing Salvador in Bahia. Forty years later the French invaded Portugal, forcing King João IV and his royal court to flee to Brazil. When João IV was able to return to Portugal, he left his son Dom Pedro to rule over Brazil as regent. On September 7, 1822, he declared Brazil independent from Portugal. Rio experienced a great economic and cultural boom. The chief impulses for the development of MPB over the next hundred years originated in Rio.

According to statistics published in the Brazilian newspaper *O Diario* on December 11, 1847, the country's population at that time was 2.1 million whites, 3.1 million Negro slaves, 1.1 million free Negroes and mulattos, 0.2 million newly emancipated slaves who had been born in Africa and 0.8 million Amerindians. As with Salvador, Rio now exerted an especially strong pull upon free and newly emancipated blacks and half-castes who hoped to find some sort of employment as domestic servants rather than remain around the plantation. They settled in the area of what was then the center of the city.

The wealthy of the city lived in salons. Heavy tapestries adorned their walls; their tablecloths were made from the finest damask satin; everything was decorated according to the latest European taste and fashion. They washed themselves in baths tiled with Byzantine mosaics and arranged their flowers in vases manufactured from Chinese porcelain. It was no rarity to find in their salons grand pianos that were used to accompany songs performed by modinha troubadours during high-society balls.

The Rua do Ouvidor, with its cafés, confectionaries, newspaper publishers and print shops was the intellectual center of the day. Men of letters, poets and artists met here regularly over coffee. On almost thirty days of the year the Rua do Ouvidor was the scene of religious processions; one could sometimes even see groups of blacks, such as the ranchos of Bahian descent. But black slaves were seldom seen, for as was said, 'Dia de santo era dia de folgar': the day of the saints was the day on which slaves worked for themselves. This period also gives us a picture of Bitu, a character still lamented today in carnival songs. Bitu was a half-caste (crioulo) who always roamed the streets, dancing and singing, in a somewhat tipsy state.

The carnival in Rio in the first half of the nineteenth century had little in common with carnival as we know it today. The Portuguese entrudo carnival, with its parades and confetti fights, was a privilege reserved for white cariocas. Masked balls first took place in 1846 behind closed doors, while the streets were filled with negradas (groups of blacks) who had their fun with limões-de-cheiro, that is, wax oranges filled with perfumed water, which they joyfully sprayed on passersby. The police banned such merriment. But who really cared anyway? Whites too were busy waging water fights, a tradition brought over from Portugal. There was nothing to hear at the entrudo balls but European music. The bohemian polka was introduced in 1845, the schottische (a type of Scottish waltz popular in the middle of the century) in 1851 and, almost simultaneously, the waltz. Mazurkas and quadrilles supplemented the repertoire. One of the main social attractions of the day was the Cassino Fluminense in the Rua do Catete. Polka fever broke out there. This new dance from bohemia became the rage after first being played during intermissions in a Rio theater.

Of course, blacks and peasants in general insisted on taking part in the carnival in one way or another. Shoemaker José Nogueira de Azevedo Paredes entered the Shrove Monday procession with a few of his friends in 1852. They made a racket with the bombo drums (modeled after the Portuguese zabumba group), which they had brought along by the score. Chronicles of the period report that the shoemaker's idea was such a success that the cry soon went up — *Viva o Zé Perreira* — celebrating the man whose bombos had introduced a disciplined rhythmic order into the carnival parades for the first time. It was just a matter of time until Rio's blacks and half-castes, already accustomed to staging street parades at family funerals, ensured themselves a place in the Rio carnival despite all bans and laws to the contrary.

The Belle Epoque

Cariocas in the nineteenth century had a special affinity for French flair. The restaurants Eldorado and Alcazar devoted themselves to featuring vaudeville acts and celebrated the operettas of Jacques Offenbach in 1869. It was inevitable that cariocas, too, would want their own Belle Epoque. And they got it. Their *bela época* occurred between 1870 and 1920 and laid the foundation for today's MPB with its basic forms: the maxixe, choro, samba and the myriad mixed forms resulting from them.

This epoch was characterized by the transition from a monarchy to a republic (1889), by the abolition of slavery (1888), by a growing Brazilian national consciousness, and by the beginning of industrialization. Brazil was in a state of upheaval, with all the economic and political problems of emerging nationhood. The emancipation of the slaves flooded the big cities with droves of blacks who were leaving the plantations. Many wasted away their lives in slum quarters, which housed the city's socially disadvantaged. All in all, it was a climate that nourished social tension. Nevertheless, or perhaps directly owing to the situation, optimal conditions were present for the creation of an urban popular music. Similar preconditions provided fertile soil for the *tango porteño* in Buenos Aires, the calypso in Trinidad, and ragtime and jazz in New Orleans.

The modinha and lundu had already managed to secure a place for themselves in Rio de Janeiro before the beginning of the Belle Epoch. The waltz and polka joined them in the first half of the nineteenth century. While the waltz offered the citizenry of the elegant salons and royal court a feeling of aristocratic dignity, the polka quickly gained a following in all strata of the populace. Polka fever spread like wildfire. *Polcar* came into use to describe a new easygoing, carefree life-style in the salons and on the streets. Most song and dance forms in Rio were combined with the *polca* (whose Brazilianization is reflected in the new spelling), resulting in ever new variations. Polca-lundus and polca-tangos (influenced by the Cuban habanera) competed for the cariocas' favor, both within the salon repertoire as well as by more popular orchestras.

Other fashionable dances from Europe soon appeared on the scene in Rio. The cariocas' turn to the European Romantic helped them discover the mazurka and schottische. But, above all, the mazurka was welcomed as the alternative to the waltz, contredanse and quadrille. Especially the latter, a successor to the minuet, and the *xotis* (or *xote*) dances, which are related to the schottische, are central to the repertoire of rural dance festivals in the *música sertaneja* tradition.

New and vigorous tones could be heard at all types of parades and processions, reflecting the growth of a national consciousness. The march was a suitable vehicle. Nevertheless, as the chronicles report, the march arrived in Brazil a bastard, born of such related forms as the *pasodoble*, military march and quick march. Brazilians played them in their own way — with somewhat more swing and a forced tempo (calling for exactly one hundred steps per minute) as *dobrado* to accompany three-part musical compositions.

It goes without saying that neither the aristocracy nor the bourgoisie could meet the demand for musicians for balls, march orchestras, theater and opera from their own ranks. As a result, the musicians best informed about the latest dances always came from the Cidade Nova, a section of the city where the lower classes lived. They played there in the neighborhood bars or in the brothels in Rua do Senado. It is hard to say whether the first fusions of their batuques, lundus and ranchos with European dances occurred here or in the concert halls and salons of the ruling class. Whatever the case, a new bastard form — the *maxixe*, a hybrid of the polca, lundu, and habanera — suddenly appeared. The maxixe was a merry dance characterized by a forced, lightly syncopated rhythm. The dancers thought up all sorts of almost acrobatic steps and figures for it. It has been surmised that the frevo, which arose in Recife at the turn of the century, still profits today from choreographic elements of the maxixe.

Where does the name *maxixe* derive from? Maxixe is supposed to have been the name of one of the dancers in the Estudantes do Heidelberg (a club for students from Heidelberg, Germany). Or maybe the name comes from *machiche*, (a type of sliding dance) or La Mattchitche, as a particular song title from the period was spelled. The maxixe which arose in 1870 represents the first urban dance of Brazilian creation.

Choro Rhythm

Popular music styles of the latter half of the nineteenth century became the melodic and rhythmic source material for a development within MPB known as *choro*. Several Brazilian musicologists even regard the choro as the only typical, independent form of Brazilian music. In view of the country's size and the great number of musical styles, one might well question this assertion. Nevertheless, it is certainly true that choro is the most interesting form of instrumental expression in Rio, and of no less importance than early instrumental forms of jazz and tango. Indeed, the choro is several decades older than jazz.

Choro music first developed at the outset of the Belle Epoque as a purely instrumental form, when the mulatto José Antonio da Silva Callado began playing popular polcas with new instrumentation. Callado's original arrangement (essentially a terno de pau e cordas) put together for the first time guitar, cavaquinho and flute in such a way that the cavaquinho played the harmonies and the guitar played back contrapuntally in the bass line the melody carried by Callado's ebony flute. (Jazz utilizes the same principle, but with jazz the melody is carried by the contrabass, and it arose much later.)

By around 1930 the pandeiro, reco-reco, and other percussion instruments customary for the samba began to back up the natural swing arising from the interplay of guitar and cavaquinho. The new sound, subtly melancholic in character, resulting from the particular interplay of instruments and from the ringing, graceful strains of cavaquinho and guitar, lent this new form its name. *Choro*, derived from *chorar*, means 'to wail' or 'to weep'. The musicians came to be known as *chorão* and *chorões*. There are indications of a possible semantic derivation from the African *xolo* dance.

The choro rhythm, where it is not identical with the polca or other playing styles, is aptly described in Waldir Azevedo's choro title 'Arraste-Pé', meaning 'dragged foot', that is walking with one foot dragging behind the other.

Improvisation was another feature of the new instrumentation suggesting parallels to jazz. Callado was accompanied by musicians who loved to improvise, and to improvise often. Because there was no such thing as a score or lead sheet, it was left up to the musician's talents and experience to recognize the correct harmonic patterns. Callado used to test young musicians during auditions by unexpectedly shifting into different, difficult keys. Those who did not recognize the modulation, or who could not follow it, would first try to hide their mistake, but eventually would be forced to give up. These difficult choro passages are known as *derrubada*.

Without rhythmic and harmonic deftness from the accompanying musicians, choro solists cannot vary and improvise on musical themes. For this reason the choro remains today the favorite form of instrumental music for many of Brazil's musicians. It would be hard to imagine contemporary MPB without it.

Callado and his colleagues Viriato, Virgilio and Luizinho took to the streets of old Rio and began playing polcas, valsas and Brazilian tangos chiefly in the proletarian district of Cidade Nova near Mangue. (The district today has been almost completely torn down.) It was inevitable that, with time, musicians would modify their musical models, especially in terms of rhythm and tempo.

Callado died in 1880. He left behind not only a large number of 'Brazilian tangos,'* but also many musicians who had come to dedicate themselves to the new music. Viriato Ferreira da Silva, his successor and composer of the popular polca 'Caiu, não disse' (with prominent derrubada passages), survived him by a mere three years.

Choro musicians began to accompany sentimental modinhas and polca serenades in this period. This finally brought them success in their own neighborhoods.

A young woman took up the task of carrying on the still young choro tradition. In 1877, at the tender age of thirty, Francisca Hedwiges de Lima Gonzaga, better known as Chiquinha Gonzaga (1847–1935), composed a piece entitled 'Atrevida' which is still in the chorões' repertoire today. Her 1899 composition 'Só no Choro' demonstrated the existence of the chorões' instrumental playing style as an independent musical form.

The daughter of wealthy parents, Chiquinha Gonzaga received the benefits of piano lessons and a general musical education. (She was an extremely emancipated woman for an age characterized by a strict moral code.) Initially, the Cidade Nova did not want to accept the fact that a woman could assume the leading position in a musical movement. 'This Chiquinha is a devil,' many proclaimed.

The success of her carnival march 'O Abre Alás' in 1899 must have won her sympathy in the eyes of the public. Several years later, active as

---

*This tango is not identical with the Argentinian tango, although it is named after it (see below).

a committed suffragette, she got mixed up in a national scandal. The wife of the President of the Republic had extended to Gonzaga an invitation to the Palace; the leading families of the nation were furious to see the composer of 'Corta Jaca' ('a song from the gutter,' they said) celebrated in the palace. The choro, after all, like all musical forms originating among the lower classes, was not considered fit for proper society.

Prior to all this, Chiquinha Gonzaga had begun calling her choros and maxixes 'Brazilian tangos'. In his *Pequenha Historia da Música Popular*, Tinhorão hypothesized that her intention was to help this new musical form along to social recognition and that, in turn, would win it a measure of popularity among the upper social strata.

Ernesto Nazareth (1863–1934) finally achieved the breakthrough into the noble salons of the bourgoisie as he began doing piano renditions of the choro (and maxixe) in classical style. Nazareth was one of the most important figures in the history of MPB. To a great degree he was influenced by the European Romantic tradition, and especially Chopin. His *tangos brasileiros* ('Brejeiro', 'Odeon'), *mazurkas de expressão* and polcas ('Apanhei-te Cavaquinho') belong even today to the standard repertoire of all choro conjuntos. In the mid-seventies Brazilian pianist Artur Moreira Lima made two double albums of Ernesto Nazareth's compositions. These interpretations give us a good idea of how Nazareth's original versions must have sounded. Ernesto Nazareth, regarded today as one of the classics in both the popular and classical musical tradition of Brazil, suffered a tragic end. Deaf and deranged, he died under a waterfall, his arms extended as if about to play another choro. Like the early tango in Buenos Aires, the history of the choro is marked by generations of its musicians. Followers of the original founders of the choro included such musicians as João Pernambuco (guitarist, 1883–1947), whose most famous composition was 'Luar de Sertão', Anaclete de Medeiros (1886–1907) and Pattapio Silva (flautist, 1881–1907) among others.

Apanhei-te Cavaquinho (Ernesto Nazareth)

Pixinguinha

Wind instruments, clarinets among them, first took their place in the choro conjuntos at the end of the nineteenth century. Rio was full of military bands in those days, and they served as important reservoirs of young musical talent for the choro conjuntos, while, in turn, the choro was adopted by the bands themselves. The arrival of jazz on the musical scene brought the saxophone to Brazil. April 23, 1898, marks the birth of the next great figure after Ernesto Nazareth in Brazil's musical history. Pixinguinha; remembered and honored as flautist and saxophonist, as well as a brilliant composer and arranger, he created well over six-hundred instrumental pieces, ranging from valsas and polcas to maxixes and chotes, not to mention sambas and choros. In the final analysis, it was Pixinguinha who established a new standard for choro music and, simultaneously, for the further development of Brazil's popular instrumental music in our century.

Pixinguinha grew up in the working-class district of Catumbi in the north of Rio as a son of the power-line worker Alfredo da Rocha Viana. The grandfather called Alfred Jr. by the African name Pizinguim (meaning 'small rogue'), which later became Pizidin, and eventually Pixinguinha.

The father was a passable flautist. His home became the focal point for many of the neighborhood's choro musicians, and by fifteen years of age Pixinguinha, along with his four brothers and sisters, was being allowed to stay up for all-night jam sessions and to play a little guitar. Still wearing short pants, he bought himself a flute and was soon to be found wherever music could be heard. One could be especially sure to find him during carnival time, which he loved so dearly. At sixteen he was already well-accepted in the music circles of the entire northern district of Rio. In addition to choro, he had a special liking for all the songs and dances of African origin that were played at festivals in the Macumba and Candomblé centers.

Pixinguinha put together his first band in 1919. In those days jobs were to be found only in the auditoriums of the newly built movie theaters on Avenida Rio Branco. More elegant strains sounded from the foyers, however, where visitors were fed a diet of classics and light entertainment music from Europe. Pixinguinha's band was called Os Oito Batutas, 'The Eight Whizzes'. Like Pixinguinha, all eight musicians were blacks from Rio's lower-middle class.

Pixinguinha's band was soon touring throughout the country, and it made guest appearances in Argentina and Paris. In 1922 several cariocas made a ruckus over these appearances: 'It's humiliating for Brazil that our first cultural mission abroad should be conducted by a black band. What will they think of us?'

Naturally, Oito Batuta's European tour was a huge success. The Brazilian musicians used the opportunity to meet European and American musicians playing in Paris. The similarities between the ragtimes and foxtrots played by United States blacks and the Brazilian choros were so great that Pixinguinha's band was introduced several times as a jazz group. In Paris Pixinguinha began to take a liking to the saxophone. So he bought one and began practicing popular shimmies, ragtimes and charlestons in order to introduce them in Brazil at a later date.

Pixinguinha seldom appeared as soloist, limiting himself instead to melodies and harmonies on his flute or saxophone. He enjoyed accompanying other soloists much more. Pixinguinha's larger significance rests in his work as a composer and arranger. Antonio Carlos Jobim regards Pixinguinha as the founder of a new epoch in MPB, which until then had been strongly influenced by Chopin. Like Jobim, many musicologists today consider Pixinguinha to be the first arranger in MPB. In fact, this is one of the main reasons so many Brazilian musicians nowadays honor him as a genius.

At the time of Pixinguinha's birth choro musicians utilized nothing more than a kind of leading arrangement that determined the various melodic parts, breaks, intervals, harmonies and bass line (of the guitar). This minimal understanding was sufficient for the musicians, and they simply began playing. But times were changing. Pixinguinha's friend and colleague, Donga, had written the first arrangement for a samba in 1917, and the two were the first in Rio to hear one-steps and foxtrots imported from the United States on shellac disks. Before that, Ernesto Nazareth had written his memorable choros, raising popular music to a higher plane. All this had an influence on Pixinguinha, stimulating him to compose pieces with complicated harmonic structures and elaborate sequences. Nevertheless, he was never able to win the recognition for his art in the first decades of the century that he has today. 'Lamento', one of his most famous choros, was strongly criticized in 1926. Its harmonic structure was, to be sure, well ahead of its time.

By the thirties Pixinguinha had become one of the most desired arrangers and directors in the burgeoning record industry. His help enabled a number of young musicians and composers to their first hearing before the general public. His main influence consisted in writing the arrangements for their sambas and choros and providing the instrumental background for many vocal productions with his orchestra. This orchestra, known as Pixinguinha's Velha Guarda (Old Guard), has a legendary character today.

In 1933 the self-taught Pixinguinha was finally persuaded to attend the conservatory in Rio. But he soon left after receiving bad grades. Baden Powell recalled a music professor in Rio telling him how Pixinguinha had later come to him to make another attempt at learning. The professor had answered him: 'Why, Pixinguinha? You have nothing more to learn, and there isn't anybody who could possibly teach you.' Another professor stated that he learned the most about counterpoint and polyphony from Johann Sebastian Bach and from Pixinguinha. The latter, the professor continued, had taken the tendencies toward modern counterpoint present in the early choros of the nineteenth century and had developed them further. Other musical forms of MPB also benefited from Pixinguinha's work.

Choro Musicians and Conjuntos

Choro's popularity began to wane as phonographs and radio (1935) came into widespread use. Only vocal stars could succeed in the new media. Instrumental ensembles offered little opportunity for mass identification with the artists. Moreover, for house balls and other musical events a *vitrola* (victrola) was cheaper in the long run than the musician's already low salary. 'Musicians eat and drink too much,' the rich would complain. In general, a musician had to play eight hours before he was allowed to take his first break in the early hours of the morning. It used to be that they were not even paid. Instead, an oxcart would drive into the Cidade Nova now and then to dump its cargo of beans, rice, flour, pork and chicken for the musicians.

Choro musicians finally found their way into orchestras, accompanying such samba singers as Mario Reis and Carmen Miranda. They were, in fact, quite welcome additions here; for of all the instrumentalists active in popular music in those days, they were the best versed and most experienced. This new sphere of activity led the conjuntos to take up a number of percussion instruments from the samba instrumentation. Tinhorão regards this moment as the birth of the *conjunto regional*. And while its musicians continued to play in sound studios and in theater orchestras accompanying the singers, for many years authentic choro was only performed in the suburban underground by these *conjuntos regionais*. Choro regionais had sprung up in São Paulo and other metropolitan areas as well.

Public taste, always subject to foreign influence, especially demanded sambas and samba-canções with big band arrangements and modern orchestration in the forties. At the same time, Luiz Gonzaga's baiões had made the sanfona so popular in Rio that the accordion came to replace the cavaquinho or bandolim in many pieces.

Only a handful of choro musicians were able to make a career out of their trade at this time, a vital necessity if the choro was ever to secure a continual, albeit small, presence on the music scene. One of those who did was Jacob 'Pick' Bittencourt, better known as Jacob de Bandolim. He was born on February 14, 1918. His father was a pharmacist; his mother came from Lodz, Poland. At twelve, Jacob began playing the popular valsas and samba-canções of the day on his fiddle. This was not enough for him, and he soon changed to the bandolim. Chorões had already used this Neopolitan instrument (a mandolin with a flat sounding board) for solo parts at the end of the nineteenth century. Jacob achieved a perfection in performance yet to be equaled. Despite his success, which was aided by the radio, Jacob never wanted to become dependent on his music. So during the day he worked as a drugstore clerk; evenings he went to the Radio Guanabara Studio, where he even accompanied the legendary poeta-da-vila Noel Rosa. In 1940 he won a competition that earned him a life-long pension.

In the forties and fifties Jacob de Bandolim composed a great number of choros, chorinhos (quick choros), valsas and polcas, including such standards as 'Isto é Nosso', 'Alvorada', 'Diabinho Maluco', and 'Flor Amorosa'. He made a number of records together with his conjunto Época de Ouro, but only after 1947. There had been very few recordings of choros produced since 1902, the year when flautist Pattapio Silva played 'Zinha' and other polcas, which were the first phonograph records produced by Casa Edison in Rio. Jacob's shellac discs made use of breathtaking instrumental technique and, most important, extremely imaginative improvisations in order to enliven the authentic choro, a project which Pixinguinha had already begun. Jacob's improvisations and those of other choro musicians often sounded like melodic parts in and of themselves. In contrast to the improvisational choruses in jazz, the chorão never departs from the melodic line.

Musicians regard choro as difficult to play. 'What's necessary are honest musicians,' says one chorão. The following description is based upon musicians' statements in characterizing their genre: Choro is an expression of a culture. Choro musicians are born, not made; choro is in their blood. The chorão is also always an extraordinary musician. He knows his instrument as no one else does. Syncopations and harmonies typical of the choro can only be correctly played with *his* instrumental technique and *his* improvisational talents. The chorão is always prepared to play. He has no troubles beginning to make music. His problem is not being able to stop. Competition among chorões is totally foreign, as are aspirations to stardom. The love of their music stands above all.

The chorões are the aristocrats of MPB. Curiously, many of them have full-time jobs as public servants. In those years when the choro was rarely played in public, a whole generation of musicians arose which was unable to support itself from choro alone.

Even Waldir Azevedo, the other important choro mainstay of the forties and fifties next to Jacob de Bandolim, was a white-collar worker at first, until his great compositional successes (such as the baião 'Delicado' and the chorinho 'Brasileirinho'*) brought him sufficient income as a musician.

Waldir Azevedo was born on January 27, 1923, five years after Jacob. He had tried a variety of instruments in his youth, including flute, banjo, four-string guitar and bandolim before he finally decided upon the cavaquinho, and thereby achieved a mastery of his instrument on a par with Jacob. In 1945 the well-known flautist and composer Benedito Lacerda (1903–1958) ended his conjunto's contract with the Radio Clube do Brasil. Dilhermando Reis, one-time master of the Brazilian guitar, was commissioned to put together a new group for singer accompaniment. It was a lucky coincidence that a cavaquinho player was missing, and Waldir Azevedo was chosen. As already mentioned, it was a difficult period for choro musicians. The end of the Second World

---

* Known as 'Amorada' outside Brazil.

War signaled what practically amounted to an invasion of musical imports into Brazil. North American foxtrot, jazz, beguine and Cuban boleros largely determined the musical scene of the day. Brazilian big bands were busy jealously copying their North American counterparts.

Only Severino Araujo and his Orchestra Tabajara from Recife remained true to the traditional repertoire of sambas, frevos and choros, although they, too, used elements from big-band jazz for their arrangements. In this period the careers of Jacob de Bandolim and Waldir Azevedo had their start. Waldir told me how he wanted to play a melody for a few neighborhood kids back in 1947, but had left his cavaquinho at the studio. He had only an old cavaquinho at home, and it had but a single intact string. Using this string, the uppermost, 'Brasileirinho' took form, the forerunner, one might say, to Jobim's 'Samba de uma nota só'. In 1950 Azevedo composed the baião 'Delicado', his second piece to achieve world renown, in a sense as a response to the bolero's great popularity at the time.

Until his death in 1980 Waldir Azevedo resided in Brasilia, which served as his home base; from there he and his conjunto regional could travel to their many engagements around the country. Many years ago Azevedo made a guest appearance on one of those 'Brasiliana' shows that have been around in Germany for decades. He came to Germany again in 1978 in order to appear on a television show hosted by Caterina Valente. Another chorão, Abel Ferreira, introduced the choro to Europe. He notes today, many years later, 'We were a hit all the way to Russia.' But in the same breath he lets us know, 'Finally, after thirty-five years of musical experience, they are discovering here in Brazil that I know how to perform Brazilian music.'

Choro instruments have not only been expanded over the decades, but also improved upon. Horondino Silva noticed he needed a lower tone on the guitar that offered him a wider range of playing possibilities, as well as a fuller sound. So he constructed the first seven-string guitar (*violão-sete-cordas*) and became, quite naturally, its best player. Dino emerged as his successor in the seventies. Jacob de Bandolim constructed a violinha, a vibraplex, a tuba de codas, a bariton de cordas and, finally, his bandolim brilhante, with which he made most of his records.

Parallel to this new instrumentation, and resulting from an affinity to other MPB stylistic forms, new varieties of choro music developed. Among them were the *brejeiro* (see the choro-tango from Nazareth bearing the same name), *jocoso* (e.g., Victor Correia's 'André de sapato novo'), *choros románticos* (modinha influence), *choros ligeiros*, *samba-choros*, and *choros clásicos* (also called *choros erúditos*). Best-known of the latter are certainly the fourteen choros by Heitor Villa-Lobos (1887–1959). Radamés Gnatalli (born 1906) attempted to improve upon folkloristic and popular playing styles, propagating a very elaborate responsory chant form using the choro rhythm (Radamés Gnatalli e a Bossa Eterna). Altamiro Carrilho, the leading choro flautist of his day, occasionally employed European classical models (for example, Bach) for his choros.

And, finally, lyrics were also written for the choro. While the vocal version of the somewhat slow choro is oriented toward the samba canção and modinha (often reminiscent of the Portuguese fado), chorinho vocals closely approximate the original character of choro music. The voice assumes the role of the flute, saxophone, or clarinet, with all the tone leaps customary for the choro, and keeping to the sequence A–B–A–C–A. There are only very few really good choro vocalists. The rapid chorinho, in particular, demands extraordinary voice control, sometimes requiring a leap from contralto to soprano and falsetto at breathtaking tempi.

Ademilde Fonseca (born 1921) is esteemed in Brazil as 'Queen of the Choro Song'. She is, in fact, the only singer who can perform Waldir Azevedo's' Brasileirinho with the same virtuosity with which the composer originally conceived it on the cavaquinho. Elisete Cardoso (born 1920), the grand old lady of the samba-canção has made recordings of Pixinguinha's choros ('Lamento,' 'Carinhoso') with an expressive force not yet matched by any other singer. Contemporary MPB singers ranging from Baby Consuelo to Nara Leão have also performed chorinhos on their albums, but without ever achieving the real master's touch.

The appearance of the bossa nova on the musical scene was a great discouragement for choro artists. Anibal Augusto Sardinha from São Paulo, famous as Garoto (1915–1955), was still attempting to lift the choro out of its stagnation, but no one was willing to follow his lead. At his death he left behind a tape recording of eight choro pieces dominated by chords that would later show up in the bossa nova. As a Brazilian musician who also played the electric guitar, North American swing, and the foxtrot, Garoto had tried to integrate elements of North American dance music into the choro. Alas, it was all in vain.

Jacob de Bandolim passed away on August 13, 1969. By then, countless honors had been conferred upon Pixinguinha. His comrades from earlier days were dying off one by one, leading Pixinguinha to confess, 'My biggest fear is that one day I won't be able to meet anyone from my time.'

On February 17, 1973, Pixinguinha wanted to attend the famous parade of the Banda da Ipanema. He made a quick stop beforehand at the church where he was to be god-father of a friend's child. He gave a handwritten manuscript of his choro 'Carinhoso' as a gift. At that very moment, as the parade of the Banda da Ipanema was commencing in front of the church and about ten thousand people were beginning to sing and dance in the streets, Pixinguinha collapsed in the church and died. A torrential downpour suddenly began outside, but that did not trouble the musicians and dancers. Yet as the news of Pixinguinha's death became known, Sergio Cabral's biography, *Pixinguinha*, describes how, 'the sweat of the dancers became mixed with tears.' Song and music subsided.

Pixinguinha's friends say he was a saint. It was only fitting that he should die in a church. When Jesus Christ closed his eyes, stormy weather was brewing as well.

Brazilians have honored their São Pixinguinha since the end of the seventies with the Projeito Pixinguinha, an annual state-sponsored festival in which artists give hundreds of concerts throughout the whole country.

By the middle of the seventies choro had acquired a new significance. The baianos' *tropicalismo*, or *tropicalia*, had created a sensation throughout the country. The Clube de Choro, under its founding director, Celso Cruz (Brasilia), made good use of the ensuing calm after the storm to revitalize the choro. One of the most devoted members of the club was Paulinho da Viola. He described himself as having been raised with escola de samba (Portela) and choro, producing a unity of *tristeza* and *alegria* in his music. Paulinho's childhood home was always full of choro musicians coming and going. His father, Cesar Faria, was, after all, a guitarist in Jacob's legendary conjunto Época de Ouro for many years. The Época de Ouro still exists today, thanks to the efforts of the Clube de Choro. Happily, many young people today are rediscovering the choro as an independent musical creation of their country that has been preserved throughout its hundred-year existence almost in its pure, original form. The choro never really was in danger of being commercialized. Its natural swing and improvisational flair make it a national parallel to jazz, even with its individual peculiarities. Paulo Moura, who feels equally attracted to both choro and jazz, told me: 'We live in an age in which everybody plays alike, the same style, the same rhythm. Choro gives a musician the chance to develop himself further, in his interpretations and improvisations.' This statement, of course, also reflects the hope that new talent will offer fresh impulses to the choro's musical development, as was the case with jazz. Several musicians, however, commented in the mid-seventies that the choro's stagnation reflected the country's social stagnation.

For all that, Brazil's choro musicians are not at present forced to seek their fortunes abroad (as Altamiro Carrilho did in Mexico), nor are they compelled to look for work in dance orchestras, or even to change their calling. Since the campaigns put on by the Clube de Choro in the form of concerts, festivals, and media and television promotion, Brazil has rediscovered the choro. Even the record industry has combed through its archives and released new issues of Jacob, Waldir Azevedo and Pixinguinha for the public. For the first time in many years, new choro records have been produced. The premier example has been Marcus Perreira, whose small record firm specialized in the seventies in authentic MPB productions. Musicians who for many years had been respected as excellent choro instrumentalists finally got their chance to record long-playing albums. Abel Ferreira, Raul Barrios, Copinha, Evandro belong to this group.

There is also no lack of young talent. On top of the list are bandolim players Deo Rian and Joel Nascimento, a student of Jacob's, and the many young musicians following in the footsteps of Canhoto (Francisco Soares de Araujo), an important choro guitarist. Around 1980 the federal 'Projeito Almirante' (named after the famous singer and MPB chronicler) promoted the young ensemble Camerata Carioca, which in collaboration with Radamés Gnatalli and Joel Nascimento learned by heart the music of Vivaldi and Astor Piazzolla as well.

Musicians, composers and singers of today's MPB have always been aware of the choro's significance, even before Brazil's public began to awaken again to the choro. In numerous record productions, ranging from Tom Jobim ('Choro') and Chico Buarque ('Meus Caros Amigos') to rock musicians (A Cor do Som, Moraes Moreira) and progressive musicians such as Hermeto Pascoal, choro has once again secured a place in the repertoire.

Kinship Bonds

A final look at the choro's significance in its Pan-American context could prove illuminating. The tango, choro and jazz (or its precursor, ragtime) all have their roots in the latter half of the nineteenth century. The tango arose under the direct influence of the Cuban habanera, the choro from the habanera via the maxixe, and ragtime right by the Caribbean in New Orleans. All three musical forms were born as mixed forms of different cultural spheres within the neighborhoods of underprivileged social groups: the tango in the Orillas of Buenos Aires, the choro in the Cidade Nova of Rio de Janeiro and ragtime or jazz in the French Quarter of New Orleans.

Jazz and choro most certainly arose with African participation, whereas the tango, as a consequence of its kinship to the habanera and the small African populace in Buenos Aires, can only be regarded as having a minimal African element.

Tango, choro and ragtime: all three were primarily purely instrumental forms. The following elements common to the three are striking:

1. Small, mobile orchestras.
2. One or two melodic instruments accompanied by stringed instruments playing the harmonies and bass lines. Percussion.
3. Collective performance.
4. Improvisation.
5. Musicians of each genre's early period are honored accordingly: Guardia Vieja (Argentina), Guarda Velha (Brazil), Legends of Jazz (USA).
6. Rhythmical characteristics: Choro and ragtime can be easily confused with each other. The tango rhythm, too, exhibits the *braking effect* typical of choro and ragtime. All three are frequently characterized by a predominance of sixteenth notes.
7. Injection of the musician's personality. Tango, choro, jazz (ragtime), in their original forms, were always influenced by the musician's personal mannerisms, means of expression and disposition, through which he communicated himself to his audience.

These are only a few common traits which I find noteworthy. It should be mentioned that many choro musicians do not like the tango, which they find too sentimental; ragtime musicians may take the choro for a copy of their own music; and tango musicians were never too pleased about Ernesto Nazareth calling his choros *tango*.

Another possible parallel one might draw from the apparent common line of descent, as evidenced by the named correspondences, would be a kinship between the samba and rock-'n'-roll.

Chapter 4

The Samba

Origins

In 1987 Brazil had a birthday to celebrate: the samba had turned seventy. That is how long it has been since Ernesto dos Santos presented his carnival hit 'Pelo Telefone' to the public. A year before that, he had the title officially registered and printed under the new name 'Samba Carnavalesco'. As we will shortly see, Donga (as Ernesto dos Santos was known) had not created a new musical genre with a new rhythm with this title (from 1916–17). It did however mark a turning point in the popular music culture of Rio and other large cities, enabling other musicians to develop the new samba music, and that, in turn, brought forth further stylistic offshoots.

It has never been satisfactorily resolved (and probably never will be) where the term *samba* originated. Since it occurs in sources and documents of Brazilian cultural history exclusively within the context of Afro-Brazilian folkloric forms, it could undoubtedly be of African origin. One thing is certain. Donga did not invent the name. Silvio Romero calls our attention to a coco in his collection *Cantos Populares do Brasil* that was published in Lisbon in 1883:

Que pra dançarem o samba

Romero added that *samba* is used as a synonym for a number of dances, including the *xiba, catereté, baiano, fandango* and *candomblé*. In the same work Romero reports that 'in the sambas, in the sound of the viola and baiano he had heard improvisors from the hinterland composing motifs using a constant refrain.' In 1928 Rodrigues de Carvalho published a book entitled *Cançioneiro do Norte* containing the song title 'O Samba' from the Ceará region:

> Since the people did not receive permission
> To dance the samba
> The commanding sergeant
> Had them all tied up in chains.

Other earlier sources mention a *semba*, an *umbigada* from Luanda (Africa), that was supposedly popular in Brazil during the latter half of the nineteenth century. Vasco Mariz expresses the belief in his *A Canção Brasileira* that the sambas which became popular in Donga's time were already extant much earlier, such as the songs 'Fadinho de Sabina' in 1888 and 'Bendengo' in 1898. There are also theories that maintain the samba existed among Amerindians even before the Africans' arrival in Brazil.

Most deserving of our attention are Edison Carneiro's studies. He has traced both the name and basic musical-choreographic features of the samba back to Afro-Brazilian batuques.

It is likely that numerous batuque forms (such as cocos, jongos and sambas) were brought to Rio by 'internal immigrants' arriving from all parts of the country. This immigration began in the middle of the nineteenth century, at the latest with the emancipation of the slaves. These people had left their plantations, fazendas or drought-stricken areas in order to seek better opportunities in the capital. They brought with them a wide variety of chant forms from Afro-Brazilian lundus, worksongs and songs from Afro-Brazilian cults. Three distinct song forms in the samba family were distinguished at the time: *samba raiado* (a simple form with satirical, humorous texts), *samba corrido* (narrative), and *samba chulado* (rhymes, found in the large cities).

During the Belle Epoque there was, basically, only one occasion in the year when a walk through Rio's different districts would bring one into contact with all the song and dance forms of the time, with all their various origins. That was carnival. Zé Perreira the shoemaker and Chiquinha Gonzaga the composer had proven that it was possible to offer the carnival public a single song or rhythm that all could celebrate together. This never succeeded on any large scale, since the different social classes celebrated their carnivals separately, and since the lower classes were heavily restricted in their activities by the rules and regulations imposed upon them by the elite. In response to this situation, as well as in imitation of the upper class's carnival organization, they began to form their own groups. Thereafter, Rio's street carnival was conducted through two organizational forms. The lower classes came together in *cordões*; the lower-middle class formed *blocos* of residents from a street or neighborhood who kept to themselves during the festivals and played their polcas and valsas.

The cordões were often identical to groups that participated in the Catholic holiday processions and that, at the same time, were in contact with the centers of Candomblé and Macumba. Chiquinha Gonzaga wrote their *marcha rancho* 'O Abre Alás' for the cordão Rosa de Ouro in 1899. *Ranchos* were the cordões' processions. Their origin is generally ascribed to Bahians who settled in Rio with their semi-religious processions. Until Chiquinha Gonzaga's marcha rancho, rancho participants simply sang and played just about anything that came to mind. 'O Abre Alás' united them for the first time around a common rhythm (a slow, syncopated march) and a common song. The cordões and their ranchos made their home in the morros in the city districts of Estácio and Catête.

Chiquinha Gonzaga's marcha rancho, which was usually played without wind instruments and with a lot of percussion, was taken up by brass bands, but it could never succeed as a secure fixture at carnival. 'Vem Ca, Mulata', a mixture of tango, polca and chula became popular in 1906. 'A Vassourinha', a frevo, was the big hit of the 1910 carnival in Recife. According to Edigar de Alencar's *O Carnaval Carioca atraves da Música*, there were even non-Brazilian influences working upon Rio's carnival music at the time. In 1913 a sentimental melody taken from the American song 'Caraboo' by Sam Marshall was well-liked. It was said to have been brought to Brazil by blacks from Jamaica. While the First World War did not have any influence thematically on MPB, historians have detected an increasing nationalism at that time. In 1916, for example, the 'Código Civil' was officially proclaimed, which they regard as a modernization of social structures. At the same time, hostile positions were taken against non-Brazilian influences, especially those of Portugal. The birth of the samba in 1917, however, could be considered as coincidental.

When Pixinguinha put together his first band, Donga his friend was also a member. Donga also frequented the home of Tia Ciata, a Bahian and Macumba priestess in the Cidade Nova with his colleagues. Tia Ciata's house on Rua Visconde de Itauna 177, right next to the Praça Onze, was a meeting place for musicians, composers and lyricists. Lundus, choros, maxixes, candomblé, ranchos and many other musical forms were played, written and discussed here. Such meetings occurred in great numbers. Bohemians in Rio met at Tia Tereza's, Bahians at Tia

Tetéa's. During the day, these *tias* (aunts) sold their *comida baiana* (Bahian food) in the streets. At the same time, Tia Tetéa's and Tia Ciata'a homes served as an information centers for the cordões and their musicians (the sambistas) in the city neighborhoods.

Most Brazilian musicologists agree that the birth of the *samba-carioca* (samba carnavalesco) cannot be ascribed to Donga alone. Ary Vasconselos believes Donga was able to combine different musical forms in circulation at Tia Ciata's into a single form. Tinhorão, on the other hand, attributes the creation to a collective of Bahian musicians working together at Tia Ciata's.

After publication of 'Pelo Telefone' a quarrel cropped up over the copyright. Donga and his lyricist, Mauro de Almeida, were accused of having 'borrowed' the text. In the same year 'Samba Carnavalesco' was recorded on phonograph by the singer Bahiano.

Donga & Mauro de Almeida

Pelo Telefone

The master of the follies
Had me advised on the telephone
Not to quarrel with pleasure
If I wanted to have fun
Ai, Ai, Ai
Leave your worries behind you, my boy
Ai, Ai, Ai
Be sad if you succeed and you'll see.
I hope you get a thrashing
So you'll never try again
To take a woman away from another
After you've performed your tricks.
Look, the turtledove,
Kind sir, kind sir,
It is outright embarrassed.
The little bird
Kind sir, kind sir,
Has yet to dance a samba,
Kind sir, kind sir,
Because this samba,
Kind sir, kind sir
Gives you goose bumps
Kind sir, kind sir
And makes you weak at the knees

Kind sir, kind sir
But it's great fun

The following is one example of the many parodies arising from the copyright dispute:

The master of the follies
Had me informed
Over the telephone
That everywhere
Fidalga beer
Can be purchased

Donga's song was a success, but it didn't make him rich. He remained a musician in Pixinguinha's various ensembles — Os Oito Batutas, Orquestra Tipica Pixinguinha-Donga, Grupo da Guarda Velha, and Diabos do Céu. Donga died in 1974 and left behind him a great number of compositions.

The samba carnavalesco of Donga and his colleagues, soon also known as *samba-carioca* or *samba da cidade*, took form over the next twenty to thirty years, finally consolidating into a new musical genre.

Rhythm of the samba (after A. Vasconsellos)

The composer Sinhô (José Barbosa da Silva, 1888–1930) was fundamental in the beginning phase of this consolidation. He came from a musical family among whom the choro flautists Callado and Pattapio Silva rated high. Sinhô was a pianist and a frequent guest at Tia Ciata's. His sambas and marchas were the top hits of the carnival season eight times from 1918 to 1928. This earned him the title *Rei do Samba* (King of the Samba). He was also one of those involved in the controversy with Donga over the authorship of 'Pelo Telefone'. Sinhô's colleague Heitor dos Prazeres (1898–1966) accused him, on the other hand, of publishing other people's compositions under his own name ('He's the King of my Sambas'). Sinhô's first row with Pixinguinha, Donga and friends came in 1918, when he had a small group sing in public 'Quem São Eles?' ('Who are they really?'). The defendants countered with the songs 'Fica

Calmo que Aparece' ('Stay Calm, It'll Soon All Be Clear' by Donga),
'Não Es Tal Falado Assim' ('You're Not On The Tip of Everyone's
Tongue', Hilario), and 'Já Te Digo' ('I'll Tell You Something', by
Pixinguinha and China). Sinhô replied with a new song, 'Tres Macacos
no Beco' ('Three Apes in an Alley'), undoubtedly referring to
Pixinguinha, Donga and China.

Pixinguinha
I'll Tell You Something
(Já Te Digo)
One of them is me
And who is the other, that I don't know
He suffered ...

None of you know who he is
But I'll tell you
He is an ugly character
Who speaks of danger without
Fear or anxiety
One of them is me
And who is the other, that I don't know
He suffered ...

He is tall, lean and ugly
And toothless

At the end of the twenties, Mario Reis, a 'discovery' of Sinhô's,
became the first important singer of the new sambas and, simultaneously, of the new media forms of radio and phonograph. Sinhô died
in 1930 on a ferryboat in the Bay of Guanabara. All told, he had written
about 150 songs, of which about 100 were recorded. His funeral was a
colorful mixture of personalities — soldiers, prostitutes, thieves, *macum-
beiros*, serenaders and choro musicians, street vendors of Bahian
candies, actors and chauffeurs. Sinhô's death marked the end of a period
in MPB. Almost simultaneous with the Belle Epoque, Ary Vasconselos
identified the years from 1889 to 1927 as the old, primitive or heroic
phase.

The Birth of the Samba Schools

Contrary to often-heard assumptions, the chief impulse for samba carnavalesco's development did not originate in Rio's favelas on the slopes of the morros. Let us not forget that Pixinguinha's father was a power-line worker and Sinhô's father a housepainter. But both were musicians in their free time as well. As the samba became popular, more and more composers and songwriters from the bourgeois middle class took part in the musical events between Ash Wednesday and the carnival of the next year. As much as the people from the favelas and around Praça Onze liked to think of themselves as the true guardians of the samba ('O Samba não tem dono, é nosso': 'The samba does not have an owner; it is ours'), they still could not prevent this new musical form that arose in their midst in 1917 from capturing the attention of those who were only thinking of profits — music publishing houses, theater and concert agencies and radio stations. Nevertheless, while upper-class money may have promoted the careers of composers and singers from their own class, it was unable to take away from the blocos and cordões the enthusisiasm for *their* music. It could even be that the participation of these upper classes indirectly influenced the formation of larger organizational forms that united the blocos and cordões at the end of the twenties. These more tightly organized, disciplined *blocos carnavalescos* were officially founded in 1928 under the name *Deixa Falar* ('Will you let them speak!'). Shortly thereafter, the name was modified to *Escola de Samba Deixa Falar*. It is assumed that the name *Escola de Samba* was taken from a samba written in 1923: 'There's no samba school like the Estácio de Sá' (a city district). Around 1930 the term *batucada* came into use, meaning three things at the same time:

— A festival and party with batuques
— A percussion group
— A compositional form (Sinhô had already entitled one of his songs 'Marcial Batucado'.)

The *bamba*, a black or mulatto figure who distinguished himself as a musician and singer, either in *partido alto* (improvising verses) or in the *batucada de perna* (danced) as a batuqueiro, first appeared with the batucada. The bamba was subject to a strict code of honor, as was the capoeira dancer, from whom the batuqueiro figure is said to be taken.

The blocos carnavalescos had no regular meeting place at that time. They met sometimes in a sambista's home or practiced in the streets and squares of the neighborhood. As samba schools began springing up like mushrooms in North Rio, favela residents recognized that they could show the world, through their own cultural traditions and presentations, that they were also somebody and that they could distinguish themselves from neighboring districts of the same social class with their samba schools.

Besides the two samba schools, Deixa Falar and Mangueira, the *Escola de Samba da Portela* was also beginning to make a name for itself by the end of the twenties. The credit belonged especially to Paulo da Portela, the founder and brains behind the whole operation. He is still known today as the 'civilizer' of the samba. He reorganized the Portela's processions at carnival, making them into lavish spectacles prepared and thought out down to the last detail. Known as O Principe Negro (the Black Prince), Paulo da Portela introduced allegorical scenes into processions. In the thirties he formed within his samba school the Academia do Samba where he trained musicians and issued diplomas.

Moreover, the Black Prince was a brilliant PR man, adding much to the popularity of his own school. We are indebted to his first-rate press work for the first well-founded newspaper reports covering the new samba schools.

The samba schools, which began with about a hundred musicians and dancers (later with as many as a thousand participants advancing onto the Praça Onze), grew rapidly in importance in the thirties to such an extent that Rio's city authorities intervened, imposing compulsory registration upon all samba schools. The city fathers recognized clearly that the attraction that these organizations exercised over the city's northern residents could be used, if necessary, to influence the masses politically and even to mobilize them.

It all began when the authorities (Getúlio Vargas's first dictatorship lasted from 1930 to 1945) rejected the original name chosen for the Portela: Vai Como Pode (Come As You Are). The name struck them as sounding too democratic, as well as conflicting with Vargas' intention to force the people to see things his way. The school renamed itself Gremio Recreativo Escola do Samba Portela (Recreational Corps of the Portela Samba School). The Vargas regime meant to exploit the samba schools in line with its own interest of strengthening patriotic fervor in the populace. In accordance with this aim, the regime let it be known that patriotism should also 'inspire' the samba school's songs. Thus as early as 1936, Mangueira patriotically took its 'Brazil's Hour' to carnival. In fact, the samba schools have more in common with governmental apparatus than they do with the anarchy of the suburbs. The parades, for example, are nearly as well-organized as those of the military. And there is a rigid hierarchy within the samba school, from the directors down to the ordinary folk.

In the meantime, members of the middle class, at least those living in the Portela, Mangueira and Vila Isabel districts, were gaining entry into the samba schools. They were sought for the social and financial connections they brought with them. Music and lyrics also benefitted from the admission of the new musicians. Whether by private or academic means, most had acquired a superior musical background and so were often able to smooth over the rough edges of many a coarse samba arrangement or to contribute a greater poetic elegance to the lyrics. This led to a change, however, in the samba's role as the voice of the morros: middle-class composers such as Lamartine Babo and João de Barro contributed hymns of praise to the dictator Vargas in the thirties, even as late as the fifties.

Two years after the putsch of 1930 in São Paulo, the constitutional revolution to overthrow Vargas began. (It was put down by the military only months later, but managed to effect new elections and a constitutional convention in 1933.) Authors from São Paulo modeled themselves on their colleagues from Rio when they wrote satirical sambas like 'Gosto que me enrosco': 'I would love to hear that the dictatorship is ending and that the courageous Getúlio has the grace to hide himself.' At the end of this song, a Figueredo is sworn in as the military saviour of the constitutionalists — the father of later president João Figueredo.

In Bahia the blocos of afoxé had established themselves firmly as a part of carnaval. They originated in the region of the Candomblé, likewise the home of the maracatú. Afoxé groups are made up exclusively of percussion instruments. The melody is carried alone by the chorus of blocos. The tie to the Candomblé manifests itself in a ritual celebration before the parade begins, in which Exú's blessing is asked.

The Golden Age of the Samba

The first period of samba-carioca, what Vasconsellos labeled the Heroic Age, was followed by an epoch of about 20 years generally considered to be samba's Golden Age (Época de Ouro). Important composers, songwriters, and the first vocal stars brought the samba into the limelight of nationwide public favor. It was also an age, however, in which the financially powerful got a whiff of the gold buried in the samba treasure chest. The record industry had already taken its first cautious steps toward recording national music (at Casa Edison in 1902 by Fred Figner) around the turn of the century; the first movie theaters were built in Cinelândia on the Avenida Rio Branco; and in 1923 Roquette Pinto, Rio's first radio station, was opened. Then, as now, radio was an important medium for introducing and popularizing MPB songs. But in those days a considerable part of the music program was produced in the station itself, enabling it to exercise its influence over the repertoire at the point of production. And the fact is that those people busy multiplying their capital via the new medium were not necessarily interested in sending their talent scouts into the morros or the samba schools' quadras. Rather, they sought their composers, songwriters and singers from within their own social milieu. Businessmen, lawyers and musicians from the bourgeoisie founded copyright organizations that also merged with music publishing houses. Through this channel, and with the help of inadequate copyright laws, they were able to turn the intellectual products of the morro's sambistas into profits, even if they were generally unwilling to present these people to the public. And lastly, at this time the foundations for the economic organization of the carnival were laid, as it was soon seen how the processions, which the samba schools kept improving, could be profitably diverted into the tourist industry. The blocos, cordões and escolas de samba had little idea of the powerful economic interests operating behind the scenes. A sambista who received a month's pay in cash for one of his compositions never thought to inquire whether he would be better off with a long-term royalty.

The next novelty to appear at the carnival after the samba carnavalesco was the *marchinha* (in 1920), a lively mixture of march, polka and North American ragtime. Marchinha and marcha soon outdid the new samba in popularity. (Sinhô had already written a number of successful marchas do carnaval.) Partisans of the march were known as marchistas (also ironically as 'marxistas'), samba adherents as sambistas. Sambas tended toward a more poetic, sentimental, philosophical tone while marchas and marchinhas tended to be lively, humorous, satirical and even pornographic (these were later banned).

The samba was enriched with a new variant around 1930 as composers from the upper class became active through the new media. The *samba-canção* appeared as a successor to the already forgotten modinha. The new variant took its song-like lyrical character from the latter, its rhythm from the samba. Percussion, though, takes more of a back seat than it does in samba carnavalesco, reminding us instead of the gentle swing of the choro conjunto. In 1929 Henrique Vogeler (son of German and Brazilian parents from Catumbi) presented Brazilian audiences with their first *samba-canção*, entitled 'Linda Flor' (identical with 'Ai, Ioiô') and sung by Araci Cortes. A year later Vogeler became the artistic director of the Brunswick and Odeon record companies and later on he worked as Villa-Lobos's assistant at the conservatory.

The second samba-canção was created by the pen of the Mineiro Ary Barroso (1903–64) and was entitled 'No Rancho Fundo'. Barroso, a doctor's son, came to Rio in 1920 to try his luck at law. His habit of traveling in bohemian circles quickly used up his money, forcing him to earn his wages as a pianist in the silent cinema. Mario Reis, Sinhô's protégé, was one of Barroso's fellow students. This was his entrance ticket into Rio's music scene and ultimately his road to fame. With hundreds of sambas, marchas, samba-cançãos and valsas to his credit, he was Rio's most successful composer. His 1939 composition 'Aquarela do Brasil' remains today the single most performed Brazilian musical title in the world.

Lamartine Babo (1904–63), his partner in 'Rancho Fundo', also came from the Tijucas middle class in Rio. As a journalist and humorist Babo had easy access to the media. He also wrote a huge number of sambas and marchas (partly in collaboration with Noel Rosa, H. Vogeler, Pedro Cabral and others), many of which became popular both in the carnival and outside of it: 'Teu Cabelo Não Nega' (1932), 'Linda Morena' (1933), 'Grau Dez/Foi Ela' (1935) and many, many more.

Noel Rosa (1910–37) began his career as a guitarist and singer in the Colégio Batista and in a music group in the Vila Isabel district. He suffered from poor health from birth and this fact may have sharpened his critical faculties. He was a bohemian, a caricaturist and essayist; a critical chronicler of his age, his songs reflected this in caustic, humorous, satirical and even lyrical language. His total production during his short life amounted to 212 compositions. Even today he is honored as a creative genius. The cariocas think of him fondly as their *poeta da vila*. He was a philosopher of the samba. Numbering among his greatest hits were 'Palpite Infeliz', 'Feitiço da Vila', 'Tres Apitos', 'Fita Amarela', 'Quando o Samba Acabou' and many others written in the period 1931–37. Forty years after his death Noel Rosa has become the focus of a personality cult, with church services, exhibitions, publications and postage stamps bearing his portrait.

Noel Rosa

Yellow Ribbon
(Fita Amarela)

When I finally die
I want neither tears nor candles
I want a yellow ribbon

Embroidered with her name

If a soul exists
If other incarnations are possible
Then I would like the mulatto girl
To tap-dance upon my coffin

When I finally die
I want neither tears nor candles
I want a yellow ribbon
Embroidered with her name

I wish neither flowers
Nor a crown of thorns
I want a choro with flute
Guitar and cavaquinho.

Other important composers of the thirties were João de Barro (born 1907, the composer of a lot of film scores and collaborator with Noel Rosa for a time in the famous Bando de Tangarás), Ataulfo Alves (1909–69), Custódio Mesquita (1910–45), Herivelto Martins (born 1912), Ismael Silva (born 1905), and Benedito Lacerda (1903–58).

In 1939 Barroso's 'Aquarela do Brasil' added yet another variant to the samba family, the *samba-da-exaltação*. Its effusive, panegyrical lyrics were not unsatisfactory for the Vargas regime. These new sambas departed from traditional samba themes of wine, women and love, and from the poetic flavor that Noel Rosa contributed, in favor of Homeric-like renderings of Brazilian history. In contrast, today's samba lyrics are very short. It was also the custom back then to fill out long melodic passages with call-like formulae like *oi, oi* or *ai, ah*, that facilitated the singing of the refrains.

Ary Barroso

Aquarelle from Brazil
(Aquarela do Brasil)

Oh, open the curtains of the past
Fetch the black mother from the mountains
Put the Congo King into the congado dance
Brazil!

Brazil!
Let the troubadour sing once more
A song to the melancholy moonlight
A song of my love ...
I want to see the lady

Passing through the salon
Dragging her dress with lace trimming behind
Brazil!
Brazil!
For me
For me

The new samba, and composers like Ary Barroso, even caught Walt Disney's attention. He invited Barroso to Hollywood in 1944 to compose the film music to *Have you Ever Been to Bahia?*

Carmen Miranda

Carmen Miranda, legendary singer from samba's golden age, also spent a lengthy time in Hollywood. She is the only Brazilian woman in the long history of MPB to have achieved world fame so far.

Perhaps only the older generation has memories of Carmen Miranda: of medium height, a graceful, delicate figure with a taste for individualistic head dress and clothes, large painted lips and sharply outlined eyebrows. She was a beauty with excellent taste. Her clothes, hats, jewelry and accessories, made from the finest materials, had an exquisite beauty, and she designed them herself. (They can be seen today at the Museu Carmen Miranda on the Bay of Botafogo in Rio.)

Carmen was a wonderful singer, dancer and actress. Her contemporaries praised her unique personal qualities and her humanity.

When the chorinho 'Tico-Tico no Fubá' (which Carmen later turned into a hit) by Zequinha do Abreu was composed in 1917, Carmen was just eight years old. She was born in Portugal on February 9, 1909. One year later, her parents emigrated to Brazil. There, in Rio, her father opened a hairdressing salon. At a time when the cinema was still in its infancy, and Pixinguinha and Sinhô were still going at it, Carmen was attending elementary school at the Escola Santa Tereza in Rio. In 1920 she got the chance to recite a poem during the state visit of the king of Belgium to Brazil, and soon afterwards she began appearing on radio shows for children. Years later she was the darling of her Catholic high school. The nuns took a liking to the 'sweet little girl with the pretty voice.' Carmen is quoted as remembering in Abel Cardoso Jnr.'s biography *Carmen Miranda*: 'My childhood was the most peaceful time of my life. I was always a quiet child and sad. I was always busy playing with my puppets, a real nestling, until I went to the Catholic college.'

Carmen's family moved into another house in 1925, turning it into a private hotel. Carmen was then fourteen. She worked as a saleswoman in a tie store, and there learned hat-making, for which she developed a great talent. Even then, surrounded on all sides by hats, she is said to have sung and dreamt of a career as a film star. But as a singer she was first discovered at a song festival in 1929. In that very same year she made her first record.

She stayed at her first record company only a few months before changing to RCA. Their hope was to build Carmen up as the female rival to the market's big star, Francisco 'Chico' Alves. One of Carmen's promoters advised RCA to have her sing only Brazilian music. That meant no tangos, no Portuguese songs. The Brazilian character of the recordings had to be underscored. And so Carmen Miranda became Brazil's first female recording star. Pixinguinha wrote arrangements, and other well-known musicians from the Velha Guarda took part.

The following years saw the start of a career known today as 'a Brazilian legend'. They were packed with festivals, tributes, concerts and records. An anecdote stemming from this period deserves recounting. In 1930 the ensemble to which Carmen belonged staged the premiere of a musical revue. For the first part of the show dazzling props and lighting effects were installed, something customary for American and European audiences. But here the public's reaction was so cold that it was decided to do without the effects in the second part of the show. Carmen went out onto an empty stage, only to be greeted, unexpectedly, by boos and whistles. Carmen broke down in tears. But instead of leaving the stage, she pulled herself together and began to sing. She received a thunderous ovation.

'I want to conquer eighty per cent of the female public,' she observed in Edgar De Alencar's *O Carnaval Carioca atraves da Música*. If thirty per cent of the men admire me, I'm happy. Why? When women are excited about me, then they want to share that enthusiasm with someone and they bring someone with them along to the show. The men don't. They come alone.'

Between 1930 and 1939 Carmen had droves of hit records. For years she occupied the number one position in all popularity polls. She was called *rainha*, the queen.

During her first concert tour Carmen also sang in Salvador, Bahia. In the audience sat an eighteen-year-old youth who would later join Carmen Miranda in Rio to celebrate his first hits. For Carmen, Dorival Caymmi wrote the samba 'O Que é Que a Baiana Tem'. ('What is it that the Bahian woman has going for her?'). Carmen Miranda had long dreamed of dressing up like a Bahian. This song, written in 1939 for the film *Banana da Terra*, gave her the chance. The costumes, as always, were her own designs.

In the same year that the film appeared in the movie theaters, Carmen's friend Sonja Henie arranged a meeting for her with a Hollywood agent. In 1940 she was already before the cameras in the Twentiety-Century-Fox film *Down Argentine Way*. In the coming years Carmen appeared in fourteen American films with such stars as Betty Grable, Don Ameche, Vivian Blaine, Perry Como, Groucho Marx, Elizabeth Taylor, Dean Martin and Jerry Lewis. Her best-known films are *That Night in Rio* (1941), *Weekend in Havana* (1941), *If I Am Lucky* (1946) and *Copacabana* (1947). In many cases, characteristics peculiar to MPB were replaced in Hollywood movies by stylized Mexican costumes, instruments and musical arrangements. The officially proclaimed policy of 'Good Neighbors' towards South America in those times (and still continued to this day) inhibited the authentic representation of cultures further afield than Mexico.

In 1940 Carmen returned to Brazil for a short visit to find that many Brazilians were not at all happy about her international career. Malicious, venomous press reports accused her of becoming Americanized, of denying her Brazilian heritage. In reply, Vincente Paiva and Luiz Peixoto wrote for her the following samba:

Vincente Paiva, Luiz Peixoto
They Say I Came Back Americanized
(Disseram que voltei americanizada)

They say I came back Americanized
With a lot of dollars
That I'm very rich
That I no longer can stand the pandeiro's break
And that I get goose pimples when I hear a cuica
They say that I'm busy with my hands
And I know there's a rumor about
That I've lost my rhythm and hot-blooded temperament
And there are even no necklaces left over
Why is such poison thrown at me?
It might be that I'm Americanized
My life began with the samba, and now
In my evening twilight
I can hold out the whole night long at the old batucada
In the world of the demimonde, which I still prefer
I still say *eu te amo* and not *I love you*
As long as there is a Brazil.

In the hour for dining
I prefer crab ragout with *chuchu**.

One year later Carmen called it quits in Brazil. She resettled in Hollywood, married the American David Sebastian, had a miscarriage, and repeatedly threw herself overzealously into film work and concert tours. In 1951 she stood at the peak of her career and is said to have been the highest paid performer in the United States. She also toured Europe and other countries.

In 1954 Carmen Miranda once again set foot on Brazilian soil for a short visit, incognito. Rumor had it in Rio and São Paulo that she was weak and sick and that she had come in order to die in her home country. But Carmen surprised these prophets of doom with her exuberance and vitality. Her return was a triumph. She later told a reporter, after her return to Hollywood, 'I'm content in the United States, but I have never stopped being Brazilian. I am happy as never before. Thank you, everyone; you haven't forgotten me. I swear, I have never forgotten my country. Look at my green eyes. They are still the same.' But Carmen Miranda was already sick, overworked and suffering from the effects of previous heart attacks. In her last interview she said, 'There is only one therapy for me — the love of the Brazilian people.'

Carmen Miranda died of a heart attack in her Beverly Hills home on August 5, 1955. She was only forty-six. A week later her body was flown to Rio. For thirteen hours sixty thousand cariocas paid their last respects, and the next day an estimated half million mourners attended the funeral. It was the largest burial ever seen in Rio, and certainly not surpassed even by the funeral of the tango king Carlos Gardel twenty years earlier in Buenos Aires. On this day one Rio hospital alone registered 182 patients in need of treatment for shock.

Years later Carmen Miranda busts were installed in many places. A museum was erected in Botafogo. As the journalist Pedro Bloch said, the Brazilian people, Brazil as she sings and dances, was embodied in Carmen Miranda.

Altogether, Carmen Miranda recorded 281 songs on disc. Among them are three rumbas, two foxtrots, and an Argentine zamba. That left 275 Brazilian titles, certainly no reason for Brazilians at the time to distance themselves from her, or to level an accusation that would hurt any Brazilian: that of *not being Brazilian*. More recently, similar attacks have been leveled at Antonio Carlos Jobim and Sergio Mendes.

───────────────────

*A type of vegetable

The Samba-Choro

The increasing popularity of radio and records led to the use of even more choro musicians to accompany samba singers. It was inevitable that the two genres would give birth to a new hybrid form. In the *samba-choro* the voice took the lead role of the melodic instruments (flutes and stringed instruments), although they continued to phrase in the same manner. Vasconsellos regards the composition 'Amor em Excesso' by Gadé (1904–69), which appeared in 1932, as the first samba-choro to be recorded. Other singers included the choro in their repertoire later on. In 1934 Carmen Miranda sang Heitor Catumbi's (1895–?) 'Comigo não!' The difference between samba-choro and samba-canção are sometimes minimal.

In 1936, the samba-choro was joined by another variety known as samba-de-breque. Translated literally, the words mean 'break samba', and the similarities to the American jazz 'break' are strong. Singer Moreira da Silva (born 1902), also called Kid Morengueira, was the inventor of this novel form of samba-choro. At short breaks between the beats the singer makes an impromptu remark or wisecrack in normal speech, as we know it from old time jazz, for instance. Until the end of the fifties the samba-de-breque remained fairly popular, cultivated mainly by samba-choro singers. The rediscovery of the traditional samba and its past greats in the seventies lent the samba-de-breque (with Nelson Cavaquinho and others) new importance.

The Marcha-Rancho

The carnival of 1917 established the conditions for the development of the samba-carioca. The evolution of música de carnaval on the streets of Rio made vigorous strides forward, parallel to the development of new samba forms in the first half of the century. Composers such as Lamartine Babo and Noel Rosa (with his unforgettable 'Pastorinhas') brought the marcha-rancho new prestige. And later on, a younger generation of composers took to writing marcha-ranchos: Carlos Lyra and Vinicius de Moraes with their 'Marcha de Quarta Feira e Cinzas', Chico Buarque with 'Noite das Mascarados' and 'A Banda' and Luiz Bonfá's world-renowed 'Manhã de carnaval'.

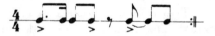

Rhythm of the marcha-rancho

Rio's Penha festival and Salvador's Senhor do Bonfim festival were centres for the marcha-rancho of the period. Around 1914 many musicians who would later play samba and choro (Pixiguinha, João Pernambuco, Donga and others) took part in the Penha's religious processions. Here, too they were already playing choros, valsas and maxixes. A number of composers who would later become successful with the samba were on hand in this circle of Penha musicians.

Ary Barroso's first composition was entitled 'Vou á Penha' ('I'm going to the Penha') even though it had little in common with the festival or with the saints. This was true for almost all Penha sambas. Still, the Penha has remained until today a musical gathering place, especially for choroes and sambistas from the lower classes. A side trip to the Penha in North Rio is well worth the visitor's time. Here, on a weekend evening, you can still hear the best of Rio's choro musicians.

Morros Samba

Samba schools, with the Portela leading the way, began presenting around 1940 their first *enredos*, professionally staged carnival processions. Fantastic costumes, allegorical scenes and well-trained drance groups were brought together under the motto of the year's campaign by the samba schools during carnival time. Silas de Oliveira (1916–1972) may be considered one of the most successful exponents of samba-enredo among the samba schools. He grew up in the Serrinha district of Madureira Rios, where a few families created the small samba school 'O Prazer da Serrinha' in the early 'thirties. Silas de Oliveira was particularly influenced by Angolan traditions, which had been preserved by the descendants of former Bantu slaves in the Madureira/Serrinha quarter. One of these traditional forms is the *jongo*; an anti-clockwise round dance to *pontos* improvised on different subjects. De Oliveira combined jongos with the Morros samba. Later in 1984, sambistas, unhappy about the dictatorial government, left the Serrinha district and founded the 'Imperio Serrano' samba school which soon became one of the leading schools in Rio, thanks to Silas de Oliveira's compositions.

Composers and songwriters from the Escolas de Samba developed their own lyric style. They completely rearranged the usual syntax and introduced paraphrase. The themes of the enredos in the thirties and fourties were taken above all from Brazilian history. Reports say that samba schools at the time always had ready a repertoire of two songs: one was the *samba do terreiro*, a battle song for the triumph in the procession; the other was improvised by the lead singer when he encountered a rival samba school and wanted to provoke it.

In the sixties, shorter lyrics with more vigorous themes supplanted the long, patriotic texts (often containing over thirty verses). The enredos became quicker and more exciting. The appearance in 1967 of 'Carnaval de Ilusões', by Martinho da Vila from the Escolas de Samba Unidos de Vila Isabel, introduced a new orientation toward Brazilian folkloric themes. This samba contained motifs from the rural ciranda. A year later the samba school Académicos do Salgueiro presented 'Bahia de Todos os Deuses'. Tinhorão reports that at the end of the song enredo dancers performed figures from the Bahian capoeira. In 1971 and 1972 Jair Rodriguez popularized two sambas having Bahian themes, 'Festa para um Rei Negro' and 'Tengo Tengo'. They were also performed by the Académicos do Salgueiro.

The return over the course of the years to the shorter texts of the enredo sambas was most certainly influenced by the authors' sympathy for the Rio Branco public, which had to hold out through lyrics of epic length until the samba school had finally passed by.

The samba schools produced many composers, songwriters and singers who used their carnival hits as a springboard to careers outside the school. Cartola (1908–1980) was called Rei da Mangueira, King of Mangueira, until his death. In 1928 with his friend Carlos Cachaca, Cartola founded a carnaval bloco. One year later, this bloco became the second samba school in Rio, the Estação Primeira de Mangueira. Cartola immediately became the first director of the harmony section. He was highly regarded outside his samba school as well. Cartola was best known for his samba-canções, expressing day-to-day experiences and the sufferings of love (the so-called 'dor-de-cotovelo' style, concerning jealousy). Middle-class samba stars such as Mario Reis and Carmen Miranda recorded his songs. Even the great Mario Reis had to persuade Cartola to sell him a composition for 3000 reis, in order that he might earn a handsome sum himself by singing it. Cartola found it incomprehensible that sambas could be bought and sold. Certainly one did no such thing with the wind and water …

By the thirties Cartola had already become a legend in the morros of Rio. The carnaval sambas he composed for the Mangueira led the school to triumph.

Of course, the competition amongst the samba schools was continual. At one point the founder and so-called 'prince' of the samba school Portela, Paulo da Portela, became dissatisfied with his own troupe and hinted to Cartola that he might like to join the Mangueira as director. He was flatly rejected.

When Cartola's first wife died in 1952 he left the Mangueira, contracted meningitis and recovered, fell in love with Zica and began to compose again. Financially he stayed solvent by washing cars, until friends encouraged Zica and Cartola to open a small restaurant with samba entertainment, which they did in 1963. The bossa nova was almost passé again by then and students had begun to comb Rio, searching for the musicians who had actually made the bossa nova possible: the sambistas. Ismael Silva, Cartola, Nelson Cavaquinho and Zé Keti became samba's Big Four, for an intellectual audience as well.

In Zicartola in Rio's Rua Carioca, Zica prepared food and Cartola was the center of the action. Sambistas from all samba schools were regular guests. Young composers of the post-bossa-nova generation made their appearances. Zicartola was the ideal meeting place for black and white — the samba of the morros and the modern Música Popular of middle-class sons from the respectable southern region. Paulinho da Viola did his first public performance at Zicartola in 1964, and when Camus made his film *Orfeu Negro* in Rio, Zica took care of the ironing of the costumes.

Zicartola existed for only a few years; in 1974 it was re-opened in the Villa Formosa quarter. That same year, Cartola's first record was released. Cartola said at the time, 'The true sambistas are those who don't earn much money: Nelson Cavaquinho, Ismael Silva and I. People who do good work don't get rich. But on the other hand, it's a good thing. Sometimes success comes, and perhaps you don't even realize it and you get swept away with it and end up acting important.' 'I'm a nobody,' said Cartola once, 'but I exist. I am Cartola. When I sing with a voice like broken sugarcane, the whole world applauds. Ah, oh, Cartola. So, I am full of myself. I exist.'

The *partido alto* deserves mention. It numbered among the original forms of the rural samba dating back to before the turn of the century, similar in many respects to the Afro-Brazilian jongo. Donga: 'The refrains of the partido alto (and jongo) were sung by the participants in improvised fashion while standing in a circle. The rhythm was simultaneously supported by hand-clapping. The women danced the *miudinho* to the music. The art of the dance consisted in moving a foot slightly angled from the hip in a easy, shaking motion, while the dancer had to hold her body erect and was not allowed to move.'

In the modern-day samba de partido alto the once improvised refrains are usually determined in advance, but are now sung alternately with solo parts. The lead singer, the partideiro, must continually come up with new verses. Xangô da Mangueira is regarded today as King of the Partido Alto and, consequently, Rei dos Bambas.

The *pagode* is an early samba variant, related to the samba de partido alto, which was revived in the mid-eighties.

Bahia in Rio: Dorival Caymmi

A young lad who left Bahia at the end of the thirties and headed for Rio is honoured today as the greatest folksinger Salvador ever brought forth. Dorival Caymmi was born in 1914. Jorge Amado wrote in his foreword to Caymmi's *Cancioneiro da Bahia*, a book of his songs:

> Anybody can make a samba using the musical words of the Nagô language and macumba melodies. But only he can write the samba from Bahia and the Bahian song; only his melodies are Bahian, the body and soul of the black people and mestizos from the macumbas, from the wharfs and ferryboats of Bahia. That is the difference. He goes much further than the simple picturesque. At each and every moment one can feel, in music and text, the colossal strength of the Bahian Negro — that instinct for freedom which is so deeply rooted because it was born in chains — that reaction to prejudice against skin color, unbounded imaginative power, courage and love for adventure. All these qualities are present in his music.

In addition to sambas having a very personal flair, Caymmi's work includes many canções about the sea, fishermen and folkloric themes. His 'Samba da Minha Terra' is very popular.

Dorival Caymmi

Samba from My Region
(Samba da Minha Terra)

The samba from my region
Makes the people weak-kneed
Everybody's shakin'
No one rests
I was born with the samba
And raised with the samba
And from this damned samba
I have never parted
Whoever takes no pleasure in the samba
Is not a healthy person
There's either something wrong upstairs
Or his feet ache

Dorival Caymmi comments: 'This samba was inspired by the samba de roda, in which the refrains occur with *bole-bole* and *requebrados*, which most certainly originated in the ardent, sensitive hip movements of the black Bahian women.' Caymmi also told me how he once caught sight of a candomblé priestess in the marketplace in Salvador and spontaneously came up with a song for her, 'Ai, Minha Maẽ, Minha Mãe Meneninha.'

At nineteen in Salvador, Dorival Caymmi began to compose toadas and marchinhas. In 1936 he won first prize at a competition of carnival song. In 1937 he came to Rio and, two years later, he was famous. The songs he wrote for Carmen Miranda (and sang with her in duets, such as 'Roda Pião') gave his career a big boost. But the best performer of his sambas and canções is still Dorival Caymmi himself. Now a resident of Rio, his musical style is inimitable as a product of the encounter between a folksinger from the Afro-Brazilian milieu of Bahia and the samba of the cariocas, which already had developed to a great extent from Bahian source material.

Caymmi once again: 'My permanent inspirations were the blacks and mulattos whose lives are so intimately connected with the sea. I know of no drama more powerful than that of wives waiting for the always uncertain return of their husbands, who go out upon the sea each morning in their light fishing boats and wonderful wooden rafts.' Success did not change this Bahian cançioneiro. He is, and will remain, what he always was, and therein lies his greatness: the singer of Bahia and its people.

Dorival Caymmi's children — Nana, Dori and Danilo — are all successful artists in their own right. Dorival also looks after young musicians and singers seeking his advice. 'It just so happens that I'm a Bahian.'

The Northeast in Rio: Luiz Gonzaga

Dorival Caymmi came to Rio in 1938. A year later Luiz Gonzaga (1912–1989) followed him from the small village of Exú in the semi-arid zones of the Sertão. At that time, Brazil stood in the shadow of the Second World War, and foreign musical imports dominated the pop music scenes in Rio and São Paulo. The samba had temporarily lost some of its importance in the world of show business. Amid this general crisis for MPB Luiz Gonzaga was the first to succeed in turning the cariocas' attention to the music of Brazil's Northeast. Gonzaga's father Januario was himself a famous sanfoneiro in Sertão, on the edge of the Serra do Araripe. His mother sang novenas, or prayers of request, in church.

The 'moleque' Gonzaga showed an early interest in the sanfona, a type of accordion: 'I made my own expeditions into the mysterious world of sound,' he says in Sinval Sà's *O Sanfoneiro do Riacho da Brigada* 'I invented melodies.' His mother Santana forbade this but 'Lula' always found an excuse to steal away to a festival or the marketplace where he practised on the sanfona of other musicians. Word spread, and because his father refused to play for the neighbors for free, Lula was called upon; first secretly, then finally with his mother's approval.

One day Gonzaga left home. A distinguished gentleman, passing through, took him on as an employee and taught him to read and write. Gonzaga saved the few reis he was paid and bought his first sanfona.

When he fell hopelessly in love and wished to marry, he fell out with his family. He reported for military duty, left Exú and came to Minas Gerais. There he purchased a new sanfona and played for the officers. In 1938 he left the military and went to Rio. He made contact with other musicians from the Sertão living there and earned a little money playing samba-canções, polkas and valsas in cafes and bars. One day some young people approached him in a cafe: why do you play only gringo music? Why don't you play your own music? So Gonzaga began to think back to his origins and his music, and at the next performance for Radio Tupi, the following scene took place (according to his autobiography, recorded by Sinval Sà):

> — Luiz Gonzaga!
> — Ready!
> — Again? You're getting to be a regular, aren't you? Which valsa is it to be today?
> — No valsa, no, Mr. Ari
> — You're going to play a tango? That is also a tango instrument.
> — No again, Mr. Ari. I'm going to play something from the North, Mr. Ari.
> — What's this something called?
> — 'Vira e Meixe'

The station recorded the song, played it, and it found wide appeal among its listeners. One day Gonzaga wanted to sing as well: 'Above all I wanted to prove that something more than badly arranged emboladas came from my homeland; instead the true music of the Sertão: the Sertão of the full rivers, but the Sertão of the desert as well, of the green corn, of the cattle that die of hunger, of the singing *acauã*, of the white wings (Asa Branca) — crying in the *quebradas*, of the mills of the magnificent *forrós*, of the good smell of the mulatto women, of the missions and *cangaceiros*. But at first they forbade me to sing. "That wasn't part of the arrangement," said the head of programming.'

In the meantime Gonzaga had found the first partner to write texts for him, Miguel Lima. But even RCA wanted only his instrumental music at that point.

In 1945 he met Humberto Teixeira, who came from Ceará, in the Northeast. Together they began to write songs with new rhythms, little known in the South and East, that soon became known, both in Brazil and abroad, as baião. Gonzaga himself denies being the creator of the baião, noting its earlier presence in Northeastern folklore. Gonzaga:

> I have picked out a certain rhythmic phrasing used by the guitarist

(violeiro) who accompanies the baião singer and his improvisations.

Along with this baião rhythmic structure Gonzaga also brought the sanfona to Rio.

Succeeding Teixeira as Lula's partner was a young medical student from the Sertão: José de Sousa Filho (Zé Dantas). Gonzaga's influence had three major effects: first, the popularization of the Northeastern baião in urban regions; second, the new prestige that Northeastern music gained in the South and East; third, the influence upon young musicians, who suddenly wanted to play the sanfona. Gonzaga also took the rhythmical group which he would later use in his band from the original folkloric form, namely the *zabumba* and *triangulo*.

Brazil's large cities welcomed the baião. Many musicians and composers embraced the new stimulus from the Northeast. Gonzaga had many imitators. 'Delicado', a baião by Waldir Azevedo, became world famous. Lima Barretto's film *Os Cangaçeiros*, which was awarded the Golden Palm at the 1953 Cannes Film Festival, featured a song, 'Mulher Rendeira,' based on a folk song from the Sertão that Gonzaga and his songwriter Teixeira arranged for the film.

However, Gonzaga maintained that the band headed by the cangaçeiro Lampião used to perform it earlier. The song was subsequently heard all over the world.

And just like Lampião, that notorious bandit from the Northeast, Gonzaga outfitted himself for performances in a Napoleonic tricorne made of leather, vaqueiro style, and the heavy leather jacket of the cattle herder.

Another big hit from the Gonzaga-Teixeira team was 'Asa Branca', a toada with baião rhythm.

Humberto Teixeira/Luiz Gonzaga

White Wing
(Asa Branca)

As I look out over the scorched earth
St. John's fire before my eyes
I asked myself, ai
God in heaven, ai

Why so much wickedness?
What a blaze! What an oven!
Not a single plant anywhere
Due to lack of water
My cattle have died

From thirst my fox
Has left the earth

Today, miles away
In my sorrowful loneliness
I wait for the rain
To fall again
So that I can return
To my Sertão

When the green of your eyes
Is spread over the plantation
I swear to you
Don't cry
Then I will return again
My dear

Caetano Veloso, Luiz Gonzaga Jr. and many others have recorded this piece. Among Gonzaga's most popular songs are the *xamego* 'Vira e Meixe' (xamego is a Northeastern variety of choro), the *calango* 'Dezessette e Setecentos' and the baiões 'Paraiba', 'Juazeiro', and 'Assum Preto'. In recent years Gonzaga, has also recorded pieces by young composers (Gilberto Gil, Caetano Veloso, Dori Caymmi) who themselves have credited Luiz Gonzaga with having been a major influence on their development.

Baião by Luiz Gonzaga

To visit O Rei do Baião the 'King of the Baião' while he was alive, you had to drive toward Galeão airport and exit left; a complicated route through semi-swamp and lake dwellings brought you to the Ilha da Governador.

Luiz Gonzaga lived here in a small suburban house with his wife and daughter. In 1978 we wanted to engage him for a film. Gonzaga apologized right off for only being able to offer us local whiskey. But we knew the Baião King was not rich. He presided over a following of millions, with a popularity in Brazil at least as great as Johnny Cash in the United States. We were served peanuts while Gonzaga's wife told us why she had to hold on to Luiz's salary. Otherwise he would immediately fly off to the Sertão, his homeland, and squander all his money in benefits for his people. The telephone rang. Mrs. Gonzaga came over to me and said, 'Gonzaguinha would like to speak with you,' I followed her through the small house, through the living room and into the bedroom. It was all furnished in spartan fashion: a double bed, a closet, a chair, a chest of drawers, all scrupulously clean. Hanging on the wall were pictures of saints, Luiz Sr., and the children. Gonzaga Jr. was on the phone. 'Listen, Claus. Be gentle with my father. He is old and doesn't always understand everything anymore. Explain it to him as often as necessary, until you're sure he's understood everything. I love my father and wouldn't like him to do anything if he hasn't understood what it's all about.' I reassured Gonzaguinha and then returned to Gonzagão. After several hours everything had been said. His majesty needed time to think. We were to call him the next morning. Of course, he would discuss the matter with Gonzaguinha and his colleagues. Eventually, he agreed, and the filming could begin.

In 1944, Brazil sent troops to Italy to fight with the Allies. Upon their return a year later, the songs in the subsequent carnivals were infused with enthusiasm and pride in their victory. However, 1945 augured the end of Getúlio Vargas' dictatorship. The defeat of fascism in Europe, together with calls for a more liberal political atmosphere – even from Vargas' own friends — were in direct contrast to his style of leadership. Although there was a flowering of the Morro samba in the new samba schools at this time, the staid sambas heard on the radio and released on record sounded old-fashioned compared with the newly imported music from abroad. Especially for the big city, they were regarded as *quadrado* — 'square'. In 1948, Vasco Mariz's *A Canção Brasileira* gave an account of the samba's topography: 'The samba arrived in Rio's center from Bahia, was formed in Praça Onze, was cultivated in Estaçio, ascended to the morro of Mangueira, and then came down once again to the plain.' To complete the story it remains to be said that the samba then retreated once again to the morros, only to be dug up again in the sixties, beginning in the southern districts of Rio. Again and again, the middle-class samba combined with other musical styles from North and South America. The *sambolero* (from 'samba' and 'bolero') and *sambalada* (from 'samba' and 'ballad') are but two examples. The Cuban bolero enjoyed great popularity for a long period of time, although it never occupied a musically important place within MPB. Waldick Soriano, Brazil's best-known bolero singer, would probably disagree. The pro-

tagonist today of *sambolerock*, sentimental, lightly rock-oriented sam-
boleros, is Roberto Carlos. At that time *música brega* became established,
brega meaning kitsch, of shallow sentimental appeal.

In August 1940 the American conductor Leopold Stokowsky came to
Rio with the All-American Youth Orchestra. He received an MPB
delegation on board the *Uruguai*, which had docked at the Praça Mauá
pier. Upon Stokowsky's request, his friend Villa-Lobos had selected
material so that Stokowsky could make recordings for his Columbia
label with a broad cross-section of Brazilian music. Villa-Lobos had
sent on board Donga, Pixinguinha, João da Baiana, Jararaca, Luiz
Americano, Ratinho, Cartola, a delegation from the Escola de Samba
Estação Primeira da Mangueira, Zé Com Fome and many others. Over
one-hundred titles were recorded on board. Stokowsky chose sixteen of
them for a two-album set, each consisting of four shellac discs and,
released them under the title *Native Brazilian Music*. The Brazilian
musicians did not receive so much as a cruzeiro for their efforts.

Nelson Cavaquinho, like many samba stars of the thirties and forties,
was overlooked for a period of twenty years. He is mentioned here as
representative of all those who suffered a similar fate. In the forties
Nelson Cavaquinho (born 1910) had his compositions sold to publishing houses, always for a small fixed sum 'so that I could eat for the week.'
He worked together with Guilherme de Brito, and his sambas, samba-
canções, samba-choros and samba-de-breques first became popular in
1950. Nelson himself, however, regards his colleague Cartola (1908–82)
as 'the greatest'. Originally discovered as a composer, singer and
songwriter way back in 1930, Nelson fell into oblivion thereafter, only to
be unearthed in 1950 once again working at a carwash in Ipanema.

As jazz and rock were making their appearance on the big-city
musical scene in the fifties, and as Jobim and Gilberto were beginning to
introduce modern sambas (bossa novas), people like Cartola and
Nelson Cavaquinho disappeared into obscurity, until Carlos Lyra and
friends helped them make a comeback that has lasted to this day.

The end of the forties also saw the start of a singing career that never
became known outside Brazil. Today, Nelson Gonçalves is still a star,
above all to older Brazilians. Actually he comes from southern Brazil, a
fact audible in his rolling 'r' and his rather Spanish style of singing.
Nelson Gonçalves has, so far, recorded over 1,233 songs, and sold 35
million records.

The middle-class samba stars of the thirties and forties were better
able to compensate economically for their shrinking popularity. One
example is Aracy de Almeida, who died in 1989 at the age of 74. As a
singer her peak was in the thirties and forties, when she became known

above all for her performances of sambas by middle-class composers. After that she still performed sporadically; for many years she appeared as one of the jury in 'A Buzina do Chacrinha', which was, until Chacrinha died, the most popular TV show in Brazil. She was really the last grand old lady of a golden age of samba.

With the return of Vargas in 1951 came another resurgence of pride in the songs of the samba schools. Brazilian history was praised in the carnival parades, with Vargas as its hero. But the hopes of the thirties, when Vargas' reforms had improved general social conditions, began to dwindle in the face of growing economic problems.

Although his second presidency tended toward dictatorship and ended with his suicide in Catete Palace, Getúlio Vargas continued to figure in the imagination of the public and therefore in the imagination of conformist middle-class composers as well. Vargas' last words echo in several sambas until the beginning of the sixties.

A new samba variety developed in São Paulo toward the end of the bossa nova era. The sambas of Jorge Ben were a mixture of Afro-samba, bossa nova and rock elements, mainly carried by a new, vital rhythmical *balanço* from Ben's guitar. Many musicians have attempted in vain to copy this rhythm. Ben's melodies, by way of comparison, are simply structured ('Mas Que Nada', 'Pais Tropical', 'Chove Chuva' and 'Fio Maravilha.)'

Samba-Batucada

Chapter 5

The Bossa Nova

The Pre–Bossa Nova Period

The end of the forties can be regarded as the beginning of the pre-bossa nova phase. North American bebop was taken into the repertoire of Brazilian dance orchestras, influencing the rhythmic accentuation of the bass players. The Cuban-influenced sambolero had a similar effect. However, there were musicians in Rio whose interpretative styles heralded the start of something qualitatively different. Dick Farney sang his samba-canções decidedly 'cool'; Johnny Alf sang his 'jazzed-up'. The popular vocal group Os Cariocas borrowed stylistic elements from the North American group The Pied Pipers, producing a sound with unorthodox harmonic sequences and dissonances. Lucio Alves, Nora Ney and Doris Monteiro were among those singers who made the switch from the expressive, extroverted samba-da-exaltação to the *samba-coloquial*, a quieter samba-canção that mixed bolero with jazz elements and colloquial lyrics.

Antonio Carlos Jobim

An album appeared in 1954 with the Sinfonía do Rio de Janeiro by an unknown twenty-nine-year-old composer named Antonio Carlos Brasileiro de Almeida Jobim. He grew up as Garoto de Ipanema, son of the diplomat Jorge Jobim. Antonio was only eight when his father died in 1935. His friends later called him Tom, but pronounced in the Brazilian way making it sound like the word for sound or tone. The mother remarried, and the stepfather allowed Antonio to study architecture. But Tom was usually found sounding out the grand piano that his stepsister Helena had received as a gift. Jobim's stepfather must have sensed Tom's musical talents, since he sent for Hans-Joachim Koellreutter, a German-born musicologist (born 1915 in Freiburg) and from 1937 a leader of Brazil's avant-garde in the *música viva* movement. The time spent with Koellreutter proved to be very important for Jobim's musical development. Other musicians from MPB (such as Gilberto Gil and João Gilberto) also received their musical training from him during his time as director of the Goethe Institute in Salvador and Rio.

Jobim met up with his university pal Billy Blanco from Pará in 1953. However, both were more attached to their music than to their books and they were soon writing their first sambas together (such as 'Teresa da Praia', recorded on disc by Dick Farney and Lucio Alves, accompanied by Jobim and his band). In 1954 they composed *Sinfonia do Rio de Janeiro*. It was Billy Blanco who first came up with the idea for this naturalistic trilogy, in essence a tribute to the mountains, the sun and the sea that make up Rio's beauty. Billy Blanco wrote almost all the melodies of the symphony. Tom contributed only small parts. Nevertheless, the symphony bears the indelible stamp of his future compositional style. Jobim was heavily influenced by the European romantics, especially Chopin and Debussy, and the symphony has always remained his favorite genre. The *Sinfonia do Rio de Janeiro* was recorded in the same year under Radamés Gnatalli's baton, with Dick Farney, Gilberto Milfont, Elisete Cardoso, and Os Cariocas. According to musicologist Brasil Rocha Brito, Jobim's 'Hino ao Sol' contains history's first bossa nova, four years before the actual beginning of the movement.

Jobim was exposed early on to a number of factors that enriched his later work. He benefited from a classical music education with, among others, a Russian piano teacher who lived 'in a small room on, above, and under his grand piano.' His uncle played Bach's guitar music. He was acquainted with Ary Barroso, Dorival Caymmi and other renowned Brazilian composers. And he was a natural talent himself. All these factors were significant in making Antonio Carlos Jobim the chief figure of the pre–bossa nova period.

Beginnings

The musical scene in the following years shifted, in concentrated form, to the Zona Sul Rio, that is, Copacabana, Ipanema and Leblon. Tinhorão observed this regional concentration and formulated a theory which explained the events of the period as a reaction by the white middle class to black dominance of the traditional samba; an argument which is borne out by the existing divisions within society. The fifties witnessed an extreme polarization within Rio's social strata. The poor, mostly blacks and mulattos, lived in the morros and the northern districts of Rio; the white and the wealthy could be found in the South, the Zona Sul. Although the bossa nova always had a light, rarified character to it, it was never popular among all strata of society and finally, in its isolation, it lost all connection to real life in Brazil. It cannot be regarded as a conscious criticism of certain social groups residing in Rio. At least, I could deduce nothing of the sort based on musicians' comments concerning their motivations. Still, Ronaldo Boscoli, journalist and songwriter, reports a talk he once had with André Midani, former head of Brazil's Odeon. Midani had taken note of how Anglo-American pop music and its Brazilian counterparts had practically cornered the record market, and it was time to reply with a new Brazilian music. Boscoli is quoted in De Mello's *Música Popular Brasileira* as saying, 'We founded the Movimento Bossa Nova with the intention of defending MPB against the specter of rock music, which at the time controlled 70 per cent of the record market.'

So we see there may have been a number of motives that finally brought together a clique with a common goal — reviving MPB.

Vinicius de Moraes

The poet Vinicius de Moraes came to Rio in 1956 to put on his *Orfeu de Conceição* in the Teatro Municipal. Without knowing it, he had created the conditions for the birth of a new song genre that would soon be capturing the public's attention as modern sambas.

Marcus Vinicius da Cruz de Mello Moraes (1913–80) was a modern poet of the people, at home both on the international stage of diplomacy as well as on the impassable dirt paths of the favelas. He was a poet, diplomat, singer, journalist, romancer and dramatist all in one.

Had he lived a century earlier, he might well have wandered the streets of old Rio as a seresteiro, or a troubadour singing modinhas and lundus. Had he been born in the Sertão in the Northeast instead of in Rio, he might have become one of the many anonymous authors of the *literatura de cordel*.

Music and poetry always represented an indivisible unity for Vinicius. Even before he received a scholarship to study at Oxford in 1933 he had composed his first songs at the age of fifteen. To be sure, his literary production was strongly influenced by Manuel Bandeira and Carlos Drummond de Andrade, two of the great poets of Brazilian modernism. Still, Vinicius's poetic genius always remained open to the most diverse tendencies imaginable. His language reflects the sensitive melancholy and irony of the bourgeois sambistas (such as Noel Rosa), as well as the lively vernacular of the everyday life of the morro dwellers and the spiritual world of Afro-Brazilian cults. His drama *Orfeu da Conceição* unites all these diverse elements. 'One day I was sitting at home reading a book on French mythology. I suddenly heard some Negroes playing their batucada from the hills nearby, and everything seemed somehow connected. I felt that there was a story to tell about these people from the morros who live suspended between love and violence.'

This was at the beginning of the forties. Vinicius wrote the first Act that very day. He did not complete the piece until 1956, during a diplomatic mission in Paris and Los Angeles, where *Orfeu* had its debut on September 22 of that year, with stage sets by Oscar Niemeyer, the architect who later designed Brasilia.

Before this, however, Vinicius had already begun looking for composers who could write the music for his work. He was introduced to Antonio Carlos Jobim in a bar. Vinicius asked if he wanted to take part. According to *O Som do Pasquim*, Tom countered, 'Do I get paid for it?' The question was understandable, since in those days musicians like Jobim earned peanuts, usually surviving by moonlighting as piano players at the corner bar. This meeting was the start of a long friendship, lasting until Vinicius's death in 1980. It was a fertile friendship as well, producing a host of songs, and was yet another major factor in the bossa nova's rise to fame.

Vinicius and Jobim's first song was 'Se Todos Fossem Iquais ao Voce' ('If only everybody were like you'), a samba-canção that sounded almost like a bossa nova. 'Se Todos' and a host of other songs born of the Tom-Vinicius partnership ('Lamento no Morro', 'Um Nome de Mulher', 'Mulher, Sempre Mulher') were premiered the same night that *Orfeu* had its first performance.

Orfeu echoes Vinicius's personal philosophy — as expressed in his book, *Pra viver um grande amor* — which demands nothing more from the world than love:

> To experience great love, you must be convinced of the truth that there is no love without devotion — if you are to experience a great love. Whoever fills his love with vanity does not know the freedom, that immense, indescribable freedom, that only a great love can give you.

Anyone who knew Vinicius, a man who loved many women and broke up with just as many, leaving them with the house and possessions, anyone who experienced Vinicius the grandfather at home in Gavea with his children and friends, knows that what he demanded from life in song and poem was lived out with the utmost verve and intensity. 'Pedro, my son,' Vinicius wrote many years ago, 'for me poetry was a cruel woman, in whose arms I threw myself day after day, without ever apologizing to all those women I abandoned for her.'

Love was his life. He never ceased trying to share it, nurture it, communicate it. And it will certainly remain as fresh as the message of his work. For me, Vinicius was a Brazilian Orpheus suspended between the love flourishing in his heart and the cruel violence of our world.

Meetings: Encontros

Before meeting Vinicius, Antonio Carlos Jobim had written several samba-canções together with Newton Mendonça (1927–60), whom many people regard as the leading songwriter of the bossa nova. One of their first songs was 'Foi a Noite'. Others, such as 'Desafinado' (1958) and 'Samba de uma nota so' (1960), have become bossa nova classics.

Jobim has insisted in many interviews that he should not be regarded exclusively as a bossa nova specialist. On the contrary, he says, 80 per cent of his compositions have nothing whatsoever to do with the bossa nova. He wrote primarily *canções da camara*, film music, symphonies, *samba-canções* and choros. Furthermore, Jobim categorically rejects the claim that his bossa novas arose under the influence of jazz:

> Americans call almost anything jazz, from Cuban rhythms to all kinds of Latino music. They say, that's Latin jazz. If that's true, then everything is jazz. African samba rhythms would also be jazz.... But the Americans would never accept the bossa nova if it was only a jazz copy, because too many people today copy jazz and they don't like that. They simply assimilate new things, as they've always done — like bossa nova, Einstein....

There were a number of musicians who actually did play modern jazz, or at least jazz-like music in the bars of the Zona Sul. At the Plaza, singer-pianist Johnny Alf played American music with a few Brazilian ingredients thrown in. His partners were amateurs — pianist Luiz Eça, harmonica player Maurício Einhorn, guitarists Carlos Lyra and Roberto Menescal, singer Silvia Telles, all of them names soon to become famous.

Johnny Alf describes how important it was to the owner of the Plaza that they improvise a lot and play jazz, even if there was no great demand for it as that time. (Menescal and Lyra later were also directors of a music school with over two hundreds pupils.)

The musicians from the different bars knew each other. When they were finished playing for the night, many would band together and go to other night clubs to hear friends play and to talk with them. Singer Nara Leão's apartment on Avenida Atlântica in Leme was often a central gathering place. Here they discussed their ideas and plans and rehearsed, learning from each other's tips and criticisms. Most were the children of wealthy parents and therefore free from economic hardships. Still, the spark had yet to ignite.

João Gilberto

In the same year that *Orfeu du Conçeição* received its stage premiere, a young Bahian named João Gilberto joined up with the young music circle. He was the spark that the group needed. He was able to offer it answers in its search for something new. Jobim commented later, 'In no time at all he had influenced a whole generation of arrangers, guitarists, musicians and singers.' It is no exaggeration to say that neither the bossa nova nor today's popular music scene in Brazil would be imaginable without João Gilberto. Now many of today's popular Brazilian musicians belong to a second generation influenced by him.

As several of the circle's musicians had wound up in the dead-end of simple jazz imitations, Gilberto was able to guide them out by showing them new rhythmic possibilities. Many new songs were harvested from this fertile soil cultivated by Gilberto's novel guitar accompaniment.

Gilberto came from Bahia. He was born in 1931 in Juazeiro as João Gilberto do Prado Pereira de Oliveira. He sang as a crooner in Salvador's bars until coming to Rio in 1949 as a member of the vocal ensemble Garotos da Lua. The first recording of one of his compositions was made in 1953 and performed by the singer Maysa. Gilberto also had occasional gigs in the Boate Plaza on the Copacabana, meeting Johnny Alf and the rest of the clique there.

João Gilberto still remained 'undiscovered' in the vocal ensemble. But as he began to sing alone, *bem pianinho* (very quietly), with only his guitar for accompaniment in the tradition of the speech-song *samba-coloquial*, but with a new rhythmic syncopation on guitar, his colleagues began to take notice. Baden Powell, who in those days played in the Boate Plaza with Ed Lincoln, said, 'I used to play my guitar off the cuff back then. But in terms of accompaniment, that there was something very different.'

It would just be a matter of time until the various groups of composers and song writers got to know João Gilberto and used his ideas in their work.

'Chega de Saudade' is the name of a Tom Jobim piece for which Vinicius wrote the lyrics. Many bossa nova musicians regard it as the first bossa nova to be recorded on disc. Elisete Cardoso sang it in March-April 1958 for the specialty label Festa, long known for its openness to all sorts of new developments and its great tolerance over questions of artistic freedom. Jobim did the arrangements, with Gilberto taking part on several titles.

It was Jobim more than anyone else who worked to get Gilberto the chance to make his own record. Rehearsals made it clear to Jobim that this young guitarist not only played differently, but also sang differently from any singer he had ever heard. Jobim says, 'At first nobody wanted to make a recording with J.G. Everybody thought, "yeah, it sounds good, but it won't sell."' André Midani, from Odeon, finally gave the go-ahead for a 78. On July 10, 1958, J.G. made his first recording with 'Chega de Saudade' and 'Bim Bom'.

Rumor had it that the Odeon rep in São Paulo was furious, cursing what the Rio office had sent him. He apologized as soon as he saw how well the record was selling.

Jobim, Vinicius and Gilberto spent almost every waking hour together. The other musicians from the Plaza clique meanwhile were still having their problems following the new *batida* (beat). Even Milton Banana, J.G.'s favorite drummer, complained in De Mello's *Música Popular Brasileira*: 'The recording sessions took a long time because J.G. was very thorough in his work, and also because none of us really knew what was next and how we should accompany the music.'

At the beginning of February 1959, João Gilberto completed the recording of his first LP, *Chega de Saudade*. (A 78 with 'Desafinado' and 'Oba La La' had come out before that.) Musicians and singers of the modern samba made their first concert appearances in this year as well. The posters for the very first concert at the Hebrew University in Rio read: 'Today João Gilberto, Silvia Telles and a bossa nova group perform modern sambas.'* The name bossa nova was born. Since the forties, whenever an MPB musician did something new, he was said to have done it 'com bossa,' something new 'with pep, talent, and swing.'

The Festival do Samba Moderno, which took place on September 22, 1959, in the Teatro Arena of the university's architecture department, gave the bossa nova's popularity a boost in student circles. Almost the entire circle was there: Tom Jobim, Silvia Telles (already with an LP on the market), Alaide Costa, Carlos Lyra, Ronaldo Boscoli, Baden Powell, Roberto Menescal, Oscar Castro-Neves and his brother Leo, Iko and João Mario, Henrique, Bebeto, Chico Feitosa, Norma Benguel and Nara Leão. Two further concerts, the so-called 'Samba Sessions', followed in the same year. Soon after J.G. recorded his second LP (with 'Samba de uma Nota So', 'Corcovado', 'Meditação', and 'Outra Vez'), Sergio Ricardo and Carlos Lyra followed with LPs of their own. On May 15, 1960, TV Record in São Paulo broadcast the first Festival Nacional da Bossa Nova.

Chief Features of the Bossa Nova

Seen in the context of MPB's development until 1958, the bossa nova is characterized by the following features:

1. A new rhythmic *balanço* (swing)
2. New text forms and themes
3. Modern, jazz-like harmonic structures
4. Novel interpretation and orchestration
5. Influence upon other fields (literature, film, etc.)

Rhythm

The bossa nova made use of the rhythm of the samba-canção: 2/4 time with the accent on the first quarter. The pre-bossa nova period saw the development of the *teleco-teco*, a syncopated variation of the same. And finally came João Gilberto's new *balanço*. Baden Powell conjecture's, in De Mello's *Música Popular Brasileira*: 'João Gilberto did the follow-

──────────────

*The singer Silvia Telles was a girlfriend of João Gilberto who later became married to Aloysio de Oliveira. She died in a car crash in 1966.

ing. He took the rhythmic figure of a tambourine from an Escola de Samba batucada, left out a few beats, and shifted the whole rhythm from one to two 2/4 measures.' I would agree with him. Of course, that does not mean that J.G. used this rhythmic figure intentionally. During my visits to Brazil I noticed again and again how easily almost every Brazilian was able to improvise an accompaniment to the samba with a matchbox or by drumming on a glass or bottle. J.G. simply offered a more refined adaptation of the same principle for guitar.

Nevertheless, the bossa nova rhythm renounces one of the central features of Brazilian music in that it reduces the customary polyrhythmic form (for example as in a samba batucada with its different syncopating percussion instruments) to a single rhythm. A consequence was that the bossa nova soon had to make room for a revival of more traditional polyrhythmic forms (samba and Northeastern music).

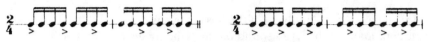

Bossa-Nova rhythms and variations

North American jazz musicians always played the bossa nova in 4/4 time. The Brazilian 2/4 felt too foreign to them. This led to a standardization of the bossa nova rhythm (especially the syncopations) which made itself felt in other areas of North American pop music.

Lyrics

Newton Mendonça and Vinicius de Moraes had the greatest influence on the new bossa nova lyrics. While the earlier samba lyrics of Ary Barroso and others had an almost report-like character, dealing with trivial happenings from everyday life or hymns of greatly exaggerated patriotism, bossa nova texts were more intellectual in orientation, more playful, poetic and even surrealistic.

An essay by Julio Medaglia, in the volume *Balanço da Bossa e outras Bossas* points out correctly that 'Samba de uma Nota Só' by Jobim and Mendonça numbers among the MPB's most ingenious lyrics. The relationship here between words and music is perfect. The singer begins the lines of the song on a single pitch. 'This is a little samba, based upon a single note.' The singer then continues, still holding the same note. 'Other notes will follow, but the basis is only one.' He then shifts to a second, higher tone, singing, 'This other is a result of what I've just said,' and then continues in the text with the initial tone.

Another song 'Desafinado' ('Out of Tune') refers directly to the bossa nova:

> When you tell me
> I have not tuned well, my love
> Please know, this hurts me deeply
> Only the privileged have
> A perfect pitch like you
> I only have
> What god has given me
> When you insist upon classifying
> My performance as unmusical
> Then I would have to lie and respond
> That this is bossa nova
> That this is quite natural

The number one subject of the bossa nova was love. Today, in translation, many of the lyrics sound banal: 'Go, my heart, for whoever does not beg for pardon, he will never be forgiven' ('Insensatez'); 'If I could only understand that love exists no longer, as your eyes tell me' ('Este Seu Olhar'); or 'As I saw you, I realized what happiness meant' ('Corcovado'). But there were others, too: poetic ones: 'Let my yearnings be gone. Truly, without her there is no peace or beauty, only tristesse and melancholy which will not leave me' ('Chega de Saudade'); humorous ones: 'The first time I met you I still harbored illusions of being happy' ('A Primeira Vez'); realistic: 'There is no end to sorrow, joy has its limits' ('A Felicidade'); allegorical: 'Once upon a time there was a wolf who wanted to eat up everyone in sight; now he trots along on a leash' ('Lobo Bobo'). But the most basic theme of many bossa nova songs was already to be heard at the famous Manhã de Carnaval ('Bonfá/ Toledo'): 'Such a beautiful morning brings forth a new song in my life.... From the strings of my guitar sounds a voice which sings of your kisses.'

Other lyrics bordered on a type of concrete poetry, showing strains of isomorphism. For example, Ronaldo Boscoli's word play, 'Rio so Rio, sorrio' which translated as, 'Rio, only Rio, I am laughing.'

As humorous, caustic or melancholy as the texts sometimes were, they were never dramatic or pathetic. João Gilberto asserts in De Mello's *Música Popular Brasileira*: 'The text must not speak about death, blood or daggers.'

Julio Medaglia groups the texts into two basic categories. One includes texts of local color that comment on particular situations or happenings. The other includes critical, politically committed texts. These arose especially at the end of the bossa nova era, and were continued by the *música do participação* and *canções de protesto* movements. But their arrival was, so to speak, announced in advance by Nara Leão's aggressive songs, Sergio Ricardo's critical commentaries, and, later on, in songs by Edu Lobo and Geraldo Vandré. The formal textual structure introduced by the bossa nova, with its tendencies toward the modern lyric, were further developed at the end of the sixties by Bahian tropicalism.

Harmonies

It may never be cleared up whether the bossa nova really did borrow its novel harmonic structuring from jazz. 'Jazz', Tom Jobim says, 'drank from many fountains, not just popping up out of the blue. And just as jazz certainly profited from Debussy and Ravel, we have to concede to the bossa nova that it, too, arose under similar influences.' Many different Brazilian composers from the last century (such as Pixinguinha for example) contributed to modernizing the harmonic structures of MPB. I believe that Jobim's contribution to the bossa nova (and beyond the bossa nova) must be seen as a continuation of this development. His classical education and encounters with contemporary European music through Koellreutter also played a role.

Different bossa nova musicians express their relationship to jazz very differently. Baden Powell, for instance, who actually had nothing to do with the beginnings of the bossa nova, says that he had heard and played lots of jazz. Vinicius de Moraes knew his way around the jazz scenes of Los Angeles and New York and says he was friends with Kid Ory, Louis Armstrong and Dizzy Gillespie. But, he adds, none of that had any influence upon his work. Edu Lobo says that he heard hardly any jazz in those days. Nara Leão, Chico Buarque, Elis Regina, Gilberto Gil, Carlos Lyra and Roberto Menescal (all of whom were either bossa nova musicians or first became musically active with the bossa nova) all call themselves friends of jazz. The fact is, however, that it was Jobim's compositions, and not theirs, that first earned the label bossa nova. Oddly, the compositions of those musicians whose affinities to jazz were readily apparent did not achieve much popularity as bossa novas outside Brazil.

In my opinion, the preoccupation of these young musicians from the Zona Sul with jazz (paralleling, incidentally, similar developments in Europe) was merely a starting point and ambience in which the long-overdue modernization of MPB's harmonic structures could finally take place. Jobim and Gilberto were there to lead the way.

Jazz has no monopoly on modern harmonic structures. In the same way, one could hypothesize that jazz was influenced by choro, which made use of a constant, swinging bass line guitar accompaniment before there ever was a jazz.

With or without jazz influence, one thing is certain: in its use of harmonies with difficult transitions, extremes of vocal range, modulations within a phrase, multiple continuous syncopated sequences and occasional suggestions of dodecaphony, bossa nova made a fundamental contribution to the revival of MPB.

New harmonies produced new melodies. An example again is 'Desafinado.' The interplay of melody and harmony gives the impression that the performer is a hairsbreadth away from the correct pitch, thus 'desafinado' (that is, out of tune).

Rhythms of some bossa nova melodies

The melodies, moreover, became simpler in character, more mellow, almost flowing. The whole interpretation became more relaxed.

By replacing the polymetric form with a constant rhythm, melody received a new and greater importance. Harmonies and chords supported both the melody and the rhythmical basis.

And, finally, we can observe an increasing use of dissonance, which was taken up especially at the end of the bossa nova era and in the ensuing movements.

Interpretation

The new musical structures permitted, and demanded, a new kind of interpretation and orchestration.

Tom Jobim declared in De Mello's *Música Popular Brasileira*, 'MPB suffered in those days from an excess of instrumentation — loads of fiddles, monstrous orchestration. We wanted to concentrate our message on the singers.'

The bossa nova reduced the orchestral size. The instrumental basis consisted simply of guitar, bass, drum and sometimes piano, with the vocalists being integrated into the instrumental arrangement. In an interview given in 1960 João Gilberto and quoted by De Mello summed up the new philosophy as follows: 'Music is sound, and sound is voice, instrument. The singer has to know how and when to draw out a high tone, or a deep one, in order to communicate his emotional message perfectly.'

The dynamics of the bossa nova musicians and singers followed in a tradition already present in MPB, as exemplified by Mario Reis and Lupiscinho Rodriguez. Performance was *bem pianinho*, that is, very soft, without extreme accents. A quasi-narrative speech-song appeared in place of the extroverted bel-canto singer of the bolero and *samba-da-exaltação*.

Impact on other Fields

This esthetic development had parallels in other cultural spheres. Graphic artists designed new and original record covers for the bossa nova. Cesar G. Vilela and Francisco Perreira supported the new artistic quality of the records with a style employing photo and text which was soothing to the eye and simple in form, using at most a single additional color set upon a black and white layout. The Odeon and Elenco covers profited especially from the new graphics.

The bossa nova was also able to secure a place for itself in film. *Orfeu Negro* (*Black Orpheus*) (director Marcel Camus), based on Vinicius de Moraes's drama *Orfeu da Conçeição*, was awarded the Golden Palm at the 1959 Cannes Film Festival. Vinicius later said, 'I like the original play more than the film. The play was a first experience with negro theater in Brazil. Until then there had been very little. There's a first time for everything.' The film's title song is by Tom Jobim and Luiz Bonfá. Lyrics were by Vinicius and A. Maria. The film's most successful songs were 'A Felicidade' and 'Manhã de Carnaval'. Both were sung for the film's soundtrack by Agostinho dos Santos, the most beautiful and best-trained voice of the era. (Dos Santos died in a plane crash near Paris in 1973.)

The film producers had placed great value upon unpublished compositions in order to be able to have part of the publishing rights. The film also won an Oscar as best foreign film.

Luiz Bonfá was also musical director for Ruy Guerra's film *Os Cafagestas* (1962). Director Glauber Rocha, working together with Sergio Ricardo, used compositions from Villa-Lobos and Northeastern folklore in the film *Deus e o Diabo na Terra do Sol* (1964), representing the closing of an era and a new thematic orientation.

A Brazilian 'new cinema' developed in proximity to the bossa nova scene. Glauber Rocha's films made use of the new music; poets and writers contributed their talents, both to film and to bossa nova composers. The new cinema, in fact, outlived the bossa nova. This was because film directors, in contrast to bossa nova musicians, chose to make the Brazilian reality an object of their scrutiny.

Journalists and music critics also penned texts derived from bossa nova songs and used the media to promote the movement. Ronaldo Boscoli is a case in point.

The bossa nova propelled many young artists onto the road to stardom. Its apparently unpretentious, simple character gave many the courage to pick up their own guitars and start singing. Many of today's leading singers and songwriters were among that original crop of amateurs so fascinated with João Gilberto's spellbinding sounds. Caetano Veloso, Gilberto Gil and others have told how absolutely overcome they were the first time they heard J. G. on the radio in Salvador, and how they raced like madmen into the city to buy the record.

The bossa nova also had effects on Brazil's music industry. Aloysio de Oliveira's new Elenco label began production with the bossa nova (Jobim, Powell, S. Telles, the Tamba Trio and others), totalling about sixty LPs in its four-year existence. De Oliveira is, without a doubt, one of the most dazzling figures in MPB. He followed Carmen Miranda to the United States as a member of the vocal ensemble Bando da Lua, only to return to Rio after eighteen years' absence at the beginning of the bossa nova era. He remains today one of Brazil's most important record and show producers.

Studios modernized their recording technique with methods borrowed from more advanced American firms.

And, finally, Lennie Dale, the best-known representative of the modern ballet in Rio at the time, tried his luck as a bossa nova singer as well. He attempted, according to Oliveira, 'to add a bodily dimension in interpreting the bossa nova.'

The Bossa Nova's Heyday

The National Bossa Nova Festival in São Paulo was followed by numerous events and activities.

In 1962 Aloysio de Oliveira initiated the *temporada* — a presentational form combining show, concert, and theater — in a series of music shows in clubs and later in small theaters in Brazil's big cities. The first was called 'O Encontro' ('The Meeting') and presented João Gilberto, Tom Jobim, Vinicius and Os Cariocas.

Fifteen years later De Oliveira once again engaged Tom and Vinicius for a show, their last, on the Canecão stage in Rio. And Tom and Vinicius told the appreciative audience how it all was back then when that beautiful young girl with the alluring gait passed by their customary bar in Ipanema, motivating them to write a bossa nova about the 'Garota de Ipanema'.

That same year, shortly before jazz flutist Herbie Mann embarked on his Brazilian tour, Sidney Frey (president of the record company Audio Fidelity) came to Brazil to put together a program for a concert to take place in New York's Carnegie Hall. It seems that many jazz musicians had learned of the new music during visits to Rio and had brought the good news back with them to New York. Frey had his problems at first, since none of the cariocas were much in the mood to travel to New York. They took some convincing, but in the end almost the whole crew went along.

On November 21, 1962, the following artists appeared in a concert entitled (incorrectly) Bossa Nova: New Brazilian Jazz: Bola Sete, Carmen Costa, the Castro-Neves Quartet, Luiz Bonfá, Tom Jobim, Agostinho dos Santos, Sergio Mendes and Quartet, Carlos Lyra, Roberto Menescal, Milton Banana, Sergio Ricardo, Chico Feitosa and João Gilberto.

That was the first half of the concert. The second half, however, had been reserved by Stan Getz and Gary McFarland for their own version of the bossa nova. João Gilberto performed for the first time with the Getz Quartet.

Jobim, Menescal and other participants are quoted by De Mello as having said of the concert: 'It was a total joke.... A black day in my career, indeed, in my life.... It was not organized one bit.... The only things that functioned were the microphones for the taping. In the concert hall they were lousy.... The organizers were only interested in getting the copyright to our music and in reaping the profits from the concert.... We didn't make anything out of it.... The whole thing was a big lie.'

As I see it, the Brazilians were intentionally swindled. Conditions were set so that they had to play mainly new compositions that the United States manager could publish. Now it is certainly true that Jobim and his gang were not the best of pals with their Brazilian publishers. Jobim relates how he had offered 'Desafinado' to a publishing house in Rio only to be rejected with, 'Really, Antonio, you're off your rocker! What do you expect from a song about a man who can't sing?' Who can really wonder then that the bossa nova people felt flattered when all of a sudden the American publishers began to show interest in them? The concert launched a tragic struggle over copyrights that lasted a decade, and was no less grotesque than the muddled situation in Brazil. In succeeding years many composers were cheated out of their author's rights by false promises, bounced checks and a host of other tricks.

The American publisher Ray Gilbert, who took a share of the initial profits from bossa nova titles, played a shady role in the whole affair. The popular duo Durval Ferreira and Maurício Einhorn (known for their title 'Batida Diferente') told me that the check they received from Gilbert's Ipanema Music bounced. Gilbert frequently even named himself as co-author or composer of the English version on the licensing statement of many records.

A run on bossa nova titles occurred. Brazilian authors, inexperienced in the international music business and with an aversion to their native publishing mafia, felt honored by the great interest accorded them. They simply signed the contracts placed before them. In this way they lost millions of dollars in royalties.

This was the actual beginning, in 1962, of the commercialization of the bossa nova.

Many musicians and singers remained in the United States after the concert; others came later. North American jazz musicians tempted them with offers too good to turn down. João Gilberto, the Tamba Trio, Sergio Mendes and Quartet, Baden Powell, Carlos Lyra, Deodato, Dori Caymmi and many others came. Even before the 'bossa nova invasion', the Tamba Trio had completed a Unites States tour, while Laurindo Almeida had become a United States citizen.

European dance schools in the sixties presented a Brazilian dance previously unknown in Brazil. To the rhythm of the twist records popular at the time, the hit parades blared out assertively, 'It's all the bossa nova's fault.' The 'jazz-samba' records of Stan Getz and Astrud Gilberto had such astronomical sales that every Tom, Dick and Harry must have thought the American saxophonist Stan Getz had created the bossa nova. This was certainly one of the reasons the American record company printed *Jazz Samba* on the record cover. They had an interest in propagating the role of North American culture in the new Brazilian music. Jazz critic Joachim E. Berendt spoke of how Rio's young musicians 'mixed their sambas with cool jazz'.

The United States recording industry's virtual monopoly of the marketing of the new Brazilian music outside Brazil itself managed to produce a host of misconceptions, illusions and ignorance. The consequences can still be felt today, many years after the birth of the bossa nova. Brazilian conductor, Julio Medaglia attests to the great affinity Stan Getz had for the 'bossa nova feeling', more so than any other American jazz musician. Medaglia noted in Getz's saxophone playing an acceptable adaption of the Brazilian *bate papo* ('chatter') which is so typical of the bossa nova. While João Gilberto tended toward a 'cool' interpretive style, Getz was more expressive. The great success of Astrud Gilberto (maiden name Weinert, divorced from Gilberto in 1964), on the other hand, was due more to chance than talent. Getz was bent on doing an English cover version of 'Garota de Ipanema'. As Astrud happened to be on hand at the studio, he asked her to give it a try. That was 1963. In the same year Astrud began singing in Getz's shows. In 1964 her version of 'Garota' was released on the Verve label, and soon fascinated millions of people the world over. Medaglia, however, left no one in doubt about what he thought of Astrud's voice: 'She sings so horribly, it couldn't possibly get worse.' That Astrud could only have succeeded in the United States speaks well of the Brazilian artists. Her style of singing the bossa nova had no rivals and no critics. Her recordings were regarded as something exotic and they sold like hotcakes.

Back to the year 1962. In Brazil the bossa nova was still far from becoming popular among the entire populace. It could not compete with the widespead appeal of the samba, bolero and frevo. The new, quiet tones were not to every man's taste. 'Tristeza', for example, a popular samba from the period, made you want to sing along. It could be sung by thousands of people in unison. That was simply impossible with a bossa nova like 'Desafinado'.

It is certainly true that the bossa nova was also a hit in other big cities besides Rio. Television broadcast bossa nova festivals and concerts. Gilberto, Lyra, *et al.* saw their records selling well. But the movement remained a concern of the youth, students and intellectuals. The financial rewards for bossa nova artists were also minimal. At the very beginning they received nothing more than a pittance for their shows. They even had to hang up advertising posters themselves. Later on, they received a modest sum for their efforts. It is hardly surprising then that the big bucks offered abroad were very tempting.

In Brazil, however, the new music was of major importance. Singer Nara Leão observed: 'We can classify Brazilian music into pre- and post-bossa nova periods.' Indeed, MPB of the sixties and seventies would not have existed without the bossa nova movement, even if its peak lasted for only a few years (1958–64). This movement, often presented as a formal musical revolution, is much more than just a musical development fostered by individual composers and musicians. It must also be seen in a social and political light.

The birth of the bossa nova fell in a period of economic expansion for Brazil. The sixties were overshadowed by a deep economic and political crisis. Despite major efforts at an overhaul, the popular regime of Juscelino Kubitschek was unable to master the problems facing the country. Unrest rose at the universities. Amidst such a social climate, the words of the bossa nova suddenly stood in sharp contrast to everyday Brazilian reality.

Even at the height of the bossa nova's popularity Carlos Lyra was casting a critical eye on the influence of jazz and the entire role of the bossa nova ('Influença do Jazz'). He explains how his work on a drama in São Paulo gave him insight into other viewpoints and methods for understanding society, Marxism being one of these. He did not accept such theories as a whole, but, he continues, his work with Glauber Rocha and the new cinema helped him become conscious of the bossa nova's isolation from society's real problems. Joining together with Geraldo Vandré and Sergio Ricardo, and with the aid of a samba school, Lyra founded the UNE (National Student Union), an institution which, like Vandré's Centro Popular da Cultura, regarded activity within MPB as political engagement utilizing all forms of Brazilian music.

Nara Leão, once apostrophized as the 'bossa nova muse', also came to take a more critical view of the bossa nova: 'The bossa nova had nothing that could be reconciled with the Brazilian reality.'

Vinicius and Tom also turned to writing more realistic lyrics ('O Morro Não Tem Yez'; 'The morros have no future'). The military coup on March 13, 1964, signaled a decisive moment for the bossa nova. The time had come for it either to shed its elitist skin and take sides or to see itself shoved aside by the new movements. Jobim had already declared in 'Globo', November 12, 1962 that 'We should stop selling the exotic appeal of the café and carnival. Subjects of underdevelopment are not ours. Let's move from a phase of agriculture to industrialization. Let's use our Música Popular Brasileira with the conviction not only of its salient peculiarities, but also its technical brilliance.'

In May 1964 'O Fina da Bossa' ('The Best of the Bossa') received its first staging at the Teatro Paramount in São Paulo. At the same time, however, this show and many others staged at the Paramount represented the end of the bossa nova era. A new orientation of MPB had set in which will be described in detail in the next chaper. Its breakup into three important movements enabled new talent orginally inspired by the bossa nova to begin their careers, 'to enter the scene'. The television shows already mentioned, as well as festivals that followed on their heels, offered them the required platform.

In the meantime, one of the bossa nova's founding fathers, João Gilberto, had settled in New York. The shy Bahian had remained true to the musical substance of his early years, expressed in one of his very first songs: '*Bim Bom. É só isso meu Baião. E não tem mais nada não.*' (Bim Bom, that alone is my baião. Otherwise I have nothing.)

Chapter 6

Offspring of the Bossa Nova

While the leading performers of this 'holy monster called the bossa nova' (Nara Leão) and their imitators were enjoying a boom in record sales, shows, tours and other activities, the movement itself was being called into question by younger musicians; the same youth, in fact, who first reached for their guitars under João Gilberto's magnetic sway. Until the mid-sixties the bossa nova had always been the exclusive property of the cariocas. Starting in 1964, three regional centers formed namely Rio, São Paulo and Salvador. According to the participants themselves, however, Rio retained its preminence as an emporium for the exchange of opinions and ideas. The new developments occurred at first simultaneously and independently from one another. Finally, they occupied the show scene in small theaters, television festivals in São Paulo and Rio and other institutions and facilities that had arisen in the bossa nova era. The TV festivals (by TV Record in São Paulo until 1969, and TV Globo in Rio until 1972) were of major importance in the post-bossa era. Many artists and composers had their first successes on them.

At the beginning of the post-bossa nova era, there were five new musical currents:

1. The *Afro-sambas* of Baden Powell and Vinicius de Moraes.
2. The *sambas de participação*, with varying character.
3. The *canções de protesto*, which are identical with several forms of number 2.

4. *som universal* and *som livre* from Bahia. Later, *tropicalismo*.

5. The *iêiêiê brasileiro*, the advance of Brazilian rock music.

As with all classifications in artistic fields, these categories are nothing more than an aid to systematization, even if the movements at the time were indeed known under these names. More basically, the movements arose from the musical and intellectual world of individuals, such as Edu Lobo, Geraldo Vandré, Chico Buarque, Carlos Lyra, Capinan, the Baianos, Baden Powell and others.

With the exception of Roberto Carlos's *iêiêiê brasileiro*, which was chiefly directed by the record companies' commercial interests, a general agreement did exist among the post-bossa nova artists on the following points:

— In both form and content, the bossa nova's intellectual isolation had caused it to lose all connection to Brazilian reality.

— Form renewal required that the bossa nova's highly stylized mono-rhythms and dreamy melodies, which stood in sharp contradiction to the pluralism of MPB should be modified. This effected a return to the older *canção urbana* (samba, marcha, rancho, modinha, frevo, etc.) and *canção rural* (moda de viola, desafio, samba de roda), using at times the modern harmonies and dissonances introduced by the bossa nova, as well as instrumental and rhythmic elements borrowed from rock music (for example, the Beatles).

— Content renewal meant overcoming the rift in communication that had existed between author-singer and the populace, and a change in textual themes to a more realistic content. One result was a demystification of traditional and rural song forms, like the *samba de morro*. This meant replacing idyllic presentations of everyday life in the favela with more true-to-life pictures.

Several statements reported in De Mello's *Música Popular Brasileira* reflect these aspects of form and content:

> Opportunism and commercialization arose with the bossa nova. At the end, the radio was playing more bad imitations than Tom or João Gilberto in the original.
>
> *Sergio Ricardo*
>
> I discovered that other people also existed, that there was such a thing as dangerous and commercial relations.
>
> *Capinan*
>
> I believe that for popular song, music must serve as a vehicle for the text.
>
> *Geraldo Vandré*

There is still another common element worth mentioning. Practically everyone from the *jovem guarda* (young guard) began his musical career playing the bossa nova. For many, João Gilberto's original singing style and novel *balanço* of guitar accompaniment represented the decisive push into the world of music. And so a number of them do not consider João Gilberto to be in agreement with the main tenets of the bossa nova movement. They charge that Gilberto was basically misunderstood by other bossa nova musicians.

> Only by returning to João Gilberto's evolutionary line will we be in a position to make a choice and be creatively active.
>
> *Caetano Veloso*

The Afro-Sambas

Baden Powell (born 1937) and Vinicius de Moraes met for the first time at the beginning of 1960. In those days Baden played guitar (Vinicius recalls it was an electric guitar) in a dance band in the boate Arpege after Tom Jobim's shows. Until then, only Baden's 'Samba Triste' (1956, words by Billy Blanco) had made a name for itself, and Vinicius took a liking to the young guitarist.

Baden Powell de Aquino was born in Itaperuna in the state of Rio de Janeiro and grew up in the Varre Sai district. He owes his name to his father's great admiration for the British founder of the Boy Scouts, Robert Thompson Baden Powell. Baden's father himself was active in the Brazilian Boy Scout movement and played guitar in his free time as well. Baden's grandfather was also a musician; he directed one of the first black orchestras that sprang up after the emancipation of the slaves in 1888. At eight Baden received his first guitar lessons from Meira, a member of the Conjunto Benedito Lacerdas. At thirteen he earned his first pocket money playing solo guitar at suburban dances. Baden soon tired of guitar lessons, preferring instead to make music with his friends from the morros in Magueira. After finishing school he got a job at a radio station. In 1955 he played at the Plaza with Ed Lincoln's jazz group, and in 1962 he accompanied Silvia Telles in the boate Jirau.

According to Vinicius, their teamwork began in 1964 when Baden came to visit and heard a recording of candomblés and Bahian folklore. He was so fascinated that he soon took off for Bahia in order to study the Afro-Brazilian music on location. Upon his return, Baden and Vinicius went into virtual seclusion for three months and wrote the now famous Afro-sambas, among them 'Berimbau', 'Samba em Prelúdio' and 'Canto de Caboclo Pedra Petra'.

Vinicius described their collaboration together: 'Baden and I were in an intoxicated state for three months, practically without interruption. But I hardly changed a line of our songs later on.' Baden had already made a careful study of the capoeira, candomblé and samba de roda, and of their instrumentation (for example, the berimbau). As a mestizo, Baden found the music (with its pronounced African elements) and syncretic cults readily accessible. They were not foreign to his temperament and mentality. 'Baden,' Vinicius told me, 'was very important in this context, because the music which we had written until then was white music. Neither of us was a Negro, and Baden was *black*. He was the first to introduce black rhythms into the bossa nova.'

Baden succeeded in transforming the chants from the candomblé into modern sambas without robbing them of their mystical quality. Occasionally he based compositions upon authentic folkloric themes, while Vinicius also remained largely true to the content of the candomblé texts sung in Portuguese or African language.

Baden also succeeded in adapting the sound and rhythm of the Bahian instruments. The best-known motif is in 'Berimbau', where the interplay of the berimbau's metal string with the resonator remains preserved in the song, as are the various rhythms that accompany the capoeira dancer.

In 1964 Baden Powell included his Afro-sambas in the repertoire of his second LP (*A Vontade*). A co-production with Vinicius, entitled *Os Afro Sambas* (arrangements by Guerra Peixe with Baden, Vinicius and the Quarteto Em Cy) developed somewhat later.

Later on, Baden continued the line begun in the African sambas when he struck up a partnership with poet Paulo Cesar Pinheiro ('Lapinha', for example).

Making the change from bossa nova to Afro-samba was simply a logical step for Baden, according to De Mello's *Música Popular Brasileira*. 'The bossa nova has its roots in the Brazilian musical tradition. That can't be denied.' Regarding the protest songs undergoing a parallel development, Baden adds:

> African music — the pain of the Negro, the laments, the sufferings he has to endure — these are things you can't ignore. Music deals with such things. Today, when someone expresses such a grievance, people say he's political. I don't believe it. When I suffer, I play a music that is influenced by my suffering. That is

highly political. Even a love song — everything arises from suffering.

The Afro-sambas treat the problems, milieu, and culture of the Afro-Brazilian population. Topical statements about the times, as in 'Berimbau', have their place too:

> Money, of which there is none
> Work, which is nonexistent

Vinicius agrees. 'For me, samba has always been a form of protest music, from its very beginnings until today. It comments upon and criticizes situations.'

Berimbau by Baden Powell

After Baden's first European tour, at the beginning of the seventies, he took up temporary residence in Paris in 1974 (there to collaborate with Claude Nougaro, Stephane Grapelli and others). His later records did not achieve the same artistic caliber as his earlier productions in Brazil and West Germany (Elenco, Philips, MPS, CBS). And songs assumed an increasing importance in his live concerts in order to hide his growing weakness at the guitar. Something was missing. This was not the old Baden. The birth of his sons and his move to Baden-Baden (West Germany) seem to have helped Baden Powell overcome his long crisis, whose roots lay undoubtedly in a drinking problem. At the beginning of the eighties Baden began making appearances in West

German concert halls once again. Time had made a difference. His style was more mature, more refined, but now had a playful quality, which, nevertheless, often succumbed to his earlier tendency to play *com raiva* (in a rage). Suddenly, one day in May 1987, Baden Powell packed his bags and left Baden-Baden to return to Brazil.

Sambas de Participação and Canções de Protesto

The new movements of committed sambas and protest songs embraced many individual activities that began in a period of economic depression and political unrest in Brazil. The military coup in 1964 exerted a decisive influence as well. Brazil was by no means alone in having given birth to such a movement. Young people the world over were identifying with songs written by Bob Dylan and Pete Seeger. In Argentina the movement Nuevo Cancionero Argentino was launched in 1963. In 1965 Violeta Parra and her children opened the Peña de los Parra in Santiago de Chile. The first festival of protest song took place in Havana, Cuba, in 1967.

Nara Leão was one of the first to turn her back on the bossa nova. On the one hand, it was a personal trait of hers to always begin something new when she considered it correct. She was not one to follow the fashions and trends of the day. On the other hand, she was a crusader in the sense of protesting against things she considered wrong, and with a desire to set them right again. For these reasons the one-time bossa nova muse devoted her first LP not to that song form to whose development she had contributed, but rather to Baden Powell's 'Berimbau' and 'Consolação', to songs by the traditional sambistas Nelson Cavaquinho and Cartola, as well as to younger, critical composers such as Zé Keti. She understood her role as complementing that of the newspapers, which, in her opinion, didn't report half of what they could. Thus her songs took on a communicative function, addressing the listener like a reporter on the radio. Her popular show 'Opinião' ('Opinion') proceeded consistent with this function. She recognized later, however, according to De Mello's *Música Popular Brasileira*, that 'the singing of protest songs alone cannot solve any problems,' since the public comes to be entertained, not to have its consciousness raised. And so in accordance with her understanding of her own role as an artist ('First and foremost I am a human being, then a woman, and finally a singer.'), she soon turned to other subject matter of a less political nature.

Carlos Lyra composed his first critical songs about the bossa nova right at the beginning of its popularity. Lyra's protest was spawned by the general discussion about whether or not the bossa nova should be considered Brazilian music. In De Mello's *MPB*, he states, 'The search for a national identity closes our memories to Villa-Lobos, Cartola, João de Vale and others.' Lyra wanted to see a return to traditional musical forms. He and Sergio Ricardo founded a working group called Música Popular da UNE (National Student Union), presenting mainly sambistas of 'yesterday' from the escolas de samba in the morros of Rio. His relationship to film producers (Cinema Novo) and poets (intimists, concrete poetry) of the period made him aware of the need to produce realistic lyrics, preferring, however, to prop them up on a foundation of traditional values. This earned him a reputation as a 'purist'. Lyra, in fact, regarded committed sambas and protest songs as all lies and pamphleteering.

The various factions of the new MMPB (*Moderna Música Popular Brasileira*) did not at first have any immediate political aims. Political engagement began with the words of Geraldo Vandré (born 1935), written while working for the UNE team. His 'Porta Estandarte' (1966 festival winner) and 'Disparada' (winner at the 1966 TV Record Festival) were, however, criticized by Caetano Veloso as a 'primitive attempt to produce an industrial, forceful Brazilian music,' similar to the way industry launched Brazilian rock music. Very few shared Veloso's scathing criticism. Despite being banned for years by the censors, 'Disparada' became an important song in the non-violent resistance movement of Brazil's intellectual youth.

Geraldo Vandré

Don't Say I Have Not Spoken about the Flowers (Pra Não Dizer Que Não Falei De Flores*)

On the march, singing, following the hymn
We are all equal, arm in arm or not
At school, in the streets, fields and on the building site
On the march, singing, following the hymn

Refrain:
Come on, let's go
Waiting means ignorance
He who knows determines the future
He does not wait for it to happen

—————————————————————

*The song was banned subsequently.

Over the fields, hunger on the large plantations
Indecisive chains move through the streets
They will compose their most vibrant refrain from the flowers
They believe in the flowers and conquer the canons

Refrain:
Come on, let's go ...

At school, in the streets, fields and on the building site
We are all soldiers, armed or not
On the march, singing, following the hymn

We are all equal, arm in arm or not
Loving in our hearts, flowers upon the soil
Confidence written across our foreheads, history in our hands
On the march, singing, following the hymn
Learning, teaching a new lesson

Refrain:
Come on, let's go ...

Vandré's successes were preceded by Edu Lobo's first honors. From his earliest youth, Eduardo de Goes Lobo (born 1943) regularly spent his vacations in his family's home region of Pernambuco in the Northeast. Vinicius wrote the words to 'Arrastão', one of Edu's earlier compositions and winner at the 1965 festival. Soon afterward, he met up with the director Ruy Guerra, an ideal song-writing partner for Edu's songs which mainly exhibit a Northeastern, Afro-Brazilian character, free of nationalist tendencies. The MMPB led Edu Lobo to re-discover frevos, reisados, cirandas, baiões and many other traditional music forms from the Northeast. As with the *canções de protesto*, Edu's songs too reflect a generalized feeling that he formulated in the line, 'All human activity is political.'

The instrumental Quarteto Novo (Hermeto Pascoal, Airto Moreira, Téo de Barros and Heraldo) also placed its emphasis on Northeastern music. In 1970 Edu accompanied their music on his LP *Cantiga de Longe*.

Edu Lobo / Guanieri

Five Children
(Cinco Crianças)

Five children without a protector
Trying to peer into the darkness
Ea, eô

Five of them, fearful of everything
In the middle of the world, brother with brother

Ea, eô

Hand in hand with their equals
Hand in hand with stones in their hands

Hand in hand, fighting with death
Hand in hand, stones in their hands

There is a place in a peaceful heaven
There is fear in their heart
Five children without a protector
Whisper a song

After the appearance of Lobo's hit songs 'Reza' and 'Aleluia' (with engagé texts by Ruy Guerra), Gianfrancesco Guarnieri invited him to participate in the musical *Arena conta Zumbi* (by Guarnieri and Augusto Boal). Lobo was already known for his collaboration with Vinicius on the song 'Zambi'. The musical narrates the story of a slave uprising led by Zumbi. It had its premiere in 1965. Lobo told me that he still wonders how it could be that, of all the songs in the show, 'Upa Neguinho' should become world-famous. Elis Regina visited him while searching for songs for her show 'O Fino da Bossa'. She insisted upon using 'Upa Neguinho', even though Edu tried to talk her out of it. The program brochure put together for the European tour of the Festival Folklore e Bossa Nova do Brasil introduced Edu with this song as a Brazilian protest singer. As will become clear from this chapter, Edu cannot be understood in this way.

The jury at the second Festival Internacional da Música Popular Brasileira in 1967 (staged by TV Record) awarded first prize to another one of Lobo's songs, 'Ponteio' (with words by Capinam). Also receiving awards that day were Chico Buarque, 'Roda Viva', Gilberto Gil, 'Domingo no Parque', and Caetano Veloso, 'Alegria, Alegria'.

Extended periods of residence abroad, including two years in the United States, have expanded Edu's musical horizons. Since then he has tended to focus his work more on composition than performance. Lobo's ambitious talents have led him into theater, film, musicals, and ballet.

Chico Buarque

Both inside and outside of Brazil, Francisco Buarque de Hollanda, better known as Chico Buarque, has the reputation as the best and perhaps the most important songwriter to come out of the country since 1966. The thirteen-year period between his first great success, 'A Banda', and the lifting of censorship on 'Cálice' in 1979 were characterized by ceaseless attempts on the part of the censors to sterilize and neutralize Chico's message.

'The world may damn me and say bad things about me. But my philosophy allows me to be indifferent.' Those are not lines from Chico Buarque. They were penned by Noel Rosa, Vila Isabel's critical poet, in whose footsteps Chico would follow. Chico was born in Rio in 1944. Soon afterwards, the family moved to São Paulo and then for a spell to Rome, where the father taught history. The family house in São Paulo was a frequent meeting place for musicians and poets, among them Vinicius de Moraes. Chico was only fourteen when Vinicius sang him his first bossa nova, 'Chega de Saudade'. When the record appeared on the market with João Gilberto, Chico was excited. He had to learn the new guitar technique immediately. A number of young musicians whom his older sister Miucha often brought home for rehearsals were ready to help him, Baden Powell and Oscar Castro-Neves among them. For a while even his fascination with the bossa nova made him neglect such figures as Noel Rosa, Ismael Silva, Ataulpho Alves and other greats of the traditional samba carioca. His goal of emulating João Gilberto left him with no time for his earlier loves of classical music, jazz and French chanson.

In 1963 Chico enrolled as an architecture student at the university in São Paulo. He was soon too busy making public appearances at student concerts even to think about completing his studies. He made his first record in 1965. Both titles from this single, 'Pedro Pedreiro' and 'Sonho de um Carnaval,' received little public attention at first. Chico then took part in the 'O Fino da Bossa' shows and in concerts organized by TV Record.

In 1966, eight years after Chico's initial encounter with the bossa nova, he composed a marcha-rancho about a brass band. It described the people's joyous reaction to the band's passing through the street. As the band passed by with its songs of love, the spectators began to laugh, dance, and sing. But when the band had gone by, each returned to his place, to his problems and sufferings. This was 'A Banda', which earned second place, behind Vandré's 'Disparada' at TV Record's second MPB festival. Of course, international versions of the lyrics ignored the real and intended meaning of the song, choosing instead to present it as a simple, comical singalong.

Dori Caymmi, who worked together with Edu Lobo and Marcos Valle in 1962, said of Chico in De Mello's *Música Brasileira Popular*:

'Chico brought a lyrical quality to the songs unheard of before. He had an ability to speak to the masses with first-class lyrics that struck you suddenly and directly. All his songs are popular. As a poet, he is of the greatest importance to our generation.'

Walnice Nogueira Galvão analyzed Chico's work as an incessant reflection upon itself. Song themes are either the song itself and its author and singer, or personal messages consisting of the author's anecdotes and experiences (see similar forms by Rosa, Sinhô and A. Alves). Galvão sees Chico's canções as an offering of brotherhood and fraternity, but without any suggestion of how they might be achieved. He poses questions (why?, for what?), but provides no answers. Chico has continued in this style up until the present, even if it is no longer so comprehensible as Galvão once observed. 'Corrente' and 'O Que Será' from his 1977 LP *Meus Caros Amigos* are evidence of a continuity in this respect.

Chico Buarque
Chain
(Corrente)*

I have composed a really progressive samba today
And believe it to be a chain
And I emphasize, consequently,
That today we have to think over the matter a little
And make sure that something decent becomes of the samba
Really only drunk or totally crazy
In order to protest and sell the mistakes
You have to be honest and straightforward
To admit that I have composed an incorrect samba
Maybe even one has to get a punch in the nose
To see that the samba has improved
There it is, but you have to look with an evil eye
When you see the dancing crowd unhappy with the samba
And it makes me sad and downhearted
So I composed a progressive samba

Galvão once more: 'Chico's perspective rejects from the very begin-ning any possibility that things could turn out differently, that human beings are the subject of history and that they can change the world.'
Chico Buarque's 1967 drama *Roda Viva*, including a song of the same

---

*The song is repeated, beginning with the second line, then third, etc. It should also be sung from the end to the beginning to get a more precise meaning.

name, was an initial signal to society that he did not intend to play the role of the obedient child so often expected of a poet. 'Roda Viva' is a song about the tumult of the times and the muzzle placed on musicians and poets: 'We swim against the current until the resistance dwindles.'

Chico Buarque frequently put his songwriting talents to use in musicals and drama; in that he was like Edu Lobo, who, in fact, wrote the musical arrangements for Chico's and Ruy Guerra's play, *Calabar, ou O Elógio da Traição*. The play was banned by the censors, and the soundtrack LP was not allowed to appear with the original lyrics and title song 'Chico Canta Calabar'. Nevertheless, the LP did come out, but now entitled *Chico Canta* — with a white cover and censored lyrics.

The constant hindrance to his work placed in his way by the censors led Chico to emigrate to Italy for two years at the end of the sixties. There he went on tour with Toquinho and Josephine Baker. But like Caetano Veloso and Gilberto Gil who had both emigrated to London, Chico did not hold out long away from home. He returned to Brazil in 1970 and wrote 'Apesar de Voce' ('In spite of you'), a passionate condemnation of the system. The song was immediately banned. The number of banned and censored pieces could be continued endlessly. Still it is worth noting that the censor could not silence Chico. Again and again repression brought forth new lyrics of the utmost poetic power, expressive of Chico's critical view of the regime. Julio Medaglia, as quoted in Campos' *Balanço da Bossa*, states:

> No contemporary composer from the morros or from the city was able to produce such magnificent poetic-musical results with such effectiveness as Chico Buarque.

But Chico refused to be classified as a protest singer: 'Certain circles use this term in order to force me into an outsider's role.' 'Tanto Mar' was composed in 1975 in the wake of the Portuguese revolution. It was banned and published again in 1979 with revised lyrics. As Chico described it, 'The song arose in the shadows of those stormy happenings in Portugal at the time. I had to shift the scene from the present to the past.'

So Much Sea
(Tanto Mar)

It was a beautiful festival.
I was content.
Soon they just let your celebration peter out
But surely
They forgot a seed
Lying in some corner of the garden

I know, many miles separate us from one another
So much sea, so much sea
You have a long way to travel to reach the sea
In order to be able to sing of spring

A music critic once termed Chico's oeuvre 'Music Against the Silence'. But it is much more than that. His lyrics reflect the perpetual struggle of a Brazilian artist within his political, economic and social environment. The folksinger lamenting his depressive everyday life is a common theme in Chico's verses. But they are also a plea for brotherhood, an expression of hope for a better day, for almost utopian conditions. In contrast to many songwriters of his generation from the Nueva Canción Chilena, Uruguay or Cuba, Chico offers us nothing in the way of political solutions. He does not summon us to direct political action.

Seldom has Chico become discouraged, despite his uphill battle. Only once did an LP appear (after many new songs had been censored) consisting exclusively of songs not his own. It is indicative of the situation that the album was called *Sinal Fechado* (*Red Light*). Chico did manage nevertheless to smuggle a title of his own onto the record under a pseudonym, something not entirely without risk since the practice is generally illegal in Brazil.

Chico also had a touch for lighter things, for example 'João e Maria', a waltz in nursery-rhyme form. Still, a few serious thoughts do creep in behind an apparently harmless façade: 'Now, I was the king and the law, and according to my decree everyone had to be happy. It is an infinite power because you came into the world without notifying me. And now I would be stupid to ask what life will make out of me.'

After re-adapting the fable of Bremen's city musicians for Brazilian conditions in 1977, Chico presented in the 1978 opera *Opera do Malandro* his Brazilian version of themes from the *Threepenny Opera* by Brecht and Weill and from John Gay's *Beggar's Opera*.

Homage to a Swindler
(Homenagem ao Malandro)

Today your everyday crook,
The professional swindler is out of fashion. Instead:
The swindler extravagantly clothed as an official swindler
Candidate swindler, federal swindler
The swindler with his portrait in the gossip column
Swindler negotiating contracts, wearing ties and with capital

While most young musicians writing engagé sambas and protest songs found an audience in the same intellectual strata that the bossa nova had, Chico Buarque was the first to be able to communicate with the lower classes. This fact was certainly significant in explaining why the censors hit him so hard.

Critics and Protest

A large number of other young musicians, songwriters and singers were engaged in protest song. One was João de Vale, the composer of 'Carcará', Maria Bethania's first hit. (The carcará is a bird found in the Sertão that attacks, kills and devours; it is symbol of the hunger and poverty of the Sertão.)

Milton Nascimento left Minas Gerais for Rio in 1965. In 1967 his 'Travessia' won second prize at the TV Globo song festival.

The critical young musicians were not accepted by all their colleagues. Ronaldo Boscoli, journalist and bossa nova songwriter, felt that protest songs were often written 'just for money' and that critical songs had become a fad. 'These leftists are frustrated romantics,' he states in De Mello's *Música Popular Brasileira*. 'What they do is good,' he continued, 'their lyrics, their melodies — good but nothing special, because they lack true roots.'

Sergio Ricardo complained that intensity and credibility were missing from what most authors were saying. Their message didn't go further than the middle class. A person couldn't sing about hunger if he hadn't been hungry himself. Edu Lobo, according to De Mello, disagreed: 'The artist's function is to demonstrate his view of the world. It's not necessary for him to experience hunger to be able to speak about it.'

Those who actually suffered from hunger became the biggest critics of the protest songs, even if they did not formulate it in words. They could not make much sense out of texts that were often too intellectual. They remained with their traditional morro sambas, or took an interest in the up-and-coming Brazilian rock. Record sales actually tell us nothing about either trend, since someone who is hungry lacks the money for records and a record player. He consumes his music either live in his neighborhood or via a *radio pilha* (portable radio).

Bahian Tropicalism

Bahia, with its predominantly Afro-Brazilian musical culture, has always made a significant contribution to MPB and its more recent development: the modinhas of Caldas Barbosa; the ranchos of Bahian groups, which influenced the birth of the samba-carioca and the carnival in Rio; Dorival Caymmi and his samba of the sea and fishermen; the Afro-sambas of Baden Powell and Vinicius de Moraes; and the musical talent of João Gilberto. In the mid-sixties a new musical movement formed around Gilberto, Luiz Gonzaga and the Beatles (representative of the entire Anglo-American rock music of that generation). In terms of importance and prominence it was almost on a par with the bossa nova.

Salvador (Bahia) had two important meeting places for young musicians around 1959. In the Cinema Roma rock musicians rehearsed and played the new styles of the day. Among them was Raul Seixas, who was to become popular in the mid-seventies. In the Teatro Vila Velha there was the Orquestra de Carlito, bossa nova devotees. Among the musicians were the students Caetano Veloso (born 1942) and Gilberto Gil (born 1942). Later on Caetano's sister Maria Bethania (born 1946), Maria da Graça Costa Pena Burgos (born 1945, later known as Gal Costa), Tom Zé, Piti and others came along.

Even if this group exhibited great enthusiasm for the bossa nova and, in particular, for João Gilberto, it did not exempt the new musical sounds from Rio from the most rigorous, critical analysis. Caetano turned his attention to the question of audience reception. To what extent can the public separate an artist's personality and style from his message? Writing in a magazine called *Anguelo* he came to the conclusion that the public's confusion would cause it to automatically attribute new developments and perceptions to stylistic innovation by an artist. From this he inferred that what was immediately recognizable in a performance, i.e. the artist's personal mannerisms, would be perceived prior to the actual information, i.e. stylistic innovations, and would occasionally be made into a fad.

If we recall that, outside Brazil, only the technique of the bossa nova has been imitated with little attention being paid to content, then we should have to agree with Caetano Veloso. In order to avoid this danger, which was seen to be intimately connected with João Gilberto's role in the bossa nova movement, Caetano and Gil made it a rule not to subject their work to any definite, formal characteristics.

The Baianos took to the stage in Salvador in 1964. They did three shows together in this first year — 'Nos por Exemplo', 'Nova Bossa

Velha' and 'Velha Bossa Nova'. For the first show they filled the program only with bossa novas. The subsequent shows told the history of the bossa nova in relation to the history of the samba. They had intended to document the bossa nova as a development from the traditional samba, rather than as some sort of new rhythmic creation or as a commercialized, media-oriented product. So the program was spruced up with sambas from the old guard. Gil had to confess they sounded dilettantish, 'though from natural impulses.'

The fourth show was entitled 'Mora na Filosofia'. Maria Bethania had it all to herself, and it became a stepping-stone on her road to stardom. She was brought to Rio to substitute for Nara Leão in the show 'Opinião' (more precisely, for her successor Suzanna Morais). Others taking part were Zé Keti and João de Vale. Dori Caymmi was in charge of the musical direction. The show made Maria Bethania famous almost overnight. Soon afterward in March 1965, she made her first record with 'Carcará' a song from this show. Since Bethania was only 18, her father insisted that she be accompanied to Rio by her brother Caetano. The 'Opinião' manager, however, was not interested in the other Baianos. He only wanted Maria. She was not happy with the arrangement, so she soon left the show and headed for São Paulo. Augusto Boal, the show's director, went after her, and she was finally able to persuade him of the necessity of doing a show together with all the Baianos in São Paulo. This was September of the same year. A month later Boal put on a second show in São Paulo, this time, however, with Maria Bethania alone, while the rest of the Baianos continued to work on advancing their own careers in São Paulo (in the Club Cangaçeiro) and in Rio (at the Teatro Opinião). It took no time before Caetano and Gil were able to make good showings at São Paulo song festivals. The big breakthroughs there finally came in the fall of 1967 with Caetano's 'Alegria, Alegria' and Gil's 'Domingo no Parque'.

This was one of those rare epochs in which São Paulo, as a focal point for new creations, discussion and radical positions, almost pushed the traditional musical center of Rio into the shadows. São Paulo provided an ideal climate in which musical developments could occur under optimal conditions: two rival song festivals (National from TV Record and International from TV Exelsior), shows in the bossa temple Teatro Paramount ('BO 65', 'O Fino da Bossa', 'O Fino'), musicals and shows in the Teatro Arena ('Arena Conta Zumbi', 'Tempo de Guerra M. Bethania'), and numerous clubs (in which the likes of Chico Buarque and Jorge Ben began their careers). Moreover, young musicians from São Paulo were more intent on creating specifically Brazilian forms of rock music than were their colleagues in Rio. The temporary shift in scene from Rio to São Paulo seemed quite natural, since the last movement, the bossa nova, had originated in Rio. São Paulo now provided neutral ground for discussion of what was and what would be. Some have interpreted these discussions as conflicts between the young guard and the bossa nova clique. People argued over whether or not the bossa nova should be considered Brazilian music. An absurd discussion, indeed. In the meantime, Brazilian rock music experts exploited the creative vacuum to gain a greater prominence on the scene.

The new Baiano movement (later termed 'tropicalism') began within this climate and, in a certain sense, as an answer to it.

The 'free, universal sound' (*som livre, som universal*), which Caetano and Gil conceived of as a musical confusion of various elements, received its finishing touches when the two young Bahians met up in São Paulo with the brothers Augusto and Haroldo de Campos. The two writers introduced Gil and Cae to the work of Oswald de Andrade a poet and leading precursor of Brazilian concrete poetry. Curt Meyer-Clason (editor of *Brazilian Poetry of the Twentieth Century*) quotes the following from the manifesto of the *Noigandres* group (see *Plano-Piloto Para Poesia Concreta*, 1958, under the 'De Campos' entry):

> *Concrete Poetry*: Product of a critical form development, graphic space as a structural agent, spatial-temporal.... The concrete poem is an object in itself, isomorphism (conflict between background and form in the search for identification). Article of everyday use.

Let's not forget, Cae and Gil wanted to do without defined musical forms. They worried that the substance of their message could be hidden by a non-musical, trick-like appeal. With this in mind they sought a literary-poetic form that would express the message without becoming a recognizable, recurring pattern. They found this form in concrete poetry. They formed a circle to discuss the new possibilities. Besides Cae and Gil, also present were Gal Costa (singer), Tom Zé (composer), Torquato Neto (songwriter), Rogério Duprat (arranger) and Guilherme Araujo (impresario).

This group produced the 'Tropicalist Manifesto': 'The present state of development of our music and the discrimination which the nationalists have proposed would confine us to a role as suppliers of raw material for other countries. It was the bossa nova that ended all this by creating something which, for the first time, Brazil could export. *Tropicalism* is an attempt to unite all possible combinations of elements. It is also called *som universal* because it unites the most recent international accomplishments (Beatles, Jimi Hendrix, the second rock generation). But it also includes choro, Noel Rosa and música caipira (rural music).'*

In this way the Baianos had found a way to take into consideration all the important developments in foreign pop music, and thus continue to hold the interest of Brazil's youth, while at the same time uniting every possible musical style of traditional Brazilian origin under one concept. They lived up to their self-proclaimed maxim of *som livre* (free sound) by using many types of sound collages, noise and musical fragments from original scenes. Gilberto Gil's *Domingo no Parque* illustrates this wonderfully. The composition and arrangements are enriched by scraps of sound from crowds and carousels.

Gilberto Gil

Sunday in the Park
(Domingo no Parque)

The king of good times — that's José
The king of confusion — that's João
One works at the market — that's José
The other at a construction site — that's João
Last week at week's end
João resolved to stay out of trouble
On Sunday morning
He left home in a hurry
And he did not go down to the river to play there
Capoeira
He did not go to the river
He went flirting
José, as always on the weekend
Stowed away his sales stall and headed off for a
Sunday walk in the park
There, nearby the river estuary
In the park, there he saw her
Juliana
He saw
Juliana arm in arm with João
A rose and an ice cream in the hand
Juliana, his dream, an illusion
Juliana and boyfriend João
The thorn from the rose hurt José
And the ice cream froze his heart

*These statements were taken from various publications,
particularly the *Journal de Mùsica*, published in Rio.

The ice and the rose — that's José
The rose and the ice — that's José
Oh, there's dancing in his breast — that's José
José, the joker — that's José
The ice and the rose — that's José
The rose and the ice — that's José
Oh, his head is spinning — that's José
Of José, the joker — that's José
Juliana is spinning — oh, spinning
Oh, on the ferris wheel — oh, spinning
Oh, on the ferris wheel — oh, spinning
Boyfriend João — João
The ice cream is strawberry — it is red
Oh, spinning and the rose — it is red
Oh, spinning, everything spinning
Look, see the knife
See the blood on the hand — that's José
Juliana on the ground — that's José
His friend João — that's José
Tomorrow there will be no market — that's José
No more construction — that's José
No more good times — that's José
No more confusion — that's João

Augusto de Campos, in his study, *Balanço da Bossa e outras Bossas*, observed similarities between this song and a film by S. Eisenstein. De Campos also provides a very precise analysis of Caetano's 'Alegria, alegria.'

Caetano Veloso

Pleasure, Pleasure
(Alegria, Alegria)

Walking against the wind
Without scarf and I.D.
In a quasi-December sun
I'm going

The sun divides up into crimes
Space ships and guerrillas
Into pretty cardinal numbers
I'm going

In the president's faces
In long loving kisses
In teeth, legs, flags

Bombs or Brigitte Bardot
The sun upon the newspaper stand
Fills me with pleasure and laziness
Who reads so much news
I'm going

Between the photos and names
Eyes full of color
Breasts full of love
Emptiness
I'm going

Why not? Why not?
She thinks about marriage
And I never went back to school
Without scarf and I.D.
I'm going

I drink a Coca-Cola
She thinks about marriage
A song comforts me
I'm going

Between the photos and names
Without books and without a gun
Without hunger and without telephone
In the heart of Brazil
She doesn't know
I have even thought about singing on television
The sun is so beautiful
I'm going

Without scarf and I.D.
Nothing in the hands or in the pocket
I will continue living love
I'm going
Why not? Why not?

In summarizing the most important points of De Campos's analysis of this song, the most telling line is '¿Porque não?' ('Why not?') The text describes urban reality, reflecting the middle-class consciousness of urban Latin Americans. It treats the problem of communication. The repeated reply, '¿Porque não?', calls into question the fragmentary scenes presented to us, forcing us to probe deeper.

Many of the songs that the Baianos wrote deal with the situation in their country and on the Latin American continent in general, for example 'America for the Latin American: *Soy Loco por Ti America*', sung in Spanish. Anglo-American rock influence is not present in every song. Gil may have been the first to play the electric guitar in MPB, but he also was able to do without it. Song forms and rhythm from Bahia and the Northeast (for example, fishermen's songs from Salvador, like 'Marinheiro Só', frevos, baiões, cocos, etc.) frequently provided the musical source material for newer music.

Caetano Veloso
Tropicalia
(Tropicalia)

Overhead the airplanes
Below the trucks
Against the wide plateau appears
My nose

I organize the movement
I orient the carnival
I inaugurate the monument
Upon the central plateau of the country

Long live the bossa-sa-sa
Long live thatched huts (palhoça-ça-ça)

The monument is made from
Crêpe paper and silver
The green eyes of a mulatto girl
Her hair hides behind the green bush
The moonshine from the Sertão

The monument has no gate
Its entrance is an old
Narrow, winding lane
And a smiling child,
Ugly and dead
Reaches out his hand

Long live the bush (mata-ta-ta)
Long live the (mulatta-ta-ta) girl

There is a swimming pool in the inner patio
With blue water
Coconut trees, voices and a breeze
From the northeast
And lighthouses

In the right hand a rose branch
Guarantor of eternal spring

And in the garden vultures
Pass the whole afternoon
Between the sunflowers

Long live Maria
Long live Bahia

A thump-thump in his left pulse
Very little blood runs through his veins
But his heart sways gently
To the samba of a tambourine

He emits dissonant chords
Over his 5,000 loudspeakers
Ladies and gentlemen
He rests his big eyes
Upon me

Long live Iracema — ma — ma
Long live Ipanema — ma — ma

Sunday, the refinement of charm
Monday means feeling down
Tuesday to the field
But

The monument is very modern
I have said nothing
About my suit's style
To hell with everything
My love
To hell with everything
My love

Long live the band da-da-da
Long live Carmen Miranda-da-da

This song lent its name to the movement in 1968.

What is tropicalism? A musical movement or a philosophy?

Caetano Veloso: 'Both. And even more than that, it's a fad. I think it's silly to assume that a person can use tropicalism to guide his actions. It's ridiculous to use the name and than go sauntering about with it. Tropicalism is a *neo-antropophagism*.'

Oswald de Andrade defined 'antropophagism' as, 'A distorted Brazilian view of the world seeking to critically adapt to foreign experiences and to rework them within a national context — similar to the cannibalism of our savages.'

The Baianos are in agreement here with their real mentor, João

Gilberto, who said, 'I refuse to folklorize my own underdevelopment and in this way compensate for the technical problems.'

In 1969 Gil and Cae went into self-imposed exile in London for a year and a half. They stood at the high point of their careers, adored especially by Brazil's urban youth. They hadn't seen eye to eye with the Brazilian military regime, which believed it could discern in their songs 'dangerous influences' on youth. Caetano was even arrested for a few months and later placed under house arrest. Henry Koller reported in the *Christian Science Monitor* of September 23, 1971 that Caetano was fuming over the fact that his Zurich concert was billed as a 'protest concert' despite his assertion that he did not write political songs. Edu Lobo's European tour in 1966 was characterized similarly.

Gil in particular used his stay in London to acquaint himself with the rock scene there and to study the instrumental art of the Anglo-American musicians. He was also impressed by jazz musicians like Miles Davis. He was able to continue these studies afterwards in a short guest appearance Off-Broadway and returned to Brazil with Caetano in 1972 with, as he asserted, 'a totally different music.'

I happened to be in Rio in March 1972 and was able to attend Gil's first concert on Brazilian soil again. The numbers hadn't changed much, consisting mostly of pieces from the period before his exile. There were a few new songs by Lennon and McCartney, Jimi Hendrix and Steve Winwood, but the new instrumentation which now tended much more heavily toward rock music, was especially striking. (I wasn't much impressed by the concert, as the voice was too often overlaid with a badly modulated band sound, a problem with which the Brazilians at that time had had little experience.)

Despite his turn to rock music, which made him popular among teenyboppers, Gil nevertheless sought to tread new terrain by orienting himself to the 'natural power of the music of the morros and the Northeast.'

Moreover, the once close tropicalism clique was no more. Maria Bethania, Gal Costa and others chose to work on advancing their own careers.

Caetano retreated more frequently now to Bahia. He had long since become a 'saint' (Roberto Carlos), a living legend. Gil was the active, forceful, agile musician; Caetano the sober, dreamy poet.

But the Baianos have still remained one big family. Even today, with their popularity hardly diminished, they write songs together and appear as guests on each other's recordings.

As Agostino de Campos succinctly put it: 'Banning the Baianos is banned!'

Iêiêiê Brasileiro

The post-bossa-nova era witnessed the rise of a Brazilian variation of rock music. This new genre called itself *iêiêiê*, adapted from — who else? — the Beatles ('Yeah, yeah, yeah').

As far back as 1957 Carlos Gonzaga's version of Paul Anka's 'Diana' sold a million singles. American musicians toured Brazil, riding the crest of the rock-'n'-roll wave. This, in turn, motivated many Brazilian musicians to form their own rock groups. Among today's popular MPB performers connected to this period are João Bosco, Milton Nascimento, Wilson Simonal and Belchior.

The Brazilian musical instrument and electronics industry was hardly prepared to meet the explosion in demand for equipment. They could barely supply five-watt guitar amplifiers in those days.

The first big stars of the iêiêiê Brasileiro were the Avalons and Tony and Cello Campello. The film *'Iuventude Trausiviadu'* (*Rebel without a Cause*) rode this wave, offering the youth (especially in the South) a new way of seeing life. James Dean jackets were in.

A remarkable single, 'O Garoto do Rock' by Eduardo Araujo, accompanied by Baden Powell and Os Cariocas, came out in 1958.

The bossa nova's exit from center stage meant that now the rock faction's *jovem guarda* had an opportunity to corner the market. Record companies sold them as an alternative to a public for whom critical, political song writers were too difficult. Roberto Carlos, for over twenty years Brazil's number one rock idol, was a product of such efforts. These same rock fans, however, would no longer consider him a rock artist since his style has evolved more toward sam-bole-rock (samba-bolero-rock).

While Edu Lobo, Chico Buarque and others largely fell back upon more traditional instrumentation, the Baianos sought out a partnership with young rock musicians. Caetano Veloso defended his 'Alegria, Alegria' at the 1967 song festival with a musical background by Beat Boys, while Gilberto Gil presented Os Mutantes as his band at the same festival. Rita Lee, later Queen of Brazilian rock, was a member of this group. She was the sensation of the festival, shocking the audience when she came on stage dressed as a pregnant bride.

The above-named groups did not, however, exhaust themselves by doing only imitations of foreign groups. They introduced elements from their own Brazilian heritage as well. Trio Mocotó did the same, with Jorge Ben presenting a rock-like samba-bossa-nova variety (e.g. 'Mas Que Nada') which brought him world fame.

Brazilian rock in the seventies did not achieve great importance.

Most of those who originally began their careers with rock music have long since moved on to regard it as only one among many possible forms of expression within current pop music. It was not until the eighties that the instrumentalists had become so sure of themselves that a number of remarkable record productions, especially in jazz rock and fusion music, could take place. Part of the credit certainly must go to those musicians who began playing in beat and rock bands, and who made sure that these musicians had both their livelihood in the band and the chance for development. Milton Nascimento is named here as representative of many others. It was not until the eighties that 'Rock Brasil' manifested itself: a movement, carried by a new generation of musicians, which proved to be so successful economically that it saved many Brazilian record companies from bankruptcy.

Talents and Hopes

The era described in this chapter is also important for the appearance of many new singers, musicians and composers not yet mentioned.

Elis Regina set new standards for interpretive style. In many respects her curriculum vitae is similar to that of Carmen Miranda. And Elis might well have been able to reach similar heights, had she not died in such a tragic manner in January 1982. Like Carmen, Elis came from a modest middle-class family; and like Carmen, she began her career in childhood, had to struggle at times against an aversion on the part of her Brazilian countrymen and developed her own personal style in costume, mime and gesture.

Elis was also connected with Carmen in her uncompromising attitude toward her work, which she tackled consciously and systematically, but always self-critically. She came from Porto Alegre in the south of Brazil (born 1945), home of the gauchos. As a fourteen-year-old child she did radio programs in São Paulo with the hits of the year in 1959. These were not, however, the bossa novas written by Jobim and Vinicius which had yet to achieve great popularity in São Paulo. Instead, she sang boleros and rock ballads in her own lively way. So one can imagine the bitter disappointment she felt upon arriving in the bossa nova stronghold of Rio. The cariocas were swinging to the bossa nova groove, leaving little room for nonconformist sounds from the South. Elis's move to São Paulo proved wise in view of the growing importance of this metropolis in the post-bossa nova era. Here she established initial contacts in the youthful scene and had the chance to help

songs along the road to success at the city's various song festivals: Edu
Lobo ('Arrastão', 'Upa Neguinho'), Milton Nascimento ('Nada Será
Como Antes') and Baden Powell ('Canto de Ossanha').

Jair Rodriguez and Elis staged the legendary show 'Dois na Bossa' in
June 1965. Listening today to the original LP cut (which can only to be
had at a high price) one can sense how liberating it must have been to be
able at last to use and hear the entire range of musical material that
Brazil has to offer.

Still remembered today is the work of Elis's choreographer, Lennie
Dale. While earlier bossa nova performers acted with conscious under-
statement on stage, called 'cool', Lennie and Elis brought it new life.

Eumir Deodato in De Mello's *Música Popular Brasileira*, recalls: 'Songs
were performed rather linearly in those days, without gestures and with
a rather prudish interpretive style. Elis Regina heralded a generation of
singers who thought about their audience presentation, and they discovered that there were other means of reaching the public than the
voice alone.'

Elis Regina brought 'show' back to the stage. She never gave a sterile
concert. The first time I saw Elis in concert the frenzy and intensity of
this woman took my breath away. It lasted 130 minutes, a nonstop
program interrupted only by a short announcement that we should not
expect a break if Elis wanted to continue.

One of Elis's biggest hits was her show entitled 'Falso Brilhante'. In
one year alone in São Paulo it was staged 200 times and attracted
211,000 music-goers.

The cariocas' affection for Elis was not always constant. She, in turn,
certainly didn't make things easy for them. She registered every musical
development in the country with a fine-tuned antenna, continually
going out on a limb by singing pieces by young, unknown talents and
critical, progressive writers, at the expense of certain success with a
more commercial repertoire. Many Brazilians held that against her,
reacting by witholding the attention she rightly deserved.

The list of other prominent names from this period reads like a *Who's
Who of MPB*: the vocal quartet MPB-4, discovered by Chico Buarque;
the vocal quartet Em Cy, promoted by Vinicius de Moraes; João
Donato; Toquinho, guitarist and singer from São Paulo; Luiz Gonzaga
Jr., the son of the baião king; Martinho da Vila; and many others to be
assessed in the next chapter.

Walnice Nogueira Galvão undertook an interesting study of the
lyrical content of *sambas de participação, canções de protesto* and
'tropicalism'. He observed that the demythologization of traditional
music forms contains in itself a new myth, whereby sung reality, truth as

a glorified 'day which will come', is directed once again into comforting, but illusory paths. Galvão regards the term *o dia* (the day) as the essential concept of the lyrics from that period. He concludes that the new lyrics embody a utopia, as if to say, 'I am not responsible; I have no opportunity to act.'

The authors console the listener by singing

— that 'the day' will not come,
— that 'the day' will definitely come,
— so that 'the day' will come.

Below are several lyrics that Galvão offers as illustration:

Chico Buarque
Marcha João XXIII

I want to see a day
Which begins smiling
And everybody
Laughs the whole day
I so much want to see a day
When the poor aren't freezing
And the rich have a heart

Edu Lobo / Capinan
Ponteio

A certain day, I know for sure
I think it won't be long now
This day, I am sure, will come

Lobo / Torquato Neto
Aleluja

Make a decision, the time has come
One day heaven will be transformed
He who has nothing left to lose
Will only be able to win

Gil / Neto
Louvacão

I praise him who sings and does not sing
Because he cannot sing
But most definitely will sing
When that certain day finally arrives
For everybody to sing

Galvão indicates finally that this perspective of 'the day' and of the individualistic solution forces us to conclude that 'singing is the only proposal that Moderna Música Popular Brasileira is accustomed to making.'

It seems to me that the repeated use of the term 'day' does have some significance. Nevertheless, it must be said on behalf of the song writers that censorship automatically imposed limits on what they could actually offer as solutions to social problems.

Chapter 7

The Seventies and Eighties

Rio or São Paulo?

For many years São Paulo had to face up to the reality that the samba, choro and bossa nova were born in Rio de Janeiro. To Vinicius de Moraes is attributed the disparaging remark, 'São Paulo is the samba's graveyard.' Sambistas and chorões under the Corcovado are still absolutely convinced of the São Paulo musicians' inability to play the samba and choro correctly. This attitude remains as strong today, even if São Paulo has been able to mount a challenge to Rio's leading position within MPB. In fact, the last fifteen years have seen just as many creative innovations originating in São Paulo as in Rio. Still, it has been some time since either city has given rise to a new movement on a par with the bossa nova or tropicalism — with the possible exception of Rock Brasil in the late eighties. Rock Brasil was certainly popular with Brazilian youth, but despite its Portuguese lyrics it was musically only a copy of international rock.

Musicians of all MPB stripes have always emphasized the importance of Rio's atmosphere — the personal, unmistakable climate of this vibrant city — for their creative work. Many commute back and forth regularly between Rio and São Paulo, with an apartment in both cities. 'São Paulo is better for concerts, Rio for living,' one can often hear. Rio's national anthem, 'Cidade Maravilhosa', written in 1934, is still valid for today's cariocas:

Wondrous city
So full of magic
Heart of my Brazil
Cradle of the samba and of beautiful song
Living in the hearts of the people
You are the altar of our hearts
Singing happily
Lush garden of love and desire
Enchanted abode
God granted you gaiety
Oh, you nest of dreams and light!

The cariocas have a wealth of songs extolling the glories of their beloved city. In one, God is said to have created Rio on the last day of his work. He moulded it from his highest quality materials to create a pearl upon the earth. But adoration of Rio is by no means unanimous. In his book *Tristes Tropiques*, French structural anthropologist Claude Lévi-Strauss compared the city with New York and found it 'despite its renowned beauty repulsive.... I feel Rio can't live up to claims of its own greatness.... All these famous peaks jut out in Rio's bay like a row of forlorn stubs in a toothless mouth.' Stefan Zweig did not agree.* 'Rio is nature turned city — and a city that communicates impressions from nature.'

Rio is, indeed, both fascinating and repulsive at once. One becomes aware of the architectural tragedy the city has undergone when one compares old photographs of the different city neighborhoods with present-day photos. You can search in vain for many of the morro hills of earlier times. They were simply leveled. Great heaps were deposited in the bays of Botafogo and Gloria in order to make room for multi-lane highways.

Fifty years ago the Copacabana was a hilly, unbuilt tract of land. The Copacabana palace stood alone amid lush vegetation in natural grandeur. Today the scene has changed. A brutal concrete skyline dominates the beach from Leme to Leblon. The ocean is a stinking cesspool in many places. A cloud of smog hangs thick over the city. Despite the many cars running on gasohol made from sugarcane, they pollute the streets where skyscrapers prevent ventilating winds from blowing through. Morro children use the opportunity presented by a traffic jam to sell their Chiclets to a waiting driver, or they earn their living cleaning

———————————————

*Stefan Zweig committed suicide in Rio.

windshields with dirty rags: a hundred cruzeiros to have your windshield cleaned; two hundred not to have it cleaned. No one crosses the street at a walk. You run because the drivers pay no attention to pedestrians. The daily trip to and from work takes hours for those who live and work in different parts of the city.

Growing crime intimidates tourists. Desperate inhabitants of the favelas rob stores and pedestrians in broad daylight. They often kill, but only from fear that the victim might try to defend himself. Well-organized bands know all too well how to exploit this type of crime. Under the pretense of hunger and poverty they plunder entire houses in grand style. At the same time, the traditional neighborhoods on the riverbanks and cliffs, such as the Estação Mangueira, are threatened by new city planning in Rio. Unrest in the favelas continues, where drug barons are honored as the Cangaçeiro Lampião once was. São Paulo is no different. Crime and environmental destruction are the order of the day.

Many Brazilian composers and musicians began their careers in Rio. Most publishing houses and record companies have their main offices there. But appearances are deceiving. The Ponta Aera between Rio and São Paulo belongs to the everyday life of nearly everyone involved in MPB.

The hinterland is a world in itself. It is not to Petropolis or Rio Bonito that the city-dwellers head on Friday nights in endless caravans for their weekend vacations. The hinterland is many many hours away, to the north, south, and east. A carioca or Paulista knows it only from TV pictures from Ceará or Piaui. In the seventies the Brazilian government made great efforts to bring the hinterland closer, particularly by presenting rural music in the cities. The motivation behind it all, however, was sheer political calculation — to whitewash the crimes of land eviction, pollution and profiteering.

Music from the hinterland has long since arrived in the big cities. Hunger, drought, poverty and land eviction forced many peasants into slum areas on the periphery of the big cities. With them came their songs and dances.

After secret service head General Figueredo succeeded Ernesto Geisel as president of Brazil, he made promises of an *abertura*, an opening to democracy. Censorship was relaxed so that many songs that had been banned for years could be published. But as the Brazilian people wanted to choose their president through direct elections, the military made it understood that too much freedom and too much democracy were not their intention.

Brazil's economic troubles are reported daily in the press. The national debt, inflation, rising prices for rice and beans and many other problems have plunged the country into a deep crisis.

The conditions in 1991 echo the headlines of 1964: economic crisis (despite a revaluation of the cruzado and a restrictive monetary policy) and shifting political pressure through different governments. The Brazilians have become uncertain. Certainly such a period has, once again, its songs. One such song is Milton Nascimento's 'Coração de Estudante' ('The Heart of a Student') which proclaimed solidarity and, during those heated days of 1983 and 1984 when the direct election of the president was being debated, advanced to the unofficial status of hymn among the intellectual youth.

Milton Nascimento

The Heart of a Student
(Coração de Estudante)

I want to tell you of something
That is the lifeblood for the hope which
lives in our breast
and rocks like the ocean.
It sleeps at our side
stroking our hands
It is the urge for freedom
Young, like love
The seed suffocated
How often has it been
How often has freedom's fate
been painfully frustrated.
But it always returns, in hope,
like the dawn each day.
We must nourish and care for this seed
so that it blossoms and bears fruit.

The heart of a student
You must treat life with care
You must treat this world with care
and friends understand.
Friends and many dreams
gleam on the greenpaths
Thoughts and feelings
Leaves, heart, youth and faith.

At the same time Milton Nascimento released a song referring to the student unrest, 'No Bailes da Vida'. Chico Buarque took up the theme a few years later:

> Dancing samba in the mud wearing white shoes, but famous, the great artist must sound the first note; the voice is hoarse, the message is good.
> But look at the samba while squatting, from the toads' point of view.
> A great artist must teach, must accept fate, must give what he has and does not have, he must be happy — to dance samba in the mud without touching the ground, to dance samba in the mud and everything is fine, to do it without scratching the varnish — isn't that what people say? The party is over, musicians to their feet!

MPB in the eighties showed signs of stagnation and creative saturation. This did not apply to instrumental music, however, whose strengthened sense of self and improving quality has helped it gain popularity. It applied particularly, however, to the many old stars and newcomers of the seventies — Gilberto Gil as well as to Elba Ramalho. Banality and superficial gloss had come to replace originality and individuality.

Symptomatic of the whole trend was the 'creation' of a new species of MPB, promoted and marketed around 1980 as *Musica pra' Pular* (Music to hop by). Basically, it was nothing more than a stew of disco, soul, rock, pop and jazz, with a dash of Brazilian feeling thrown in. Brazil had always desired entrance into the international world of pop music. Brazilian subsidiaries of international record companies have always promoted the sales of music delivered to them by their American and European parent companies ahead of their own national products. That is, after all, how the system of capital investment in the Third World works. In the eighties record companies the world over complained about dwindling sales. It was inevitable that the crisis would also rock the Brazilian music industry. Bankruptcy and merger on the one hand, and bloated salaries on the other characterize this contradictory situation.

One musical form must also be mentioned: that which the Brazilians call *música brega*, kitsch, cafona or boko moko; over-sweet, sentimental songs that almost always feature love as their content and stylistically fall into different categories within MPB. This music retains a large share of the Brazilian market, and many artists, some of whom appear in the following chapters, have produced at least a few of this type of song. The representative brega-interpreters include Ivon Curi, Agnaldo Timoteo, Jerry Adriani, Ronnie Von, Evaldo Braga, Odair José, Fernando Mendes, Os Fevers, Michael Sullivan, Sidney Magal, Roberto

Leal, Wando ... as well as the stars of música sertaneja (Sergio Reis ...) and those of Rock Brasil for the kids.

The advent of Brazilian rock with Portuguese lyrics came just in time to ease the economic pain. In the late eighties, new initiatives developed in the rock scene that aimed to gain international stature with national productions.

One thing hadn't changed, though, since the tropicalism movement; that was the vital presence of all forms of musical expression in Brazil's folklore and pop music. This variety, with its sheer inexhaustible new material, kept MPB alive. New international pop music trends and their adaptation by Brazilian artists also played a significant role. For the urban Brazilian is also a modern consumer. He desires a continual flow of new stimuli to tantalize him. He greedily absorbs new sounds, new faces and new presentational forms. The joyful experimentation of young Brazilian musicians began, around 1986, to include Caribbean music. The new forms that arose from this, however, such as fricote, lambada, or chicote (from Bahia) enjoyed only shortlived popularity.

The Samba's Development

The question of a national or non-national music posed itself less and less since the bossa nova period. The continual presence of samba and other varieties on the musical scene, for example, offered adequate space for chauvinism to flourish.

This did not mean that Brazilian artists surrendered MPB to the internationalization of music without a fight. The Brazilian mentality, environmental problems, politics, the economy and society were all subjects that their songs still dealt with.

The big song festivals of the sixties were controversial. There was intense discussion of quality and commerce, disappointments, manipulations and criticism. In retrospect, this could be easily deduced from the titles that were able to do well at the time. Songs like 'A Banda' (1966), 'Domingo no Parque' (1967), 'Memoria de Marta Saré' (1968), and 'Sinal Fechado' (1969) tell us something of the standards set at the time. Compared with these songs, which continue to be popular, the winning song at the 1970 festival ('BR-3' by A. Adolfo) suggests that in 1969 a particular phase of MPB had come to an end, a phase in which the winning songs at festivals were almost always connected to the juncture of their artist's career. At the last festival, in 1972 ('F. Internacional da Canção' in Rio, sponsored by TV Globo), Jorge Ben's 'Fio Maravilha' took first prize. But nobody bothers anymore with the following places, nor with the results of the previous year. Eight years later, TV Globo attempted to revive the concept of the competition festival by staging MPB-80. It enjoyed only moderate success.

Zé Keti

The Voice from the Hill
(A Voz do Morro)

I am the samba,
The voice from the hill.
I truly am, yes, sirree.
I want to show the world
That I'm somebody
I am the king of the wide open spaces
I am the samba
I come from Rio de Janeiro
It's me who brings joy
To millions of Brazilian hearts
One more samba, if you please
We want samba
He who requests it
That is the true voice
Of the people of this nation
Long live the samba, let's sing
This melody for a happy Brazil

Toward the end of the bossa nova era the critics began to rediscover the sambistas from the *velha guarda* within the samba schools and in the morros, and to set them once again upon the concert stage. This meant that many sambistas could now enjoy a better standard of living. But, more important it meant people started taking a new interest in them. They were heard once again. There is no such thing as a sambista who does his thing in the total seclusion of his room or exclusively in the recording studio. A sambista needs an opposite member, someone he can address with his songs. A sambista composes from the heart. His songs are not born at the piano, but rather in a circle of friends and colleagues who correct and encourage them and sing along. The sambista found such a conducive atmosphere earlier in the quadra of his samba school. But the crisis situation in which samba schools found themselves for many years, revolving around the issue of preservation of traditional values, had caused many sambistas to distance themselves from their schools. But they often found a replacement. The urban youth and many MPB artists understand the importance of these 'traditional' songwriters. A sambista from Rio does nothing different from a blues singer from Chicago; he sings to his audience about his experiences and feelings, about politics and the times. Many traditional samba schools practically ignored these time-honored carriers of the tradition. Their judgments and advice were deemed uninteresting.

Other artists wanting to learn from them appeared on the scene, and especially women, among them Beth Carvalho, Clara Nunes, Leci Brandão, Alcione, Dona Ivone de Lara and Christina Buarque, Chico's sister.

Beth Carvalho (born 1946) grew up in the Urca at the bottom of the Sugar Loaf and in the Zona Sul. She had a taste of the scene via the bossa nova and all succeeding styles, but never could achieve any success within it as a singer. At thirteen she was already a regular guest at the Salgueiro Samba School and then in Portela, until she discovered the roots of the samba in the Morros Mangueira and São Carlos in 1970. She met Nelson Cavaquinho, who helped her develop her speciality, the authentic samba. Since then her road has taken her to the top. Sambistas from many samba schools offer her their new songs first. In 1980 composers from the Bloco Caçique de Ramos offered her the samba 'Vou Festejar', 'a gift', as she put it.

Clara Nunes (born 1943) became an orphan at an early age, her father was a violeiro and folia-de-reis singer. She arrived in Rio in 1965, and there she was able to make a name for herself quickly. She had always devoted herself to traditional morro sambas and had achieved great popularity long before Beth Carvalho. Compared to Beth's somewhat coarser, less polished performance, Clara had that certain flair, which combined grace with fire. News of her death in 1983 sent shock waves throughout the country, giving rise to a heated debate in the media. Clara Nunes had died from the after-effects of anesthesia given during an operation.

Leci Brandão (born 1944), a child of the Portela, grew up in Vila Isabel, and was the first woman to be accepted by the Mangueira Samba School. She had saved money from factory work in order to attend a university law course, which she soon broke off after her first successes as a composer. Her sambas, using a style popular in the seventies, both chronicle her times and cast a critical eye on them.

The singer Alcione (born 1947) came from São Luiz de Maranhão to the samba centers in 1967. Her father had been head of the town's brass band and taught her to play clarinet, saxophone and cornet. She became quite a hit in Rio, although she is not so closely connected to the morros and samba schools as her colleagues Beth and Leci. In January 1981 she surprised her fans with a small present picked up on a trip to Angola: 'Marrom' (as Alcione is also known) openly acknowledged her African roots, wearing her hair African style with cowrie shells in her pigtails and singing Angolan folk songs.

Dona Ivone de Lara (born 1922) recorded her first LP at the tender age of fifty-five. She received her musical training at home and at samba schools. Ivone credits her 119-year-old aunt with having taught her *caxambú*. In 1965 she joined the Imperio Serrano School, where she met up with sambista-songwriter Silas de Oliveira, who became her first musical partner. Today Dona Ivone de Lara is a chief representative of the archaic samba.

The eighties were particularly scanty in terms of producing new, exciting young samba talent. Among the women, Leci Brandão was the only important new face of note. Among male singers, Paulinho da Viola, Jair Rodriguez, Martinho da Vila, and João Nogueira had the floor to themselves.

Martinho da Vila (born 1938), a carioca, entered the Aprendizes da Boca do Mato Samba School at thirteen. At fifteen he wrote his first samba. In 1965 he arrived in Vila Isabel and shook up the carnival processions there by introducing a new type of samba enredo which he oriented on the samba de blocos. In the following years Martinho had a number of big samba hits at the Vila Isabel carnival. Martinho da Vila also became known for LPs and shows that reflect his interest in the general folkloric milieu of the samba and its early rural forms. Like no other samba singer, da Vila's exuberant swinging style was able to join text and music together in a percussive song.

In many instances careers have a lot of similarities. João Nogueira (born 1941) was born in the Meier district of Rio, played as a choro regional guitarist at an early age, made connections at the Portela, where he was successful with sambas. Dissatisfied with his samba school, as were so many sambistas, he later left the Portela. João Nogueira founded the Clube do Samba in Meier as a meeting place for sambistas, where information and opinions could be exchanged.

But there were other roads as well. Luiz Melodia, born upon one of Rio's morros, mixed his sambas with blues and soul. He gathered inspiration from, among others, Jorge Ben and Roberto Carlos. His soul brother Cassiano traveled a similar route. Both also played a role in the short-lived Black Rio movement.

After more than twenty years Jair Rodriguez still remains the best-known singer of the samba-carioca. In recent years he has increasingly taken compositions by young authors from other MPB genres into his repertoire.

For many years one spoke in Rio of the 'Four Greats of the Samba': Nelson Cavaquinho, Guilherme de Brito, Candeia and Elton Medeiros. Nelson Cavaquinho (born 1910) used to play choros. He discovered the samba of the morros around 1930. He then switched to guitar, which to this day he still plays in a manner all his own: he plucks the strings with only the thumb and index finger of his right hand. Nelson Cavaquinho worked as a composer with many sambistas from the morros. Cartola, for instance, introduced Nelson at his first public appearances when he opened his restaurant Zicartola at the beginning of the sixties. One can frequently hear Nelson today playing the samba-canção he has come to master in Rio's Teatro Opinião in the Noitada do Samba.

Cartola, born 1908, died in 1980. For years he, too, was one of the main attractions for many young cariocas at the Noitada do Samba. Cartola's life was intimately connected with the Mangueira. There he worked closely together with his *parçeiro* Carlos Cachaça as a composer and songwriter. In the thirties Mario Reis, Carmen Miranda and Francisco Alves recorded songs by Cartola. He was, like Nelson Cava-quinho, a bohemian among sambistas. He was a poet and, as long as he lived, the best interpreter of his own sentimental, intimate samba-canções. He sang of everyday happenings — of love and dreams — almost like a troubadour or *seresteiro* from a bygone age. People called him the 'divine' Cartola. I remember very well many a wonderful evening spent in the Teatro Opinião. First up were Xango da Man-gueira's sambas de partido alto, then the Conjunto Nosso Samba, Baianinho, and dance solos by the Passistas. Then 'O Divino Cartola' was announced. It was so quiet in the hall you could hear a pin drop. And then he came on stage — small and haggard and almost blind, carrying his guitar with him. He was unsure how to use the microphone. Laughing shyly to the audience he began:

The Roses Don't Speak

(As Rosas Não Falam)

It beats once more
My heart full of hope
For the summer is about to end
And so I enter the garden with the certainty
That I will have to cry
For I know too well you no longer want to be with me
So I complain to the roses
How senseless, the roses don't speak
They only smell sweet
Like a perfume which they stole from you

> You should come and see my sad eyes
> And who could even dream my dreams
> Ultimately

And the audience, each and every person there, sang along quietly. Every verse.

Another one of the Four Greats, Candeia (born 1935), is no longer with us. He died in 1978. He had been an inspiration and model for sambistas, and his death left many of them with a sense of helplessness as to how to extricate the samba schools from the quagmire in which they found themselves. Candeia was not only a samba devotee. He also had a keen interest in the African roots of the samba — the *jongos*, *caxambús* and *maculelês*. In 1976 Candeia, Guilherme de Brito, Elton Medeiros and Paulinho da Viola founded the Quilombo, an alternative samba school dedicated to returning the samba and Escola de Samba to their original black founders and to sharpening black consciousness concerning the importance of preserving their true samba tradition. Candeia recalled the epoch of the slaves' emancipation in which the blacks' carnival processions served to demonstrate the validity of their own Afro-Brazilian culture, as well as to demand that it be recognized.

Almirante, too, departed the scene, passing away in 1980. Noted chiefly as a chronicler of the samba's golden age, his records and archives provide us today with an invaluable documentation of the samba-carioca. Almirante's archive can be seen today in the Museu de Imagem e Som in Rio.

The departure of so many sambistas who had been active (and often disregarded) in developing the samba and samba schools for over fifty years left an enormous dent in the surviving samba scene. If it is to continue, it will not be due to the successes of short-lived carnival sambas solely intent upon raking in the profits. The samba gets its vitality from its creators — the sambistas — on the quadra, in the bar and wherever new melodies and new lyrics arise. Beth Carvalho, Jair Rodriguez and others who enjoy the limelight would be nothing without the sambista.

The Post-Bossa Nova Artists

Bossa nova musicians and songwriters did not stand still after 1964. They managed to develop themselves and their modern sambas further. While Antonio Carlos Jobim produced records chiefly in the United

States, he was still regarded as the key figure and mentor of MPB. Tom has often been criticized for being Americanized* and for earning a fortune in the States. 'A journalist once asked me what it felt like being so famous,' Tom says. 'I told him I'd really like to know what it felt like being rich.' And it's a simple fact that for years Brazilian recording companies ignored Jobim. So he had no choice but to record his albums in the United States. Claus Ogermann arranged the majority of them, including a co-production with Frank Sinatra. But Jobim was, at that time, critical of the American music business and didn't last long there. In Brazil he is a welcome guest at his colleagues' concerts and recording sessions. He frequently writes arrangements for them or plays piano or sings for their recordings. In 1982 Tom and Edu Lobo released a very nice LP ('Tom + Edu') characterized by a sparse instrumentation. João Gilberto also remained true to his principles. In the years that passed since his 'Bim Bom' and 'Chega de Saudade' got the bossa nova movement rolling and he moved to New York, he has made return visits to Brazil.

Herbie Mann let me in on the background details to the 'Amoroso' LP. João had refused to go to a recording studio, offering instead his own apartment for the recording session. So his New York flat was wired for sound, and the entire LP was done with JG sitting before the mike in pajamas, playing only his guitar. Ogermann later recorded the strings and orchestral background separately and did the mixing. In Brazil JG gave a few concerts that were accompanied by scandal. He once let an audience wait in vain for him at the Canecão in Rio. He simply didn't show up. Another time he called off a stint of guest appearances intended to last several weeks shortly before the first show. He didn't like the way the microphone sounded. Instead, he appeared with the same show on TV soon afterward. The most important rule for those wanting to work with JG is, 'Just don't provoke him.' For all that, his concerts in Brazil were a grand comeback. JG remains the idol of that Brazilian bossa nova generation of the sixties, which pays astronomical prices to see and hear him. João Gilberto is a legend.

Vinicius de Moraes, composer of *Orfeu*, died in 1980. Brazil mourned the loss of a loved one. He had just celebrated the tenth anniversary of his partnership with Toquinho. Toquinho and Vinicius were a poetic-musical duo with a unique musical style, aspiring to be 'like a swallow in the rosy dawn of new sounds.' Vinicius also wrote lyrics for many young MPB musicians. One of his last dramas was *Arca de Noë*. In 1978 Vinicius set foot on stage with Tom one last time, (this show was also

---

*Among his critics was the musicologist José Ramos Tinhorão — a superb expert on MPB, but with chauvinistic tendencies.

presented at the Palladium Theatre in London) He sat down at a table and waited for the concert to end before emptying his decanter full of gin and water. He sang, too, with a warm, rough voice. He majestically recited poetry, with lots of hand gesticulation. He chatted with the audience and with Tom and the other musicians as if they were all visiting him at his home in Gavea. Vinicius lived there, surrounded by children and grandchildren, and was often visited by friends and colleagues into the wee hours of the morning. The partnership with Toquinho helped Vinicius to overcome at last the stylistic limitations present in his previous work. A new music was born, made up of thousands of facets of Brazilian pop and folklore, poetry and prose. Many young musicians found in Vinicius a partner with a bubbling, youthful vitality. His lyrics propounded generally understood truths, especially his philosophy of love. Vinicius lived to be only sixty-seven. Shortly after his death, Edu Lobo told me he had had many friends, but few knew the real Vinicius. Those who knew him best felt that at the end he had lost his will to live.

After the bossa nova, Mário Albanese from São Paulo introduced the *jequibau* (a variety of batuque), a 5/4 rhythm he developed out of Afro-Brazilian music from Minas Gerais. Despite recordings by Andy Williams, Vic Damone and Charly Byrd to his credit, Albanese's jequibau could not prevail.

Astrud Gilberto tried to make a comeback in the United States in 1983, but with no success. An art critic from the *New York Post* once commented upon one of her appearances in that city: 'Ipanema is not forever.' That aside, Astrud Gilberto did profit from a small bossa nova renaissance in Europe, which was initiated by artists such as Sade Adu and Matt Bianco with their bossa-inspired songs. Antonio Carlos Jobim was rediscovered internationally as well. After being honored by an American copyright firm in 1989 he made a European tour; in the United States the old jazz versions of the bossa nova, from Bud Shank to Charly Byrd, were being played once more.

Twenty-five years after the bossa nova, an anniversary which was nearly overlooked, the cultural bridge between the United States and Brazil was opened again. David Byrne dubbed himself the champion of MPB in the United States, but produced with his first 'Brasil Classics' only poorly researched anthologies. His own Brazil-inspired album 'Rei Momo' left many connoisseurs of Brazilian music cold. Byrne also helped Margareth Menezes, from Bahia, to gain international acclaim. Sarah Vaughn, Manhatten Transfer, Mark Murphy, Herbie Mann and others have extensively included Brazilian compositions in their recordings. As a producer, Quincy Jones has for many years been a loving promoter of MPB in America.

This new interest in MPB after the bossa nova epoque found many Brazilian artists in doubt as to whether they should also record their songs in English for the international market. As far as I have been able to find out, the sales of such recordings did not exceed in their native language.

Brazilian-born Arto Lindsay and Paulinho da Viola appeared together on stage in Rio, while Paul Simon preferred to send scouts with DAT recorders into the streets of Bahia to gather inspiration for his album 'Rhythm of the Saints'.

Samba performers — be they modern, traditional, pop-oriented, or folkloric — don't put their programs together based on the latest fashions and trends. MPB is rich in material. Sambistas choose from it what they like and, frequently, what their colleagues present them. Partnership plays an important role in MPB. Artists work together in writing songs and recording them. One example is Chico Buarque's 'O Que Sera' from 1976.

Chico Buarque / Milton Nascimento
What Could It Be?
(O Que Será/A Flor da Terra)

What could it be
What could it be
That they sigh in nooks and crannies
That they whisper in verse and song
That they decide upon in the darkness of the caverns
That stirs the mind, what travels from mouth to mouth
When they light up a candle in an alleyway
What they shout out in the taverns
And scream at the marketplace
That certainly lies in nature
Can that be
What has no certainty and never will have
What cannot be mended and never will be
What has no size
What might that be
That lives in the minds of lovers
That mad poets sing about
That the most drunken prophets swear
That is the pilgrimage of the cripple
That is in the fantasy of the discontented
That is in the everyday life of the prostitute
In the plan of the criminal, of the helpless
In every sense and meaning

Can that be
What has no decency and never will have
What cannot be censored and never will be
What has no sense
What might that be
That all regulations cannot prevent
Because all smiling will challenge it
Because every bell will ring out
Because every hymn will sanctify it
And all youth will rage
And even the eternal Father, who has never been there
Will, when he sees this inferno, give his blessing
What a government never had and never will have
What has no shame and never will
What has no reason

Such cooperation promotes musical quality and prevents isolated artistic developments.

Some MPB stars are more reserved. Edu Lobo, for instance has rarely given concerts in the years since his big initial successes, and his record releases have occurred with relatively large time lapses betwen them. He has chosen instead to concentrate his energies on musicals, ballets and film music. When I asked him in 1972 who his models were, he replied, 'Gil Evans is, in my opinion, the most perfect man in popular music I've ever heard. And Miles Davis. In other areas, Cat Stevens, James Taylor and Chicago.' Regular visits to Europe and the United States have kept Edu abreast of all the latest developments. In 1978 an LP with Ferreira Guillar's 'Poema Sujo' and music by Edu Lobo on it was banned. Five years later Edu wrote the music for Guillar's drama *Dr. Getúlio* (song lyrics by Chico Buarque). His ballet *Gabriela* and Naum Alves de Souza's ballet *Grande Circo Mistico* (lyrics once again by Chico) appeared that same year. De Souza also choreographed Edu's ballet *Jogo de Dança*, which had its debut in Curitiba in October 1981. Edu called this new task a 'lonely leap into the dark.'

The first time I saw Luiz Gonzaga Jr., he was standing on the small stage of a suburban theater in Rio chatting with the audience. He was telling them of having read in the newspapers that a German impresario had come to Rio in order to engage him for a concert tour in Germany. That really was written in the *Globo*. Gonzaguinha explained to his listeners in Marechal Hermes, 'It's all so silly. People there understand just as little of our language and problems as those American tourists who come to the Sertão and declare, "They need rain here"!' Everybody laughed. I approached him shyly after the concert. I told him who I was, and we shook hands and decided to go for a drink together. Out of the short drink came a long discussion that led us in the early morning hours from the suburbs to a bar in the city.

On another occasion I visited him at his home in the Rio district of Tijuca: toys, papers and musical instruments lay strewn all over the place. Gonzaga seemed more haggard than ever. His cheekbones were more pronounced than usual. His eyes were bleary. He was nervous and inattentive. He had just completed his latest record. He put it on and left me alone with the music for half an hour. I listened to it to the sound of the telephone's ringing, children's screaming and conversations from other rooms in the house. He returned. I told him what I thought of the LP and that we should have a go at releasing it in Europe with English lyrics. Months later I received an answer from a record company in Cologne: 'The man is too good for the German market.' I wrote this to Gonzaguinha. He replied, 'Let's keep fighting!'

Luiz Gonzaga Jr. first turned up at one of Rio's many song festivals in 1969. He was born in 1945, the natural son the King of the Baiãos, but was not raised in his home: his mother, the singer Odaleia, died in 1947, and Gonzaga had quickly developed a new relationship. Gonzaguinha was fostered out to a family living in the Morro district of São Carlos. His new father, Xavier Pinheiro — 'O Baiano' — was a guitarist, and serestas took place regularly in his house. Gonzaguinha rarely saw his real father, who was forever touring Brazil. When at seventeen, 'O Moleque Gonzaguinha' ('the Negro Boy', as he called himself) wanted to move in with his father, he was turned away: they were too dissimilar, it was claimed, it would never work. Only when Gonzagão could no longer deny that his own son had become a successful and acclaimed composer and singer did he welcome him into his life, discovering many similarities between them, despite their different political leanings. 'Luizinho,' he said after their first collaborations on stage and in the recording studio in the early eighties, 'is a miracle; someone whom you can observe rising forth in full mastery of his talents … He is a worker … I believe we have a lot in common in this respect, *por ai.*'

Gonzaguinha, who died tragically in a car crash in South Brazil on the morning of April 29, 1991, always said that he preferred dealing with reality, not with dreams or divine inspiration. He always gave his music a real aggressive punch, for good measure. But Gonzaguinha also wrote about love, problems with relationships and developed autobiographical material. It was precisely these songs, such as 'Explode Coração', that were made famous by Maria Bethania and other MPB artistes.

In his song 'Sangrado' he defined himself as an artist:

When I raise my voice
Please understand
That word for word
A man reveals his heart
Through his tongue openly
And vulnerable
It is of the battles of life
That I sing
When I open my mouth
With great force
All you hear
Becomes true
And has been lived by me
Look at the gleam in my eyes
My shaking hands
My sweating body
All expressions of myself and my feelings
And when I weep
And when the sin caresses my smiles
Do not relax
But sing
As your song makes me sing
When I raise my voice
Please understand
This is how I live
And love

Gonzaguinha never became a superstar like his friend Milton Nascimento. He was more of an anti-star, but popular, nevertheless. His songs treat themes and situations that frequently repeat themselves. They made him fathomable. They gave us a continual supply of information about his personal development. Gonzaguinha said, 'There came a day in my life in which my path crystalized. But this path is a spiral. There are always points above and below the original path, and these correspond to my life experiences and to the things with which I live, which I live out, do and believe. Causes, effects consequences, contradictions. I plant the seed and harvest the new grain that brings forth fruit.' Judging by the sales of his records, Gonzaguinha reached the pinnacle of his career in 1983; but always continued to publish songs of an equally high quality.

In August 1989, Luiz Gonzaga Jr.'s father died in Recife and was buried in Exú, the place of his birth. Immediately after the funeral,

Gonzaguinha began to make one of his father's dearest dreams a reality: a cultural center for the local inhabitants of Exú, in the Parque Asa Branca on the banks of the Sertão river. Before his own death in 1991, Gonzaguinha had already provided gas, water and roads from his own fees. Under his direction, a park was created around his father's birthplace. The Gonzaga museum organizes performances for the promotion of Sertão culture, such as meetings of the sanfoneiros. In 1990 alone, Gonzaguinha gave 106 concerts throughout Brazil to raise money for the Asa Branca Foundation. A year before, shortly after the death of his father, Gonzaguinha's last LP was released. It contained many of his father's songs, some new compositions by Gonzaguinha himself and some others recorded by the two of them together, dating back some years. The song 'A Vida do Viajante' contains the lines: 'I devote my life to traversing this land so that one day I may come to a happy rest ... to evoke memories; memories of places visited and memories of friends I have left behind.'

Gonzaga Jr. worked in the MAU (Movimento Artistico Universitario), which first made the headlines in the sixties. The movement aimed to attract public attention to its politics through artistic quality. In addition to César Costa Filho and Aldir Blanc, Ivan Lins also achieved prominence within the movement. Even the television station Rede Globo, usually loyal to the government, joined in by planning a regular program for students in which they could stir up the public and give them something to think about. But nothing of the sort actually happened. Official pressure paralyzed the movement before it even started. Lins withdrew completely into seclusion and his friends in the movement, Luis Gonzaga Jr. and César Costa Filho, were simply silenced.

Many Brazilians came to regard Lins as a Communist singer and author. Such classifications, of course, are made all too easily in countries with rightist military dictatorships. Continual censorship of his work since the MAU era has forced Lins to suffer the consequences of such an identity. He is certainly a critical songwriter. He never ceased calling for the promised 'opening' to democracy, and this made Brazil's military rulers squirm.

Vitor Martins / Ivan Lins

New Times
(Novo Tempo)

In these recent times
Despite this torment
We are attentive

We are more alive and ready
To help each other
In these recent times
Despite the dangers
Of an even more brutal violence
Of the night which helps it
We are in the struggle
To survive.

In 1987 Ivan Lins released 'Mãos', an ambitious LP with a very ironic song about United States involvement in Nicaragua. Two years later Lins himself was in the United States with a new production 'Love Dance', and for the first time in years, Vitor Martins had not written the lyrics. Instead, Lins sang forgettable verses in English. The press release that accompanied this LP describes it as 'music to groove and dream to.' Music for the masses, a no-obligation consumer product from a man who, at least in Brazil, had sent completely different signals. Even prior to the LP with the song 'Nicaragua', Lins was known in the United States where George Benson recorded his 'Love Dance'; Lins gave 18 concerts in the United States, made a television show, and Manhattan Transfer recorded several Lins numbers on their Brazil album. One can surmise that in 'Love Dance' the Americans had elegantly managed to divert Lins from recording critical, ironic songs such as 'Nicaragua', in that they demanded English lyrics and then immediately provided the texts. Thus they avoided any danger of Lins' (or Vitor Martins') texts frightening the Americans off and spoiling business. Lins is, as he says himself, first a musician and a composer. One can't help hearing his affinity with American jazz-rock.

Lins became an artist who produced nice safe songs that here and there showed real musical quality — but they are interchangeable, no longer unmistakably Ivan Lins. No common reality, no shared fate connected the American text writers with Ivan Lins — only the check from the same record company. And that company even tuned Ivan Lins' voice down a few decibels, because that's not what counts in this business any more.

Música brega and Rock Brasil became areas in which investment by the music industry has been rewarded. Joining música sertaneja more recently is the children's market, where 'samplers' made in connection with children's TV-programs are sold in great numbers. Indeed, the success of Xuxa in this field was greater than all other competing MPB categories. Xuxa, who hosts a popular daily television show for children on TV Globo has, since 1987 had a series of best-selling LPs. Xuxa product is now planned for marketing in other Latin American countries.

Among the vocal groups, which established a firm tradition in Brazil in the thirties, Ceu da Boca and Boca Livre made a brief appearance. Without actually replacing the established groups EmCy and MPB-4, they did attract a youthful pop-oriented audience with their modern arrangements, an audience that then turned to the less artistic songs of Brazilian rock groups.

Several stars had their start in the eighties — among them were, however, few personalities. Elba Ramalho, a north Brazilian who showed little singing talent but a gift for sex and hopping around, became Brazil's new superstar. The purchase of her LP enabled the buyer to participate in an automobile lottery for a new model called Elba.

Elba Ramalho was already a top star by 1987. Especially noteworthy are the excellent musical arrangements of her songs. She was less impressive, however, in her reditions of typical Northeastern songs.

Similarly working his way up the charts, that is, until his death, was Cazuza, from the soft Rock Brasil scene, to which Ritchie, the English son of a soldier with a strict religious upbringing, also belongs.

Marisa Monte sang her way to a gold album in 1989. She wanted to be an opera singer and earned a living for years as a chorus girl. She was hailed as a great discovery in Brazil, as an alternative to Rock Brasil for the youth. She brings together in her repertory traditional values (from the era of Carmen Miranda to Gilberto Gil) with those of contemporary pop music from Brazil and abroad, seeking to collaborate with bossa nova composers as well as rock musicians.

The old stars such as Maria Creuza, Fafa de Belem or Alaide Costa have lost ground to the young women of MPB. Even a relatively recent celebrity like Angela RoRo, who with Leci Brandão was a proponent of a new consciousness among Brazilian women and provided refined insights into lesbian experience, has had to make room for youth's new idols.

Other figures, like Benito de Paula and Wilson Simonal, highly acclaimed newcomers in the seventies, are all but forgotten today. Even Jorge Ben has had to fight against his countrymen's faulty memories by continually releasing new versions of old hits.

Rio and Its Samba Schools

Voices from the hill sound somewhat hoarser after Ash Wednesday, and that's not only because of carnival fun.

For years a battle has been raging as to whether the hill can still claim the samba as its inhabitant. To put it more precisely, the question has been posed whether the samba schools set at the bottom of these hills (Rio's morros with their favelas) still function as a mouthpiece and communications center for the hill. Sambistas dread the very real possibility of being kicked out by the music industry. Hill dwellers are suspicious of the increasing number of wealthy people buying into their neighborhoods. The samba schools seek to avert total collapse by turning out ever more commerical products. After fifty years of being the main carriers of diverse tendencies of cultural and social development within the poor districts, Rio's samba schools today are rent by a deep crisis that might very well signal their end. The fulfillment of one prophecy seems near. 'Praça Onze', a samba perennial from 1942, states:

> Some day soon there will be no more samba school.
> Cry, tambourine, cry, world —
> Favela, Salgueiro, Mangueira, Estação Primeira —
> All you samba schools, put your pandeiros in the closet
> For the samba schools no longer take to the streets.

Morros with No Future

Morro residents live closer to heaven and God, to paradise and hell, so the saying goes. The reality of life in the favelas on the slopes of the morros is a far cry from the clichés offered us in our mass media. Images of women busily getting down to work right after Ash Wednesday preparing costumes for the next carnival hides the harsh reality of untold misery in these settlements. There is no sewage system and seldom water and electricity — that is, unless the Pope decides to pay the morros a visit. Then the favela residents' urgent demands and needs are hurriedly met — until the Pope departs, after which the 'progress' is dismantled once again.

The Morro Does Not Lie

(O Morro Não Engana)

Climb up to the hill
Climb up exhausted
Poor me

> Poor in nothing
> Hill of fear
> Hill of sleep
> Hill of asphalt

The center of the samba is not the morros alone. They have to share this role with other districts in Rio, such as Cidade Nova and various suburbs. The batuqueiro makes his home there — a figure associated with capoeira musicians who takes part today in the roda de batuque, the batucada. The much-respected *catedráticos*, (professors) and *bambas* (*o bom de tudo*), men who especially cultivate the samba de partido alto, also make their homes here. Sambistas live here, devising their sambas de quadra (samba do terreiro) in between carnival campaigns and their samba endredos just before rehearsals for the parade.

The morros are also a hiding place and base of operations for men of the underworld. Drug trafficking thrives in the favelas. There are even areas where the police themselves do not dare set foot. It's no rare thing to hear gunfire during the day.

But on Saturday evenings people meet in the roda de samba. Mondays and Fridays, however, are reserved for nocturnal macumba and candomblé rituals.

At the end of the twenties the Morro do Salgueiro, near Maracana Stadium, had become an important creative center for the samba in Rio. One could hear the following verse sung in Salguerio with a sense of pride and self-confidence:

> The Querosener are helpers
> The Mangueira is a professor.
> But in front of the band
> Salgueiro is its doctor.
> São Carlos is competent,
> Favela carries a scepter,
> But within the samba school, of all these people,
> Salgueiro is the master.

When the two blocos Azul e Branco and Depois Eu Digo merged to form a single samba school, the very existence of the Salgueiro favela was threatened. One day a man showed up in the favela with a judicial summons for default on payment. He claimed to be the owner of the land upon which their shacks were built. Azul e Branco took up the people's case. They hired a lawyer to defend their tenant rights and won.

Competition

I have already mentioned the birth of the samba schools. Soon they had selected regular domiciles for themselves. Like sport clubs, each school selected its own colors and banners so that it could be easily identified.

Their internal organization began to take on a more solid form. As new samba schools were springing up every day, the city tourist board decided to transfer the first-class samba school's processions from the traditional Praça Onze to the wider streets of Rio's downtown, and later to Avenida Presidente Vargas with its newly installed grandstand. In 1984 they paraded for the first time in Niemeyer's Praça de Apoteose (Sabucai), a very modern-looking hall that did nothing to improve the carnival atmosphere. Samba schools of 'less importance' are limited to displays at Sambódromo; others are limited to public appearances in suburban areas. Compared to the mass street spectacles put on by the samba schools, the whites' carnivals in the southern zones of the city were losing ground fast. Today they are more like costume shows, fairs for rich cariocas to exhibit their narcissism and vanity at exorbitant prices.

Rivalries among schools improved the quality of the processions, costumes and music from year to year. At the same time it meant a tremendous expense, which threatened the very survival of the samba schools's mortgaged palaces.

In 1979 a quarrel broke out between the samba schools and Riotur, the Rio tourist board, over whether to dispense with the *mestre sala, porta bandeira,* and the *commissão de frente,* the central figures in the carnival procession. The porta bandeiras are dancers who carry the samba school banners. Over the years a number of women had become permanent fixtures in this role. Suddenly they rebelled, demanding more money for their costumes.

All three figures from the carioca carnival are remnants of a past borrowed from Bahian rancho processions. Jota Efege, well-known chronicler of the samba-carioca, put it even more strongly in his book, *Figuras e Coisas do Carnaval Carioca*: 'Basically, the samba schools have nothing original about them. Everything they have they've copied from the ranchos; they haven't created a thing of their own. The main things are the Bahian women and the percussion. The allegories and every-thing else, although effective, are of secondary importance.'

The quarrel was solved with a compromise. The jury's rating system for the porta bandeira, mestre sala and commissão de frente would be reduced in importance. It was this rating system, under Riotur's control, which more than anything else had become the object of criticism over the years. The gold trophy Estandartes de Ouro (Riotur),

Scoring Categories

1. Allegory and Scenery
   (1–5 points); in addition to the allegorical wagon, the *alegorias de mão*.

2. Harmonia
   Song, directed by the *puxador*, and rhythm.

3. Mestre Sala/Porta Bandeira
   Often in Rococo costumes, Louis XV. The mestre sala dances around
   the porta bandeira and protects them from attacks by rival samba
   schools that want to steal their banners. (He sometimes has razor
   blades hidden in his fan.)

4. Fantasia
   The scenery and costumes for the *enredos* became even more opulent
   and luxurious when television coverage began in the sixties. Problems
   often arise in the samba schools when participants refuse to wear the
   prescribed costumes. (This happened, for instance, in 1954, when
   Salgueiro put on Palmares; nobody wanted to dress up like a Negro,
   since the whites' costumes with weapons and plumes were so
   popular.)

5. Bateria
   The heart and soul of the procession. Its basis is the surdo, derived
   from the Afro-Brazilian atabaque. Also guica, tamborine, reco-reco,
   agôgô, frigideiras, pratos, caixas, tárois, repiniques. It used to be that
   each samba school had its own rhythmic particularities: Mangueira
   was quick-footed with surdos (*treme terra*) and double marcação;
   Portela with the tabajará, a lively rhythm; Imperio Serrano with
   metallic sounds, etc.

6. Enredos
   The enredo is determined by the lyrics of the song written for the
   procession. Fantasia, allegory, and scenery come together in lively
   interplay.

7. Samba Enredo
   The samba, or carnival marcha (very different things in the forties), is
   a *samba de empolgação* (spirit-stirring samba) with short melodies and a
   strong refrain. Often the thousands taking part in the enredo get
   confused, with the front singing one verse, the back another.

8. Evolução
   Choreography linking dance and rhythm, conducted by the director
   of the Harmonia.

9. Commissão de Frente
   Enredo calling card with famous sambistas from the school (about 15
   people) or to particular themes.

as well as prizes from the newspaper syndicated Globo and Coca-Cola, were awarded for the first time in 1979. The Estandartes de Ouro are awarded in various categories, including audience communication, best *bateria*, dance and samba enredo. The *Journal do Brasil*, a daily newspaper, awards its Estandarte do Povo each year, also in different categories.

Thematic Material

The forties and fifties witnessed a change in the thematic material of the processions and sambas. Epic-length treatments of themes from Brazilian history had been common until then. Then shorter texts of a more humorous, satirical nature came to predominate. Brazil's folklore and ethnic roots came more and more to occupy center stage. By the sixties one could hear not only many African sambas, but also Afro-Brazilian rhythms and folkloric music of all types from the whole country.

Reflective of this, the 1973 carnival hit was called 'Tem Capoeira', composed by Batista da Mangueira. 'Mangueira will offer us capoeira from Bahia. Let's have a good carnival. Samba is our tradition. But be careful, look for cover, when Mangueira arrives: she'll blow up a storm.'

Today, samba enredo subjects can be anything under the sun. A samba school marched to the following lines lampooning major Brazilian politicians of the period in the 1979 Brasilia carnival: 'Hostages, you've brought us troubles. Figueredo has done the same. The Ayatollah will save us, and the government will be flabbergasted.' A year later, amnesty and torture were themes heard at the carnival.

At their founding, samba schools averaged one hundred musicians and dancers for a carnival. Today two to four thousand per school is common.

The Mangueira Samba School entered the 1974 parade with 144 numbers, a literal feast for the eye and ear. Everything Brazil had to offer in the way of folklore was there: Indian music, folkloric performances and festivals, gaucho music and fishermen's music, Afro-Brazilian cults: every form of urban popular music imaginable. You name it, it was there. The procession of this school alone lasted four hours!

The Beija Flor Samba School's motto in 1978 was 'The Creation of the World in the Old African Nago culture.' In general, samba schools have tended increasingly to highlight Brazil's African roots. This is especially the case recently in response to competition presented by western pop-disco music and its ability to entice youth away from the schools. This tendency can also be regarded, to some extent, as an attempt to create a conscious counterweight to the pop music interests of the wealthy youth of Rio's southern districts. Some samba schools have tried hard to adapt, even to the extent of drawing on North American soul music mixed with the sambas.

Organization

At one time the samba schools had, more or less, only a single task to perform — to prepare and perform the carnival procession. Nothing has really changed in that respect for samba school directors today. But sambistas take a different view. Martinho da Vila has said of the subject: 'Carnival — it's a spectacular opportunity — more for the tourists. But the samba school's real importance lies in the pre-carnival period.'

Martinho considers the samba schools to be of greater value to the residents of a neighborhood during those times when they are not gripped by the carnival fever. Then they function almost as community centers. People meet each other there mostly on the weekend, children receive music lessons in youth groups, projects are undertaken in various work groups, and there's a chance just to talk about everyday problems and concerns. Roughly speaking, samba schools are like clubs. And they are similarly organized.

Although the carnivals might appear to the viewer to be a chaos of movement and color, they are in fact, perfectly organized right down to the last detail. Despite this, carnival does represent, in a sense, a type of anti-structure. The poor attire themselves in the robes of the rich. Men dress as women. But the samba schools represented at the carnival do not actually offer this. They are disciplined and organized; they have their statutes, unwritten laws, administration, management, directors, and vice-directors.

The residents of a neighborhood do not automatically become members of their samba school. In general, one can distinguish between *componentes* and *sócios*, i.e., participants and members. Componentes are the creative artists who march along in the carnival route singing, dancing and making music. The sócios have more of an official function. Among sócios we can further differentiate *sócios componentes* — those who have distinguished themselves at the carnival and can thus be promoted — and *sócios fundadores*, those men who founded the samba school and therefore possess special privileges. Finally, there are *sócios especiais*, special members.

The sócios, or members, are divided up into men, women and children and assigned to individual departments, called *alas*. The alas are responsible for organizing song, dance and music groups. For example, there is an ala for composers, another, primarily female, for those who work on scenery and costume, and an *ala da bateria* — drummers, with a subdivision for children (the actual samba 'school', if you will).

A number of alas are combined to form the *alas reunidas* for the *enredo*. The various samba school departments are each headed by a directorate having president, vice-president, treasurer and secretary. A joint directorate with even more individual posts stands above them, as well as a carnival commission. One notices immediately upon entering the samba school how this complicated hierarchy is reflected in a corresponding seating arrangement in the house. Particular booths or balconies are reserved for the composers, drummers, the directorate and other dignitaries. The common members (componentes) are allowed to hang out in the *quadra*, the big training ground within the samba school. Since components and sócios alone would hardly be noticed at a carnival parade, *grupos* were added to the procession. These are loosely organized circles of friends, open to everyone and without any bureacratic entanglement with the directorate, allowing them to be a good deal more flexible.

To become a member of a samba school one must wait for a place to become free in one of the departments. This usually occurs through the death, expulsion or withdrawal of a member. The fact is, however, that a number of posts always open up after the death of a sócio, since it's the fashion to hold several offices simultaneously, even if this acts as an impediment to executing democratic decisions within the school.

Composers (like everyone else) have to apply in writing. Once accepted, they stand under a perpetual compulsion to produce hits, for this is the only mechanism by which advancement within the school hierarchy is possible. But since only one samba per year stands a chance of attaining success, composers frequently change schools from year to year.

Each samba school has its old guard — a *velha guarda* — in which the distinguished personalities from the school's early days come together. Their veneration in samba circles can take on an almost cult-like character at times. We can compare it with the adoration traditional jazz fans accord the old jazz musicians from New Orleans. There's another parallel to jazz and blues worth mentioning. You will hardly ever find a sambista known under his Christian name. Their performing names derive from particular personal qualities, background, musical instruments, etc. For example, *Cartola* means cylindrical hat. Carlos *Cachaça* could be translated as Charles Booze; *Zé com Fome*, Zé 'with Hunger'; *Pelado da Mangueira* 'the bald-headed man from Mangueira.'

Cartola was the gray eminence from the Mangueira and, indeed, became one of the most important figures in all of MPB.

Most compositions proposed by house composers for the carnival end up in the garbage can. The selection process goes on for weeks, with all the different sambas being played in the quadra. The directorate makes the final decision on a single samba, based on a kind of school plebiscite.

For the 1974 carnival 312 compositions (177 sambas, 126 marchinas, 9 frevos) were written. These choices underwent a strict selection process beforehand, being tested for their chances of marketing success. Nevertheless, the unbelievable happened: not a single title made it onto radio or TV. The reason was that a quarrel had broken out between music publishing houses and broadcasting networks due to commercial interests controlled by the all-mighty monopolized carnival organization in Rio. So the street remained the sole platform for the samba schools to present their new songs.

Discontent

The main criticisms directed at the traditional samba schools in the eighties can be summarized as follows.

First, the finances are unsound. The schools are in debt and can hardly ever cover their costs. Their carnival presentations take on ever more lavish forms without being able to pay for them. This forces them into a fateful state of dependence upon industrial sponsors, the bosses of the illegal Bicho lottery and increasing subjugation and control by the omnipotent tourist agency Riotur.

Every performance they give, be it during or outside the carnival, requires Riotur's permission and for that the samba schools get very little in return. The contract the samba schools signed with Riotur in 1976 was a disastrous one. Riotur's organization and control of the carnival processions was nothing new, but the 1976 contract signed by the AESCRJ (Associação das Escolas de Samba da Cidade do Rio de Janeiro) stipulated conditions whereby the samba schools were forced to subordinate all their activities to Riotur's schedule of events, and appearances outside this schedule required special permission from Riotur. Violators were fined. For their part, Riotur subsidized the schools — much too little, say the sambistas — but also received their share of the profits when the school won at the carnival. Moreover, several schools agreed to tie-in contracts which, with Riotur's participation, transferred the copyright for song titles (either in part or in full) to the schools during carnival. That meant, in essence, that the author of a carnival song could only find a place for his composition at a samba school (which had the best means available to popularize it) if he was prepared to sign a statement allowing the school to exploit it commercially.

The Mangueira Samba School's total costs for the 1979 procession amounted to 2 million cruzeiros. ($150,000). A single costume for the standard-bearer, for example, costs $7,000 and for the percussion group $30,000. Three thousand registered members paying monthly dues of 10 and 5 cruzeiros for men and women respectively were in no shape to finance such an undertaking. Of course, there was plenty of money floating around at the carnival. The sambistas say that the big wheels from the carnival mafia make the biggest bucks. Their methods are almost Sicilian-like. Representatives from the big collection agencies (which have since been abolished) attend the carnival balls and note down every piece that the bands play. Since the orchestras play many of their own compositions, and since these are not contractually agreed upon with the agency, they are automatically deleted from the accounts as 'Composer Unknown' and the agency pockets the money for the night's work.

Second, the samba schools are heavily 'infiltrated' by the rich and well-to-do from the southern districts. These high-toned elites have usually bought their way in through crooked means. Their different background and views are seen as disruptive of the samba school's social texture. As a consequence, sambistas and other school members feel like visitors in their own home. One of them told me, 'I feel like a tourist.'

The third problem was formulated like this by Paulinho da Viola in 1976: 'You go to a rehearsal, but it is no rehearsal. It's more like carnival. In order to please the many spectators, tourists and people from the south of the city, they've stopped playing their beautiful sambas and replaced them with trivial, mundane compositions intended to excite the audience.'

The result is an ever-growing tension between directorate and composer within the samba school. The management demands hit songs. These, however, can only be produced when composers bow to pressure exerted upon them to use the same tried and tested patterns over and over again. But most sambistas still regard the samba as their own personal form of expression, as their means of communicating with the public. In order to better understand the sambista's dissatisfaction with his school, it is necessary to know that until recently the copyright in Brazil was not handled in the author's favor. Instead, the composers received only a one-time payment, and once in a while a monthly sum, depending on supply and demand. But a royalty or any other form of further remuneration was absolutely out of the question. The publishing houses and the many copyright organizations pocketed the profits themselves. In the final analysis, composers of carnival hits ended up with little more than fame (unless they themselves were members of the publishing mafia). Theoretically, this has all changed since the advent of new laws. In practice, samba school sambistas still get peanuts. Their compositions belong in the first instance to the samba schools, who in turn sell them off to the touristic colossus Riotur or cut shady deals with record companies and publishing houses.

The Portela Samba School gained a measure of notoriety a few years back when its directorate simply passed over its in-house composers for the writing of that year's carnival samba, commissioning instead an external author team.

It is not surprising to see that samba hits from carnival sell badly on disc. Since only a small percentage of all Brazilians can afford a record player, the market is limited and also not easy to manipulate — not even among wealthy Brazilians. Even then, it is the old compositions which are played mostly. Composer Joel de Almeida commented: 'The significance of carnival songs is no different from Christmas songs. The same old pieces are played over and over again. Pure folklore.' The sixty-two-year-old composer Orlando Silva added, 'Carnival is dead. It's lost all its life.' Maestro Gonzaga is also pessimistic: 'Nobody knows any new musical compositions and nobody sings them either. When I have something new but I notice the people don't know it, I quickly signal the orchestra to play "*Mamae Eu Quero.*"' Many sambistas sought ways to help themselves out of this quagmire. Some sold fake tickets to their own rehearsal evenings. Others sold their own booze at the school. Many, however, sold themselves. Even if they won't admit it, they prostituted themselves to a country's carnival and music business which had long since swallowed up the samba schools whole. A visitor notices nothing of this in the day-to-day life of the samba school since this all happens more or less behind the scenes. The schools have lost little of their appeal for the residents of the city, even if some have stopped going due to the large numbers of outsiders milling about. *Pagodes* have taken hold in Rio again; evening gatherings in the suburbs with eating, drinking and music. Friends are invited to attend the pagode. There are even bars, such as Caçique de Ramos (entrance free), which offer pagodes as an alternative way to spend the weekend.

Pagodeiros have a vocabulary all their own:

Dia de branco — start of the work week (Monday)

Boca de ferro — iron mouth (microphone)

Jogar um creme — throw the cream (well-sung song)

Several sambistas, among them such well-known figures as Candeia, Monarcho, and Paulinho da Viola, founded the Quilombo, a samba school intent on combating the samba's commercialization and watering down. Paulinho da Viola became famous in the sixties in the Portela Samba School. His selfless dedication and support brought many samba and choro musicians from Rio's northern and southern districts closer to one another. He says, 'Today's samba is banal and of little value. I don't see a way out of this situation. An escola de samba is an institution suffering from the influence of various factors — progress, industry, commerce, tourism. I'm not saying that it's possible to flee from such things. It's an illusion to think the samba school could ever be what it once was. The worst is that the sambistas have lost sight of its value. I also don't believe that the Quilombo can remedy the situation.'

The samba school was once an honest institution, sambistas say. The year of hard work, worries and quarrels took a back seat to the common goal of becoming the best samba school of the season.

There seems to be no way out of the crisis. The best sambistas leave their schools, since they find nothing for themselves there anymore, neither in terms of ideals nor monetary reward. The samba schools seek financially sound partners to help them out of the crisis and end up being dictated to by their 'rescuers'. The partners demand commercial success, something the schools are hardly in a position to bring with any quality, since the best sambistas have long since gone. The results are sambas ranging from moderate to bad and sambas that don't sell. It should come as no surprise, then, that sambas from the good old days still rate highest with the people.

There is one thing, however, that the music industry and samba schools have been unable to pervert — that is, the rhythm of the pandeiro, cuica, agôgô, surdo, bombo and atabaque. As long as these remain, it's always possible to make a good samba — even outside the samba school.

The samba is still alive and kicking in Rio, even if the international press reports nothing but the death toll at the carnival each year. It lives in the weekly samba evenings, the *noitada do samba*, put on at the Teatro Opinao, a small neighborhood theater near Ipanema comparable to the legendary Preservation Hall in New Orleans. Nelson Cavaquinho, Catola, Beth Carvalho, Clementina de Jesus, Lupiscinio Rodriguez and Clara Nunes all made appearances here. The intent of the financially plagued organizers was to bring together morro composers and urban audiences from outside the samba school. (The 'A Fina Flor do Samba' concerts, held since 1966 in the PUC, were forerunners of this series). At the same time the organizing office would occasionally take on a managing function for sambistas performing there.

Candeia

Last Testament
(Testamento de Partideiro)

For my wife
I leave love and affection
At peace with the Lord
And for my son I leave behind
A good example
At peace with the Lord
I leave behind as legacy
Strength of mind and character
At peace with the Lord
And whoever plants love
Always leaves fond remembrance behind
At peace with the Lord
For my friends
I leave my pandeiro
At peace with the Lord
I have honored my parents
And loved my brothers and sisters
At peace with the Lord
But for the Pharisees
I leave no money
At peace with the Lord
Because a sambista
Does not have to be a member

The big stars from MPB still bestow upon the samba and its schools a respect bordering on reverence. Musicians from the schools, and especially the *velha guarda*, are welcome guests at recording sessions.

Several years ago a number of samba schools captured the public's attention as they opened their gates to a musical movement called Black Rio. Black musicians from the northern districts had discovered American soul music. They embraced this music from their brothers up north, spicing it up with that special 'samba feeling' of their own. But Black Rio was a contradictory phenomenon. Was it unaware of the presence of 400 years of Afro-Brazilian history in today's MPB? Did Brazilian blacks need black music from the United States to rediscover the feeling for their own music?

A Brazilian record company is said to have received a million dollars from its New York parent company in order to promote Black Rio and to make it palatable to the international market. The funny thing about the movement was that its musicians had not only adopted the music of their black American brothers, but also their clothes, language and ideology. They simply forgot their own culture and history on the spot. Racial unrest reared its ugly head as Black Rio people molested white visitors at concerts and abused them verbally. One can assume that the Brazilian subsidiary of the American record company mentioned above knew full well that this could happen. Several samba schools lent their quadras to Black Rio groups for performances. Commerical aspects could hardly have been the motivating factor, since Black Rio fans — mostly poor blacks — had little to spend on drinks. If publicity was the hope, then the attempt failed. Visitors stayed away for fear of abuse. Four years later, Black Rio was all but forgotten. Afro-Brazilian music has proven stronger than the United States invader.

One of Rio's most successful samba groups at the end of the eighties was called Só Preto – sem preconceito: Black Only – without prejudice. The five singers and musicians came from Rio's almost endless northern suburbs a contemporary mixture of sambas, afoxes and pagodes with noticeable, but not dominating, electronic instrumentals.

The samba has traveled the long path from the morros down to the samba schools, from there to the city center and carnival and ended in the glittery world of tourism and the music business. A real danger exists that one day the samba schools might make the voice of the morros the voice of the factory assembly line, thus robbing itself of its real lifeblood. There are still ways for the samba to reach an audience outside the samba school. According to a bulletin issued in July 1991 by the International Federation of Carnival Groups, based in London, there are about 100 gringo samba schools in Europe, more than twenty in the US and about twelve in Japan. But what's true for the samba school holds for Brazil in general. The people curse it and criticize it as far as allowed, but they love it nevertheless.

The Hinterland: a Reservoir of New Talent And An Inexhaustible Source of Raw Material

Our media are accustomed to informing us of Brazil's political and economic troubles, its billion-dollar budget deficit, its interest in nuclear energy, its large weapon export. We care more about such things than reports of another kind — about environmental destruction and genocide in Brazil. Small farmers and agricultural laborers in the

North and Northeast are forced to leave their land, often by the most brutal means imaginable. American and European firms located in Brazil have not played the role of mere innocent bystanders. The Amazonian jungles are being deforested for the profits of national and multinational firms. Primitive tribal peoples who attempt to resist the advance of the bulldozers are contaminated or exterminated. Small farmers from all parts of the country who are forced to resettle sink deeper and deeper into frustration and hopelessness.

The Brazilian government initiated a propaganda program in the seventies, attempting to cast these horrifying developments in a new light. Using the slogan of the 'rediscovery of the interior's beauty', music and folklore from the region received new media attention. Governmental organizations (like FUNARTE) initiated concert series in the cities and country, an apparent attempt to correct the imbalance between privileged cultural metropoles and the disadvantaged hinterland. The undertaking was hopeless, since Latin America's history from time immemorial has been one characterized by this polarization between town and country. Catholic missionaries since colonial days regarded the backcountry as the 'devil's domain' with, according to Münzel, a 'fanatic religiousity of hope'.

Still, these governmental programs have, to a certain extent, brought the hinterland's music closer to city musicians by delivering new information and knowledge about the *materia prima* of their nation.

Waldemar Henrique was one of many 'rediscovered' in the Amazonian areas. He was a composer who worked, in a most artistic manner, at refining the myths and legends of the Amerindian-European--African mixed culture of his region, as well as its ritualistic songs.

Indeed, big-city MPB (excepting mass productions of national and international style) is unthinkable without the music that stems from the hinterland regions. The samba rio would have exhausted itself in endless repetitive patterns, were it not for the Cearenses, North-easterners, Baianos, and Paraenses. Assimilation and competition have had the same positive result. São Paulo, with its millions of Japanese, Italians and other nationalities, would have been a city without music had it not profited from the richness of Brazil's MPB.

Música Sertaneja

A tourist might assume the samba, above all the carnival samba, to be the best-selling frontrunner of the Brazilian record industry, even though carnival sambas fare especially poorly in terms of record sales.

Música sertaneja, on the other hand, receives hardly any attention from visitors to Brazil, even though it makes up 40 per cent of the country's total record sales. It is the most popular music in Brazil's hinterland, comparable to American country-and-western music.

Although considered as a form of *música caipira* (the folk music of the countryside), música sertaneja has gone its own way, becoming so commercialized that it has little left in common with the real rural folklore of the caipiras other than a few basic forms. Today, only the real folklore heard at festivals in the South and East of Brazil is regarded as música caipira. These are songs which have a secure place within religious ritual, folkloristic performances and festivals, For this reason it is a rare occurrence to hear such songs on disc, yanked out of their original context. Big-city dwellers speak mockingly of 'iêiêiê dos caipiras' as the yokel's hit parade.

The musical material employed by música sertaneja differs according to region. In the South one hears commercialized gaucho music, in the East modas de viola and toadas, and in the Northeast forró, baião, xotes and xique-xique. Song texts are chockfull of declarations of love for the home region or extol the beauty of nature, the female species or life in the country. Composers and musicians in São Paulo imitate gaucho rhythms to lend a recitative quality to their toadas.

Toadas and the related modas are the chief material for the improvising folksinger (the violeiro or cantador). To the accompaniment of the guitar they sing and tell anecdotes from the hinterland and tragic stories of love and death. These once spontaneously improvised songs have undergone widespread dissemination since the advent of radio, television and the phonograph. These media have occasionally helped a folksinger or two to make the leap into the música sertaneja hit parade.

The so-called *duplas* appear most often in these hit parades. Duplas are male vocal duos popular in the South in the form of improvising singers at the São Gonçalo festival, and in the North at the Bumba-Meu-Boi performances and at singing contests. Among the most popular are Tonico e Tinoco, Jacó e Jacozinho, Roberto e Meirinho, and Vieira e Vieirinha. There are thousands of such duplas. If one can manage to get a foothold in this branch of the music business, i.e. to have some commercial success and sell a few hundred thousand records, then it's possible to live better than most sambistas in Rio. Even though many a piece may exceed the limits of good taste, urban pop musicians have taken an interest in música sertaneja. Commercial considerations were, after all, certainly not the only motive, because urban popular music and música sertaneja both have rural musical folklore as their common basis. But really, no big MPB star can afford to overlook the major sertanejo hits, all the more so when they also are of high musical quality. It should actually have come as no surprise to branch insiders and the public when many years ago Gal Costa became the first pop singer to record Cascatinha's 'India', one of the biggest successes of música sertaneja in the past thirty years.

In addition to musical productions there is a large offering of films, television series and radio programs dealing with the Caipiras' life: one big film hit *O Menino da Porteira*, earned $1 million in São Paulo in 1978 alone. The musical theme was a composition by the duo Luizinho and Teddy Vieira, which was also released that same year by Jair Rodriguez.

The star of the film was Sergio Reis, a name frequently encountered in the música sertaneja hit parades. One maxim holds for all sertanistas: what might sound like a consciously oversentimentalized interpretation to our ears is, in actuality, the true folkloric singing style within música sertaneja. This style necessitates a forced, almost whining voice, for it is the meter alone, not the melody, that counts. Even Jair Rodriguez has taken up this style.

Música sertaneja's chief markets lie in the South, East and Southeast. In the Northeast, which has also contributed elements of its own music, the largely unadulterated Northeastern music still predominates. Caboclos — refugees from the rural areas — brought this music to the outskirts of Rio and, even more so, to São Paulo. They erected their own dance halls (*forrós*) here. On weekends they dance all night long to the music of small ensembles made up of accordion (sanfona), bombo or zambumba drum, triangle and percussion. And as in olden days, the accordionist makes the calls. Forró has much in common with Cajun music and square dance.

Forrós are furnished with neither tables nor chairs. After passing the body search at the entrance there's nothing but dance floor before you. But nobody really cares, since there are so few breaks between dances. The ensembles on stage play on steadfastly; forty-five minutes at least until the first short break. *Xaxados, xotes, quadrilles, chamamés* and *baiões*; one well-known melody after another without a break. After a while they begin to sound like polkas, rhinelands and quadrilles, although played and danced much differently. The sanfoneiros improvise freely; they are masters of the incessant repetition of a phrase.

In the Forró Pedro Sertanejo in São Paulo the whole family works together. Pedro, a música sertaneja star, sings and plays on stage. Mother, son and daughter attend to the guests, technical matters and the till. Pedro has set up a small sound studio for himself above the stage. Despite the age of his mixer unit and microphone (which would delight any collector) records are still produced here. Discos Continental, leading distributor of música sertaneja, markets most of them in São Paulo.

A number of artists have succeeded in fusing the essential folkloric substance from música sertaneja into their modern song arrangements. One of them is Renato Teixeira from the south of Brazil. Teixeira works hard tracking down traditional songs whose melodies and lyrics he compiles in archives and at rural folk festivals.

You will have to look hard, however, to find a piece in the música sertaneja hit parades that tackles the harsh reality of the Brazilian hinterland. Love songs about home, to the sweetheart, humorous or nostalgic lyrics — but hardly ever a realistic description of the peasant's lot; land dispossession, migration from the country or a myriad other problems.

Since the sixties a younger generation of musicians has attempted to describe this reality using the stylistic means of música sertaneja. Chico Buarque was among them. He transposed into music parts of João Cabral de Mello's poem 'The Life and Death of the Farm Hand Severino,' as well as *Funeral de um Lavrador.*

The Baianos

In terms of form and content, the tropicalism circle's revolution belongs to the pages of history.

In 1976 Gil told me his viewpoint at the time: 'Tropicalism was necessary at that time, also as a kind of protest song with political reference. My public today, people from the middle and upper classes, is enlightened. So I don't have to show them the problems anymore. Instead, I sing about how I personally deal with these things. I sing a kind of Brazilian blues.' Caetano Veloso expressed similar views in a *Veja* interview in 1977: 'I admit it: I was revolutionary in 1967 and 1968. But not anymore.'

The Baianos' music had, for the time being, become more rooted in this world. The filigree of progressive elements made up of concrete poetry and universal sound increasingly gave way (especially with Gil) to a greater reliance on the percussion and the rhythms of African and Caribbean origin. Many critics were angry. They complained that the Baianos had compromised themselves by completely descending to the level of dance music. Caetano, at least, wasn't bothered at all by such criticism. He was always happy seeing people dancing and he had always enjoyed singing in discothèques.

Caetano Veloso
Let Me Dance
(Deixe Eu Dançar)
Let me dance
So that my body can remain,
My brains will remain, they'll keep themselves busy
Let me sing
So that the world can remain, it will find something to do too
So that everything will be just great, rarely everything that one
dreams of
I sing, I dance, that which will also be.

Caetano's audiences, on the other hand, remained well-behaved and
in their seats even at his concerts in discothèques.

In contrast to his friend Gil, Caetano was always seen as a dreamer
and even, at times, out of touch with reality. In 1977 he let it be known
that, 'I'm tired of being modern. Now I want to be eternal, timeless.' Is
this anything but an expression of his wish to be free from the pressures
mercilessly imposed upon the leader of a political-musical movement?
Certainly, the sensitive, fragile Caetano has been unable to forget that
period of his life when he and Gil were arrested together in São Paulo,
dragged to Rio and forced to spend thirty days in solitary confinement,
'lying on the ground, unable to speak with anyone.'

But Caetano Veloso has not given up. His lyrics ('Qualquer Coisa',
'Purificação', 'Subaê') still provide new food for thought. They are even
polemical now and then, for example, toward the choice of language his
colleagues employ. This occasioned his enthusiastic young colleague
Djavan to coin the term 'caetanear'. Caetano himself has proven to be
an artist of new word-creations. Baby Consuelo's rendition of Caetano's
song 'Menino do Rio' (1979) created quite a stir.

Caetano Veloso
Young Boy from Rio
(Menino do Rio)
Boy from Rio
Hothead, but shivering
With tattooed dragon on the arm
With pants and body moving in step
With an eternal flirt in your heart
I love to see you
Boy, idler
Suspended tension from Rio
I sing God's praises that he protect you
If only Hawaii were here

Everything you dream of
All places
The waves of the ocean
For when I see you
I long for your desiring
Boy from Rio
Hothead, but shivering
Take this song as a kiss.

Caetano Veloso continued to receive gold records with regularity. A 1983 performance by his fellow countryman and idol João Gilberto set him thinking in a new direction, and he composed a series of songs, as he put it, in a 'climate of true love'.

'Araça Azul' ('Blue Araça Fruit') — Caetano's most ambitious release to date — appeared in 1987. Uncompromising, harsh in places; abrupt shifts bring together opposing musical planes that are, at the same time, related to one another. Cae subtitled this album, 'Um disco para entendidos', 'A record for the informed'. The theme-setting piece on this LP is a ten-minute-long suite with the ironic title 'Sugar Cane Fields Forever' — a return to the Chuck Berry theme that has accompanied Gil and Cae since the beginning of their careers.

But these sugar fields are different. One can even hear them — in the sambas de roda from Bahia, which describe the work on the sugar cane plantations, original performances of which are dubbed in here — and in between, Caetano's confession: 'I am a mulatto, grew up on the coast.' In another song he states: 'Totalmente terceiro sexo, totalmente terceiro mundo' — 'completely third gender, completely third world.' On this LP, Caetano the champion of Luiz Caldas' new Brazilian-Caribbean creations, personally introduces a new Caribbean-Brazilian cross-breed the salsa-palenque. Here a priest appears on television, speaking out against the legalization of abortion and in favor of the blessing of death — and Caetano says: 'no, what twisted thinking.'

His album 'Estrangeiro', produced in 1989 by Peter Sherer and Arto Lindsay won international acclaim.

Gilberto Gil's career has taken a totally different route over all these years. In the same year that the four Baianos (Caetano, Gil, Maria Bethânia, Gal Costa) staged their show entitled 'Os Doces Bárbaros' throughout Brazil (until the authorities forced them to close it), Gil flew to Nigeria to attend a cultural festival. His LP 'Refavela', which came out a year later, reflects Gil's encounter with the African roots of Brazil's musical culture:

Refavela, like Refazenda, a poetic sign

Refavela, folk art under the tropic of cancer
And capricorn
Refavela, a small city, refuge of the migrations
Compelled by the caravels
Refavela, like Luiz Melodia
Refavela, tribal groups in a whirlwind of change
Of the city and nation, not the backwoodsman
Rather the total José
Refavela, town of singers, musicians, dancers, blacks
Whites, mestizos, a people made of chocolate and honey
Refavela, the poet's weakness, what he develops
What he says, what he sees.
Refavela
Re vela
Fa la
Ve*

Gil's phenomenal success at the Montreux Jazz Festival encouraged him to embark on an international career. He recorded his first LP for the international market ('Nightingale' under Sergio Mendes's direction) during a six-month stay in the United States in 1978. His return to Brazil in November was awaited with great excitement. I recorded the following statements by Gil at his press conference in Rio:

> On stage, live, I'm good. But usually not in the studio. But to work with these musicians, these technicians, producers, studios — absolutely everything was a positive experience for me.... Los Angeles is a dead city. When I leave my house here in Rio, I'm right smack in the middle of life. I can see it, hear it and smell it. But there you never meet anybody. Everything is dead.

Gil had wanted to work only for a few months at a time in the States in order to be able to return regularly to Rio and Bahia for longer stays. But the big break-through on the international scene had yet to occur so Gil had to modify this wish. Soon afterward, he met his African colleagues for a second time, this time at the 1979 Berlin Horizonte Festival, which was dedicated to African culture. The festival presented many musicians from that continent and, as a preview to Horizonte '82, many Brazilian artists as well (Gil, Quinteto Violado, Os Tapes). Gil hurried from hall to hall, fascinated to hear everything the Africans had

---

*A bit of word play: 'Refavela develops speaks sees'.

to offer. 'My greatest desire is to be able to make this kind of music like the African bands. It's so simple. Even with only two chords. This African music — that's me.'

Jamaican reggae music's world-wide acclaim opened up new vistas for Gil. He presented Jimmy Cliff's 'No Woman No Cry' in Portuguese ('Não chore mais'), and even sang a duet with Cliff in 1982 at Montreux. Gil says, 'My turn to reggae is simply the opening up of a new, wider terrain for me. It's like an appendix to MPB.'

'Gil,' says Caetano, 'was the driving force behind tropicalism.' We should not forget that international pop music played an important role in tropicalism. John Lennon's death led Gil to offer his condolences with a song entitled 'Dear Yoko', while his 'Chuckberry-fields Forever', an Afro-American mixture of Brazilian rock-'n'-roll, belongs to the very best of international pop music. Gil has always had an eye on the international market in which he would so much like to play an important role. His 1981 LP 'Luar' made his intentions in this respect all too clear. Still, Gil is unafraid of being shunned by Brazilian audiences for denying his identity. 'Nobody can pretend not to see the samba living in me.'

He sang 'Ela' ('Her') in 1979, winning great acclaim with it. For him Ela is not a woman but music, a music that he has yet to define formally, even after tropicalism, African juju, reggae and the polca-samba-balanço of his 1982 LP 'Um Banda Um'. 'You can't use old keys to open new doors,' is Gil's maxim.

Meeting João Gilberto once again and working with him on the 'Brasil' LP did not have the same salutary effect upon Gil as it did upon Caetano. Even as he reached the charts once again with 'Preciso Falar com Deus' in 1983, many insiders regarded his career as having reached a low point. The vitality and fire that had fed his creativity for so many years seemed extinguished. Without a doubt, Gil's producers had not given him the best advice. They knew only how to transform Gil's desire for international fame into dollars. But perhaps another element should be considered here: Gil may have become tired of the high-stress world of his international career and disoriented by unfamiliar paths between Africa, the Caribbean and the United States. But his friendship with Caetano has remained strong. Together they attempted to expose the ridiculousness of a 1981 song festival, its jury and the supposed quality of the premiered songs. Caetano and Gil also share a distaste for any governmental attempt to politicize MPB. Even so, Gil dabbled a bit in Brazilian politics himself after 1987: he accepted a post as Commissioner for the Black Culture of Bahia.

A new generation has grown up in Brazil since the days of tropicalism in the sixties. Gil, the father of five children has said: 'Caetano said recently that we have to try to avoid the negative factors of aging and to accept the positive sides of youth.' For Gil this means always addressing the pop music tastes of his young audiences.

Gil and Caetano offer clear proof that in the long run even so strong a movement as tropicalism cannot remain immune to harsh political, economic and social realities. The initial goal of creating a free, universal music encountered its natural limits both in censorship as well as in the commercial demands and benefits of the music market. In Gil's case, especially, we could term this process an adaptation to economic realities. That, however, would, still be inadequate, since it accounts only for the symptoms, not the underlying causes.

The distaff side of the Baiano four, Maria Bethania and Gal Costa, have worked successfully in recent years on building their own careers. As two singers without any ambition to write their own lyrics and compositions, they have been able to concentrate their energies on developing their performing styles. When Maria Bethania toured Europe in 1972 with her Festival Folklore e Bossa Nova do Brasil (the critics were not exactly generous in their praise), she was already known in Brazil, but not yet famous. Ten years later, after one of her shows in Rio, I worked my way to her dressing room through the usual hoarde of admirers. She sat there, somewhat tired but obviously very happy, and said matter-of-factly, 'You know, I'm now a big star here.' Although she certainly had not said anything wrong, we really had to laugh at this sentence. Each year Bethania has reaped the profits from new LPs and from the accompanying shows of the same name: 'Cena Muda', 'Pássaro Proibido', 'Pássaro da Manha', 'Alibi', 'Mel', 'Talismã', 'Alteza'. ... She releases a virtual stream of non-stop gold records. Her repertoire indulges increasingly in excessive romantic feelings and unrequited yearnings that are often difficult to distinguish from sentimentality. Seen through European eyes, Maria Bethania's love for the dramatic, which she expresses in gesture, expression, and poetic declaration, has something pathetic about it. Especially in the attitude of a queen of MPB:

Wally Salomão/C. Veloso

Nobility
(Alteza)

When my man went away
I blew a message
To the four winds
That my throne was defiled

And my kingdom destroyed,
I am a queen
Who voluntarily abdicated
Scepter and throne
And who gave herself
Entirely as I am

With her twenty-sixth LP 'Maria' (1987), Bethania became Maria, sister to a girl from Nairobi; she became sister to housewives, dancers, workers, prostitutes in Brazil — to whom the following song by Joyce is dedicated: 'Women of Brazil, found guilty like all women since the apple came to earth — protectresses of all virtue, saints and termagants, daughters of Mary or the goddesses from Hollywood — they are all sisters because nature has made them so beautiful.'

Gal Costa, too, has no trouble selling a half million records per LP release. Until 1979 she had her problems making the scene. But in that year her show 'Gal Tropical' debuted. Hearsay has it that her manager was reading a book about Rita Hayworth one day and suddenly hit upon the idea of engaging a costume designer to spice Gal up for her next show. The new styling caught many a male eye, and before long Brazilian *Playboy* was offering her huge sums to pose nude. Gal rejected the offers. Besides, she says, she lives for her fans; her highest goal is to please and entertain them. She achieves this with a clear, pure voice and cleverly arranged repertoire that until recently was puristically Brazilian, but has broadened increasingly to find a wider audience. In the mid-eighties, Gal Costa stood, at the peak of her Brazilian career. However, attempts to be more than just a flash in the pan on the international scene have so far failed. Next to Beth Carvalho, Elba Ramalho, Alcione and Fafá de Belem, she is one of the leading female vocalists in MPB. Gal characterizes this epoch as follows: 'I believe women have decided to take power. It used to be worth nothing to be a woman. Today it's only the women who are popping up new on the scene. Where are the new male singers?'

Novos Baianos Novos

While the Baianos circle was working on its *som livre* concept in São Paulo, other bands were springing up in their home city of Salvador as a result of the craze for the Beatles and Jimi Hendrix.

Pepeu Gomez recalled how in 1969 the samba was really only popular among university students. Most of the people in Salvador were rather negative about the samba. An aggressive climate reigned at the time anyway, continued Gomez, and people were complaining about everything. Guitarist Gomez, together with his brothers Jorge (drums) and Didi (bass), founded a rock band at the time. Pepeu then formed a new band that he called Os Leifs, and Jorge sooned joined in. At the same time, however, the Novos Baianos made their first appearance in Salvador in 1968. Singer and pandeiro player Paulinho Boca de Cantor had launched the group. The Novos Baianos saw themselves as following in João Gilberto's footsteps, but they also aimed at combining Bahian music, Northeastern music, and samba with rock and jazz elements. First Didi, and then Pepeu, deserted Os Leifs for the Novos Baianos, which then performed with the following arrangement: Paulinho (singer, pandeiro), Pepeu (electric guitar, substituting for Lanny), Morais (guitar, singer), Jorginho (drums), Didi (bass, guitar), Baixinho (drums, bumbo), Baby Consuelo (from Rio, singer and percussion) and songwriter Galvão.

The Novos Baianos were very successful in Brazil for a short time, until internal frictions led to the group's breakup. But the musical tradition founded by the group still lives on today in its successor formations.   .

Morais Moreira, chief composer for the Novos Baianos, began his solo career in 1975. His trademark is a swing baiano consisting mainly of forró, choro, samba, bossa nova and, to a lesser extent, rock.

Pepeu Gomez's discoverer and most active promoter was Gilberto Gil, who soon came to regard Pepeu as his preferred guitarist. In the past Gomez also released under his own name a series of LPs with a mixture of rock and Brazilian music. Gomez's life companion is the carioca Baby Consuelo, who made her debut with her first LP, entitled 'Eu Sou Baby Consuelo', in 1978, after the breakup of the Novos Baianos. In this and following productions she proved herself to be an original, natural singer unafraid of tackling even the most difficult vocal parts. The titles were written mostly by her friends Pepeu, Morais and Galvão. Despite their artistic immaturity, they did promise an original, enriching character for MPB. In the eighties, finally, she let her recording company persuade her to try out the latest, and while her punk style and colored hair may have won her a larger public, they have not improved the musical quality any.

In 1971 Dodo and Osmar founded the Trio Eléctrico in Salvador, Bahia. Making use of electronically amplified cavaquinhos and guitars, they rode through the streets of Bahia atop an open carriage, playing sambas, frevos, choros, etc., soon to become one of the main attractions at the Salvador carnival. Os Novos Baianos and Gilberto Gil took central features of the Trio Eléctrico style into their own music. Dodo has since passed away, but his son Armandinho had met his cousins Dadi, Mú, and Gustavo Schroeter during a trip to Rio. Dadi had played bass for the Novos Baianos; Mú, like Dadi for a time, was a musician in Jorge Ben's band; and Gustavo Schroeter had worked in Rio as a drummer for Gal Costa, Raul Seixas and Zé Rodrix. The four began a partnership, inaugurating the instrumental group A Cor do Som, and by 1977 they had already made their first LP. Their versatility, seen in the ability to integrate such traditional forms as choro, samba and frevo into the Trio Eléctrico sound, and then to unite this with rock structures catapulted the group to fame. In no time A Cor do Som had advanced to become one of the most popular instrumental groups in Brazil. The group's name (meaning 'the color of sounds') recalls the earlier accompanying group for the Novos Baianos of the same name. Its members, especially Morais Moreira and Pepeu Gomez (both of whom have moved to Rio in the meantime), worked closely together with A Cor do Som.

Another Bahian Raul Seixas had already left Salvador in 1967 as a tender twenty-year-old. Seixas told us in an interview of how he led Salvador's first rock band with electronic equipment way back in 1957. By the end of the seventies Brazilians were calling him their Raul Rock Seixas. A number of record hits preceded this.

The Salvadoran native Simone, daughter of an opera singer and of a pianist, left for São Paulo in 1964 and debuted with her first LP in 1973.

Bahia's greatest folksinger, Dorival Caymmi, lives in Rio. He doesn't have to worry about such things as hit parades, record sales and the like. He is already a living legend.

Bahia de Todos os Soms

In the middle of the eighties, Bahia became for a while the center for MPB. In Salvador's historic old quarter, Pelourinho, African traditions were revived, while in the south of Salvador, the fishing village of Porto Seguro, overcrowded as it was with tourists and bars, saw the creation of new variaties of Carribbean music, hip hop and Brazilian music.

Black carnival associations, called 'Blocos Afros', were established from 1974 onward in considerable numbers. They gave new impetus to the Bahian carnivals with their afoxé drum sections and developed structured organizations which were initally comparable to Rio's samba schools, but developed differently. A Bloco Afro such as 'Olodum', founded in 1979, turned itself into a 'grupo cultural' in 1984 with, for the first time in Salvator's history, a black woman as president. The image of the African woman, her garments and hair style, presided over the resurgent Africanism in Pelourinho: a conscious reversal of the old, colonial idea of 'negritude'. This African orientation, exemplified by 'Olodum's' female president, broke with the restricted information policy of former times: 'During the military dictatorship especially, there was no information on what was really happening in Africa … nothing about the revolutionary processes that were taking place in Africa or what their aims were … this was done so that we should not get the idea of imitating them and defending ourselves in an organized way.'

'Olodum' financed its own district organizations by producing costumes, allegoric edifices and instruments and then selling them throughout the world. An important contribution was made by the group 'Olodum' (with its education section for children), which Paul Simon recorded in 1988 for his album 'The Rhythm of the Saints' and later edited in the studio. 'Olodum' never accepted any money from Simon for this, the President declaring at the time that, 'for us, this is a cultural exchange'. When Simon later came to make a video for the song 'Obvious Child', the performers and musicians involved did receive a fee while 'Olodum' was also paid royalties for the song. More recently, 'Olodum' have also been invited to take part in recordings, festivals and tours by other North American and European artists.

During the Bahia carnival, 'Olodum', together with other afoxé Blocos such as Ara Ketú, Geronimo and Filhos de Ghandi parade through the streets of Salvador on mobile floats equipped with loudspeakers. Their music pays testimony to the very intensive, almost purist, recognition of African genres, such as the use of many different percussion instruments and liturgical choral songs. In 1986, the merengue, a genre rich in tradition from the Dominican Republic, was translated to the latest disco standard by musicians such as Wilfrido Vargas or Porfi Jimenez (similar to Trinidad's soca).

The career of another new MPB star took off explosively: Luiz Caldas, a protegé of Caetano Veloso. His LP 'Magia' sold over 250,000 copies upon release. His recipe for success was the mixture of Bahian and Caribbean music. One of these cocktails he called 'deboche' at first; later it was changed to the successful title 'fricote'. Fricote was one of the predecessors of lambada. Later in the same year (1987) Brazil's new superstar Elba Ramalho recorded a song by Luiz Caldas — a new combination of afoxé and Caribbean music. Four designations for it appear simultaneously on the cover: fricote, deboche, chicote and lambada.

At the Carnaval da Bahia in 1987 the frenzy to mix Bahian and Caribbean music knew no bounds. Elements of funk and even rap sung in Portuguese were added.

As soon as fricote-lambada-deboche-chicote and others appeared and breathed new life into the musical scene, the 'teenies' were quickly inspired — and just as quickly, they watered down the new rhythms, as far as the musical-melodic components are concerned.

Afoxé groups such as Banda Reflexus got into the lambada business as well, creating among other things, mixtures of afoxé and reggae, while African groups relied more heavily on a reggae-samba mixture. Chiclete com Bacana took over the soca, the calypso-disco successor.

While lambada stormed the hit parades in France, Switzerland and Germany in 1989 in a hit version by the group Kaoma, rock bands like Treblinka or Gang Bang were popular again in the trendiest discos in Bahia's Rio Vermelho, such as the Paris Latino.

The Lambada Story

Seldom have so many lies been spread about the origin of a dance, a melody and a rhythm as in the case of lambada.

If it hadn't been for the opportunistic and unscrupulous Frenchmen Olivier Lorsac and Jean Karakos, lambada would today be one of the many popular dances of Bahia's youth, and as such it would have been replaced by its successor long ago. The rise of lambada is unique in music history and deserves a thorough evaluation.

To trace the origins of lambada in Brazil, one must separate it into its components: dance, rhythm and melody. Upon closer examination the claim that lambada originated in Brazil cannot be maintained on all three counts. It does appear to be true that in the twenties or thirties in the north of Brazil, in Belém do Pará, there was a dance called lambada. The word 'lambada' itself was supposedly taken from the slang of Belem's slums. Witnesses, commenting in Brazilian magazines, agree that the lambada came into being at that time as a mixture of lundu and carimbó, with a merengue rhythm that came from Guyana.

Their descriptions relegate dance and music, however, to the category of *música brega*, shallow background music. It is also certain that there were recordings going by the name 'lambada' in Manaus, Belém and later in Bahia — before Kaoma's lambada success in Europe.

In 1987/88, Bahia's Porto Seguro became the center of the new Brazilian lambada, which no doubt recalled the merengue-import from the Amazon in its musical and rhythmic elements. The dance, however, was in my opinion a simple imitation of the mambo in *Dirty Dancing*, a film very popular in Brazilian cinemas at the time. In photo stills from *Dirty Dancing*, the leg position is identical to that for the lambada. Lambada researchers in Brazil pointed out that the carimbó-merengue-lambada in the north had already been banned as obscene some decades before, but this appears to me to be a coincidence.

In March 1988 the French film producer Olivier Lorsac came to Porto Seguro. Just one month later he expressed his enthusiasm for lambada to the music producer Jean Karakos, who had already launched Brazilian music in the United States on his Celluloid label. Lorsac and Karakos went about the marketing of lambada in a grand manner. According to their own testimony they then bought over 400 copyrights to lambada compositions as a precaution, so that they could control the expected lambada boom. They found partners in the French television broadcaster TF-1 and in industry.

Out of all the lambadas available in Brazil at that time, they chose 'Chorando se foi', which the singer Marcia Ferreira had released in 1986. Karakos did a new production in Paris and to this end, brought into being the group Kaoma: three musicians who played for the African star Toure Kunda; Brazilian Claudio Queiroz on saxophone; Argentine Juan Jose Mossalini on accordion; and Brazilian singer Loalva Braz, backed up by a chorus of one more Brazilian and one African. Although the label on the Brazilian record bore the names of the authors, Karakos and Lorsac invented an imaginary name for the creator of lambada, alias 'Chorando se foi': Chico de Oliveira. The publishing rights of this composer were registered at the French Sacem by Karakos and Lorsac through their publishing company BM Productions.

The first doubts as to the correct identity of the author were expressed in the late summer of 1989, when the Kaoma production took first France, then other European countries by storm. Karakos assured me in a telephone conversation that the name was a pseudonym that stood for the many authors and arrangers who had collaborated on the title. A few weeks before, Karakos had declared in an interview in the *Folha do São Paulo*, 'Naturally he [Chico de Oliveira] exists. But if you'll permit me, he is not a great author or composer. His only advantage is that he is registered at the Sacem ... he lives in France, ... no he doesn't live in France, he is registered at the Sacem, he's travelling...'

At this time Karakos and Lorsac made intensive efforts to extract an agreement to a publishing contract from the actual authors of the music and text. The song had in fact been recorded in 1981 for the first time, in Bolivia, by a group called Los Kjarkas. Text and music were originated by the Kjarkas musicians Ulisses and Gonzalo Hermoza from Cochabamba. Karakos and Lorsac supposedly offered the Hermozas $60,000 U.S. as compensation, in their first attempt to deal on the telephone. But by then, the summer of 1989, the song was already on the charts, and a friend of the group in Germany had warned them. On her advice, Ulisses Hermoza had already joined GEMA in Germany in 1985, which indicated on the twenty-second of September that year, that the song by Kaoma plagiarized 'Chorando se foi'. The copyright law professor Nordemann in Berlin was assigned to protect the interests of the Hermoza brothers against Karakos/Lorsac. The Frenchmen had, however, exploited the Hermozas' legal inexperience to the extent that they possessed two contracts (signed in Rio and Buenos Aires) and felt quite secure.

For the Hermozas, the success of their song was a painful experience from the beginning. The five Hermoza brothers have played in the group Los Kjarkas for about twenty years and given concerts all over the world. The Kjarkas are dedicated to the research, documentation and presentation of traditional Bolivian music.

The Hermoza brothers also work together on a bioenergy project in Bolivia. Near Cochabamba they, together with the local residents, supposedly revived a bioenergetic association with nature, in the tradition of the Quetschua. They bought land in order to reforest it. Seeds from trees all over the world with high biologic information were brought there, in order that, according to their German friend Almut Kowalski, the trees later would be 'in constant energetic contact' with the native trees.

The one member of the Kjarkas group somewhat versed in legal matters, Gonzalo Hermoza, who had also written the text of the song, was not invited to Rio to meet with the Frenchmen. Almut Kowalski suspects that his presence was specifically avoided, because in Rio, the Frenchmen showed Ulisses a contract written in French that transformed the plagiarism into a legally contracted situation. Ulisses signed it and took a copy back to Bolivia so that his brother and lyricist Gonzalo could also sign. Gonzalo recognized the situation and refused. On the day following the signature, Almut Kowalski telephoned Ulisses and was dismayed at his condition. Her comment: 'They must have gotten him drunk.'

In the meantime a Bolivian record company sealed a pact with Karakos in France. Ulisses Hermoza's song had first appeared there.

According to the claims, the copyright was transferred at that time, and the Lauro label now had control of it.

All this occurred in the final months of 1989 — as Kaoma's hit spread like an epidemic throughout Europe; it must have accumulated millions of dollars in copyright fees.

The showdown finally came in La Paz. The Bolivian government provided two lawyers and three translators for the discussion with Karakos, who had previously annulled all pending contracts. Lorsac/Karakos would now only receive a percentage of the royalties for the arrangement of the song.

In January 1990, the final signing of the contract was to take place in Paris. However, an agreement was reached there with EMI Music, by which the publishing conglomerate acquired copyright to the title and promised to represent the authors' interests in the courts. The French Sacem had already frozen all the song's earnings. At the MIDEM Convention in Cannes, the Hermozas appeared to be relieved. For them, the end of an era had come, when even their families had received threats to jail the brothers if they did not give up their claims on those involved in the plagiarism swindle. For the Hermozas, money was never the central issue. To their way of thinking, the origination of a song can never be equated with money. The whole disagreement brought unaccustomed dissonance into their lives. The moral side, the loss of their integrity, concerned them more than the millions of dollars. In a word: the unscrupulous machinations of Lorsac/Karakos must have seemed completely alien to them.

Karakos and Lorsac, incidentally, were never called to legal account. Finally Lorsac received a reprimand from the French Sacem. In Bolivia the affair at least motivated the government to stand up more decisively for the rights of Bolivian authors in the future.

The feedback from Kaoma's success (4 million singles and 2.5 million LPs in Europe alone) in Brazil was enormous. Lambada dance schools sprang up even in parts of the country that had not previously been affected by Porto Seguro's lambada fever. A chart success, with a Bolivian melody, Caribbean rhythm, produced in Paris — all at once, Brazil was the topic of international conversation. (Even the video of Kaoma, which made lambada known worldwide, was filmed in Ibiza, not Bahia.) But for the Brazilian record companies, it meant good sales. The European record companies blindly bought everything in Brazil that could possibly carry the magic name lambada. Even recordings of Vinicius de Moraes, who died in 1980, suddenly appeared on new 'original lambada' samplers from Brazil.

In Rio or São Paulo, the lambada dance figures awakened memories of the almost forgotten maxixe and of the mambo dancers in the gafieras.

Beto Barbosa sold over one million copies of his lambada LP in Brazil, Alipio Martins sold half as many and the 'Rei da Lambada Tropical', Betto Douglas, sold the less kingly total of 140,000.

The Bahian Margareth Menezes, who had accompanied David Byrne on tour, began her international career at almost the same time — but without lambada. Her countryman Geronimo, however, swam with the lambada wave as far as France. In April 1992, Ulisses Hermoza, one of the authors of the 'lambada' hit 'Chorando se foi' died of cancer in a German hospital. His royalties were, at that time, still frozen, and EMI-Publishing had yet to realize one of its promises to promote his group Los Kjarkas both on record and the concert scene.

Mineiros

Minas Gerais which simply means 'general mining', calls to mind images of precious stone and gold discoveries, as well as the flowering of baroque culture that left its indelible stamp upon such cities as Ouro Preto, Congonhas and Diamantina. Minas Gerais gave birth to Brazil's national hero, the freedom fighter Tirandentes. Alejandinho, a brilliant sculptor from the eighteenth century, also lived here. The contemporary poets Carlos Drummond de Andrade (who died in 1987) and João Guimarães Rosa, as well as the sculptor GTO, are also Mineiros. 'Minas é dentro e fundo,' Minas is deep and within, says Carlos Drummond de Andrade.

Milton Nascimento is Minas Gerais. One could call him a 'superstar' of MPB if this term did not carry with it all the negative connotations associated with 'product', 'hit', and 'box office'. And these terms would certainly do an injustice to Milton's work, his roots, and his personality.

Elis Regina once said, 'You know, don't you, that there is no such thing as Milton?' Indeed, Milton's name is almost always mentioned with great respect in Brazil. But his songs never fail to communicate his rootedness in this world when he raises his voice in a plea for love and peace and against war, censorship and repression.

Perhaps it's his eyes, or maybe his karma, which leads so many people to believe that Milton is not of this world. Or maybe it's the cocoon-like exclusiveness his clan weaves around him that lends him a façade of inaccessibility. Milton is not sparing of words. But he also does not waste them. He can sit silently for long periods, make a joke and then

Gravação de
MILTON NASCIMENTO
na EMI - ODEON

SAN VICENTE
Milton Nascimento - Fernando Brant

N.º DE CAT. 3P - 013

return to his silence. '*A obrigação é ser feliz*', meaning 'The obligation is to be happy': Milton demands this from his fellow human beings, meaning by 'obligation' the 'right' as well.

Milton Nascimento was born in Rio de Janeiro in 1942. When he was only six, his family moved to Três Pontas, a small city in Minas Gerais. His stepfather, a mathematics professor, decided that the life of a bookkeeper would be right for Milton. His stepson, however, did not agree. After working at it for a while with great reluctance, he soon gave it up to dedicate himself to music. Between the ages of thirteen and fifteen he was already performing as an accordion and bass player, and later as a guitarist and lead singer. His first idols were João Gilberto, Dorival Caymmi and Henry Mancini.

At nineteen, with an initial capital of ten dollars in his pocket, he left for the provincial capital of Belo Horizonte. There he got a job as a guitarist and singer in a Japanese bar. In succeeding years he met Marcio and Lô Borges, Elis Regina, Wagner Tiso, Fernando Brant and Toninho Horta (the legendary Clube da Esquina, or Club on the Corner) — all of them musicians who have worked with him again and again since then.

In the next period Milton worked with the vocal group Evolussamba, with a jazz trio with Wagner Tiso and with the Sambacana Quartet, with whom he recorded an LP in Rio in 1965.

In 1966 he came fourth at the TV Excelsior song festival in São Paulo with Baden Powell's (and Lula Freire's) 'Cidade Vazia.' In the meantime Elis Regina had begun her career, recording that same year his song 'Canção do Sol.' A year later Milton entered three compositions in TV Globo's International song festival in Rio: 'Travessia' (second place), 'Morro Velho' (seventh place) and 'Maria, Minha Fé'. In Rio Milton met up with Agostinho dos Santos and Eumir Deodato, who became friends and promoters of his work. In 1968, Deodato took him to the United States, where he recorded 'Courage', produced by Creed Taylor, Milton's discoverer at the Rio festival. A follow-up tour in the United States and Mexico did not bring the desired success.

Dark clouds hung over MPB in 1969. Many artists were going abroad to escape censorship and political persecution. Others were leaving because of lack of work. The small Theatro Opinão in Rio presented a series of concerts that year entitled 'Milton Nascimento e Som Imaginário' with Wagner Tiso, Zé Rodrix, Tavito, Robertinho Silva, Luis Alves and Nana. In that same year Milton's first LP appeared in Brazil ('Milton Nascimento'). Luiz Eça and Deodato did the arrangements, Fernando Brant wrote the lyrics. Musicologist Geni Marcondes wrote on the cover: 'Bold harmonies, a flair reminiscent of the Spanish and

Portuguese troubadour, new harmonic ideas inspired by the bossa nova, his own special style in singing the toada, rural rhythms mixed with modern, samba syncopation.' The LP 'Milton' followed in 1970 with a song addressed to Lennon and McCartney of the Beatles, whose influence upon his work Milton never denied. The later LP 'Minas' is considered by many to be Milton's 'Sgt. Pepper'.

L. Borges / M. Borges / F. Brant

Song of America
(Canção da América)
For Lennon and McCartney

Because you know nothing
About western garbage
You no longer need to be afraid
You don't need to be lonely,
Every day is a day for living —
Because you haven't seen it
My part in the West
Does not need to be afraid
Does not need to be shy
Every day is a day for living —
I came from South America —
I know you couldn't possibly know that
But now I am the cowboy,
I'm made of gold, I'm you
I come from this world,
I am Minas Gerais.

In 1975 Milton recorded the LP 'Milagre dos Peixes' ('The Miracle of the Fishes', who are silent and yet so eloquent). As practically every lyric was banned, Milton simply recorded the pieces without words — voiceless songs, bird songs and other noises. Despite the initial handicaps 'Milagre dos Peixes' was chosen best record of the year. A live LP followed shortly, recorded at a concert under the same name, bringing Milton into the Brazilian charts for the first time.

Milton was soon a star in Brazil and began receiving invitations from abroad, especially from the United States. Jazz fans, musicians and critics took a special liking to him. Wayne Shorter engaged him for his 'Native Dancer' album. It is no doubt true that jazz musicians are specially tuned to musical fine points; but Nascimento is no jazz musician. Caetano Veloso once described Milton as *Mil tons*, 'a thousand tones'. Milton's work draws from the most diverse sources — from the sounds of the Três Pontas dance bars, to work songs and ritualistic slave hymns, to Gregorian chants from Jesuit missions, and Brazilian folk songs. He does not conceive of jazz and rock as fundamental parts of his melodies, but rather more as musical packaging and arrangement.

Milton has demonstrated over and over that he is, properly, a musician. In many songs he uses his voice like an instrument, especially at high pitches (for example, 'E Dai' and 'Evocação das Montanhas'). He is a perfectionist in the studio, recording again and again every sound and voice, and occasionally even filling in for a missing instrumental part with his own voice.

Milton Nascimento is also a discoverer. His songs 'Dos Cruces' and 'San Vincente' were the first to point to the cultural links between Spain and Minas. He recalled the traditional toada hymns of his home. In 'Sentinela' ('Deathwatch at my brother's body') he reminds his listener of the magnificent Gregorian chants in the baroque churches of his home.

Milton seldom writes the lyrics of his songs alone. But he also does not let others simply hand him completed lyrics that say nothing to him. He prefers to work together with a small circle of songwriters with whom he is able to engage in an intense, lively interchange about his work, his compositions, and his aims. Fernando Brant, a childhood friend and one-time reporter for a local Belo Horizonte newspaper, is a member of this circle, as are the Borge brothers, film director Ruy Guerra, Tulio Mourão, Ronaldo Bastos and Ferreira Guillar.

Together with D. Pedro Casaldaliga and Pedro Tierra, heads of the Igreja Renovadora Brasileira (Brazilian Reformed Church), Milton wrote the *Missa dos Quilombos*, a requiem mass commemorating the suffering and resistance of the African slaves in Brazil. Lacking in the mass are the usual splendor and opulence of Catholic tradition. It received an open-air premiere in Recife in 1981.

In the Name of God
(Em Nome de Deus)

In the name of the son Jesus, our brother,
Born with light-brown skin
Of the tribe of Abraham
In the name of the Holy Ghost with the banner
Of our hymn, with the awe of celebration.
In the name of the Trinity, in the name of the people
Who expect — in the mercy of their destiny —
The voice of Xangô
To liberate Quilombo Palmares.

In the name of a people continually dragged into
Suppressive exile over the ocean.
In the name of the people
Who established its own palm groves
Its free republic
Of runaway slaves.

Dom Helder Camara, who collaborated on the mass, contributed the following prayer at the end, abridged here:

Mariana, mother of God
Mother of all humanity
In the name of all races
Mother of all song on our earth
Beseech your son
Not to let our celebration end.
It is important for the church leaders
Not only to talk
Not only to applaud
But for the bishops' conference
To start solving the mountain of problems
The blacks have to face.
The same holds for the Indians.
Unmistakably, we want politics,
Subversion
Communism
And the gospel of Christ,
Mariana
The sufferings the blacks endure
Belong to those major problems
Humanity is facing
The injustice of oppression
The damned fabrication of weapons.
Let peace be manufactured instead.
An end to injustice.
Fifty million die of hunger.
Peace for every day
An end to slavery
A world without masters and slaves
A world of brotherhood
A world of brothers and sisters bound by truth.

The history of the African slaves in Brazil and the genocide perpetrated upon so many Indian tribes are themes that Milton treats repeatedly. Of late he has widened his vista to include the Pan-Latin American dimensions of the problem. Milton has recorded Violetta Para's songs and sung together with Mercedes Sosa and Pablo Milanés.

Milton has sung works from the *nueva canción* movement of neighboring countries in their original Spanish versions. The LP 'Clube da Esquina 2' includes a song calling for Latin American unity, performed by Milton and Chico Buarque. With such recordings as 'O Quera Será', 'O Cio da Terra' and 'Calice', this duo has presented important and timely commentaries in recent years on present-day Brazilian reality. Milton dedicated his song 'Menestral das Alagoas' ('Minstrel from Alagoas', a Brazilian province) to Senator Teotonio Vilela: 'Whose is this righteous anger, this civic soundness, which, while making music at the fair, discovered Brazil anew?' Vilela became a symbol, embodying the political hopes of the Brazilian people. He himself called the song 'our Marseillaise'.

In 1983, the direct election of a president still seemed as far away as ever, and many Brazilians lost hope that democracy would ever come. Against the backdrop of student unrest at the universities Milton composed three songs that were spontaneously adopted as hymns by the movement. 'Coração de Estudante' calls for solidarity with the students. 'Caçador de Mim' ('Hunter of Myself') reflects upon the difficulties faced by the songwriter in Brazil, imprisoned within his own songs and seeking truth, but always confronted with struggle, fear and violence. Fear as a way out? Wherever he may land, he will discover what makes him feel as he does. He will encounter the hunter hunting himself.

In 'Nos Bailes da Vida', he demands, in allusion to events at demonstrations: 'each artist must go, with muddy garments and soul incrusted by the soil, to where the masses are.'

Milton has always resisted being labeled an intellectual artist and thereby being forced into the role of an outsider. He lives, so he says, wholly from within and tries to make honest music.

Milton works in Minas Gerais on a politico-cultural level as well. He and his Quilombo colleagues direct a music school in Belo Horizonte for which the youth of the region are charged nothing to attend. Through concert tours and radio stations (thirty in all) his Música de Minas attempts to effect a decentralization of MPB away from its coastal centers, and to achieve greater recognition for the culture of his home region.

Milton also composes music for theater, film and ballet. He has turned to acting roles in film, as in his small role in Werner Herzog's *Fitzcarraldo*.

April 1984 witnessed a high point in Milton's career at home. Seventy thousand people celebrated his appearance in Rio's new Praça da Apoteose (built by Carlos Niemeyer). Soon afterwards, 120,000 came out in Belo Horizonte to rejoice with the Bituca from Três Pontas and to join with him in song. In 1985 Milton became an honorary citizen of Minas Gerais.

Milton's switch from Brazilian Polygram to CBS had the greatest affect on his international career. The first CBS LP 'Yauarete' appeared in 1988 in many countries simultaneously, and CBS made it possible for international stars like Paul Simon (title: 'O Vendedor de Sonhos'), Herbie Hancock, Wayne Shorter and Quincy Jones to collaborate. Originally a black panther graced the front cover. The record company became stubborn over the title and consulted zoologists. A panther is no jaguar, and so it moved to the back cover and beneath the album's title came the subscript: 'Panther'. The effort could have been spared, because in the language of the Xingu Indians, the word 'Yauarete' actually means panther.

João Bosco was born in 1946 in Ponte Nova, Minas Gerais. His mother and sister played violin and piano. As a boy he tried out singing, and at thirteen he formed his first rock'n'roll band, concentrating with his acoustic guitar and maracas on a repertoire from Elvis and Little Richard. In 1962 he began studying engineering in Oûro Preto. The bossa nova wave had already arrived in Minas, and that meant the end of Elvis and Little Richard. João Bosco, by now a singer and guitarist fully devoted to bossa nova, met up a few years later with the poet Vinicius de Moraes, and he invited Bosco to Rio. Their collaboration produced three songs: 'Rosa dos Ventos', 'Samba do Pouso' and 'O Mergulhador'. After completing his engineering degree, Bosco settled down in Rio in order to continue his partnership with songwriter Aldir Blanc. In the meantime, however, the bossa nova was practically passé among the cariocas, forcing him to try out new forms.

The Bosco-Blanc duo's first hit was entitled 'Bala com Bala', recorded that same year by Elis Regina. Since then she has laid great importance on Bosco and Blanc's writing her new songs. A year later João Bosco released his first LP. Others were soon to follow. Not until 1982 did he have a big sales success with 'Commissão de Frente'.

João Bosco is a well-rounded composer, equally versed in bossa nova, samba, ballads and rock. Besides his outstanding guitar playing, the creative possibilities of Bosco's voice are most riveting. He balances, slurs or abruptly changes to falsetto in a percussive manner around the offbeat in the best tradition of the African, European, and Amerindian vocal art. João Bosco swings with every beat.

Aldir Blanc's lyrics exhibit a constant poetic quality. At the center of the songs are man and his life. Perhaps that is why Blanc and Bosco so often use the vernacular, that is, the jargon of the streets and hinterland — to make the message understandable to a wide public.

The Borges brothers Marcio and Lô of Belo Horizonte, also belong to the MPB Mineiros. Prompted by their father Salamão Borges, they made their first public appearance (along with five of their nine brothers and sisters) in 1981 as members of Os Borges.

The Mineiro Eduardo Araujo, born 1945 in Juaima in Minas, is considered to belong to the *jovem guarda* of the sixties. Once called the Rei do Rock de Minas (the King of Minas Rock), Araujo released a series of records in the late sixties and seventies, but was unable to build upon these earlier successes.

The Northeasterners

The Brazilian Northeast is widely regarded as a treasure chest of folk music gems. Northeastern music first found a home in MPB in the forties through Luiz Gonzaga's baião. With the end of the bossa nova epoch, Geraldo Vandré, Edu Lobo and, later, the Baianos were chief figures in taking up Northeastern rhythms and sounds. Since then, central features of Northeastern music have established themselves firmly within the MPB tradition. The amount of folkloric primary material is truly inexhaustible. Instrumentalists, above all, are fascinated with the material at their disposal, turning again and again to structures from baião, xaxado, frevo and xique-xique. The number of musicians from the Northeast who travel south to Rio or São Paulo to make their careers is also large; the Quarteto Novo (Hermeto Pascoal, Airto Moreira, Téo de Barros, and Heraldo) started in São Paulo in 1966 as Geraldo Vandré's accompaniment, only to dissolve three years later. Keyboard and accordion player Sivuca comes from the Northeast, as do composer-songwriter Billy Blanco, Zimbo Trio bass player Luiz Chaves, rock musician Ednardo, singer Vital Farias, pianist Tania Maria, and finally Djavan from Alagoas. His 1975 song 'Fato Consumado' was his first big success. Djava Caetano Viana was twenty-five when he came to Rio from Maceio, where he played guitar in pop bands at dances. He went to become one of the most successful international stars of MPB. Most of the compositions recorded by Manhattan Transfer on their Brazil album were his. Djavan himself played as guest soloist on the album. Today, like Milton Nascimento or Gil, he produces the majority of his LPs in the United States. Earlier, in the heyday of the bossa nova, for example, it was the case that Americans engaged Brazilian musicians to lend an authentic touch to their American versions of the bossa nova. Now the top Brazilian stars hire American musicians for their expertise in rock and funk.

Djavan's strengths lie chiefly in composition, of both words and music. With his connection to a North American record company, it wasn't long before sporadic attempts were made to include English texts on the LPs. But what is an English song on a record with ten or eleven Portuguese songs, if not simple vulgarization? Or is there such an important message there that the Anglo pop crowd absolutely must understand? For Djavan (LP 'Birds of Paradise') there were only cliches, such as palm trees on a beach, moonlight, blue lagoons — 'and the two of us'. He sings about the things that Americans might not like in his native tongue; about New York, the Big Apple — where he fell into difficulties, into the quicksand of this very different metropolis, where so much comes together from all over the world, including its negative aspects.

Robertinho de Recife and Alceu Valença are also from the Northeast. Valença follows in the tradition of the cantadores, the itinerant singers at the markets of the Northeast. He joins elements of their singing style with the explosive structures of rock, all based upon original Northeastern rhythms. The thematic message reads: 'Everything is political; nothing is political.'

Alceu Valença

Rhyme with Rhyme
Rima Com Rima

Cantador
Your improvised airs
Reach the loftiest heights known to the creative spirit.
Your verse possesses a matchless power
Fatal, perfect, precise
Oh, bard of our collective unconscious,
You sing the praises of the people and their vexations
And the hope
Which springs eternal.
Forge verse and hymn
In the toada rhythm from Alagoas
In the meter of Martelo Alagoano.

The Quinteto Violado was formed in 1971. For half a decade Northeastern musical folklore drew its chief popularity from (next to the Movimento Armorial and the Cearenses) the work done by these five musicians. From their hometown of Nova Jerusalem (Pernambuco) they traveled through the whole Northeast noting down what they heard at folkloric performances, desafios, and festivals. Marcelo Melo, Toinho Alves, Luciano, Sando and Fernando (Sando was later replaced by Zé Flauta) dressed up baiões, forrós and frevos in modern arrangements without altering the basic character of the original piece, thus avoiding the crime of robbing it of its authenticity. It was Gilberto Gil, by the way, who first discovered Quinteto Violado and helped them get started.

In 1976 Quinteto Violado presented its best and, in my eyes, most important work. Entitled *Missa do Vaqueiro* ('Mass for a Cowboy'), it commemorates another mass written for the vaqueiro Raimondo Jacó, who was murdered in 1954. The original mass is still performed each year on the third Sunday of July in Serrita, Pernambuco state, on the site of the murder. The story is a moving one. Priest João Cancio lived in the city and came to recognize two things early on. First, the Sertanejos were imbued with a very deep religiosity. Second, their vocabulary was not big enough to follow complicated sermons and seminars. Father João began to devote all his time to studying the habits and customs of the vaqueiros, soon becoming a key figure in their lives. One day he met up with Luiz Gonzaga, who, together with Nelson Barbalho, had composed a hymn on the vaqueiro's death. Both were appalled by the misery the vaqueiros had to endure, and so they decided to write a mass for the murdered man as a living symbol for the people of the Sertão. A simple altar was erected on the site where Raimondo Jacó was found. In front of it the vaqueiros, dressed in the leather garments for which they are noted, paraded their horses in ceremonial fashion. The vaqueiro aboio commenced the mass to violeiro accompaniment. In the offertory, each vaqueiro laid a small piece of his clothing in front of the altar. Luiz Gonzaga sang, demanding justice for Jacó's death. A liturgical communion followed, with each vaqueiro eating his customary daily meal of dried meat, cheese and a few lumps of brown sugar.

This mass has changed much over the years, but its essential character has been preserved. After attending the mass, the Quinteto Violado arranged a meeting with Janduhy Finizola from Caruaru, the composer of several pieces from the work. Finizola was commissioned to write a new *Missa do Vaqueiro* for the Quinteto, which received its first performances in 1976 in theaters across the country. I had the good fortune to attend a performance in Rio. Though a foreigner to the inner world of Brazilian thought and feeling, I could not help being overwhelmed by the work. At the end of the piece we all rose from our seats and silently made our way to the exit, reflecting upon the significance of what we had just experienced. The mass had gone beyond simply communicating the Sertanejos' deep religious fervor and their almost helpless plea for atonement of the murder. It painted a vivid, horrifying picture of the Sertão's squalor, characterized by poverty, hunger, wasted lives and the destruction of human potential.

Luiz Gonzaga is also to be credited with having discovered a great new talent in MPB. In 1948 the baião king gave a seven-year-old accordion player in Garanhuns (Pernambuco) his address in Rio and a few hundred cruzeiros. Six years later, the thirteen-year-old Dominguinhos showed up at Gonzaga's doorstep in Rio. The first thing he did was buy the boy a new accordion. Dominguinhos made a career with it, even though the bossa nova wave had brought the guitar to the forefront of public interest. Gonzaga and all the Baianos employed him for their recordings and concerts and helped him record his first LP, after which other successes followed.

Movimento Armorial

Arte Armorial arose in northern Brazil in 1970. The initial impulses came from within a circle of artists under the direction of writer Adriano Suassuna, working in the fields of ceramics, painting, theater, sculpture, poetry and music. The movement aimed to distance itself from certain customary conformist pressures that they saw dominating art in all of Latin America — from the muddled new paths of the avant-garde, from routine and from incorrect or just plain bad interpretations of tradition. Their credo states: 'We are not out to produce some sort of romantic, sentimental, or fabricated new fashion. Arte Armorial must be an expression of our people and our times. We desire neither dogmatic realism nor a return to the morbid cults of a dead past.'

An exhibition of plastics in October 1970 was the occasion for the Armorial da Camara orchestra to put on its first concert in a Recife church. Almost all the musicians belonged to the Recife conservatory. They identified themselves with the basic tenets of the movement as they attempted to recreate 'the realistic and magical spirit of the romanceiros from the Northeast.' The sounds of improvising repentistas in responsory verse, of the troubadours and cantadores of days gone by, and the viola, rabeca and pifano music that accompany them, were all part of the orchestra's repertoire. The Armorial musicians also made use of the simple woodcut motifs from the literatura de cordel to decorate their record covers. The musicians set themselves a further goal. They wished to break down the barriers that separated serious and popular music in favor of a music closely oriented to the realities of Brazilian culture. The result was a hybrid music, classical in its conception and performance, popular in its roots.

Four instruments typical of the Northeast determine the sound produced by the Orquestra Armorial under Cussy de Almeida's direction. However, not all of the original instruments are used. Their sound is reproduced in part by conventional instruments. Six violins and two violas stand in for the rabecas, transverse flutes for the pifanos (wooden flutes), a cello (struck with the bow) for the berimbau de lata. Zabumba percussion instruments — bombo, surdo, drums and cymbals — are still used. The Quinteto Armorial, conducted by Antonio I. Madureira, utilizes original instruments to a greater extent.

Both ensembles rarely draw their musical material from the original, authentic folklore, although their music, in terms of sound and character, is hard to distinguish from it. Composers of modern music, such as Guerra Peixe and the members of his orchestra, write their own cheganças, reisados, revoadas and romances — all musical forms known in the folkloric performances of the Northeast.

Cearenses

In 1877 the inhabitants of Ceará state fled high up to the North, to escape a drought that had struck their region. At the end of the seventies Fortaleza in Ceará was the center of a vital musical and literary movement. Continuing the tradition of this nineteenth-century movement of young intellectuals in Fortaleza ('*Fornecer pão de espirito aos sociais em particular e aos povos em general*': 'furnishing spiritual bread for friends in particular and for the people in general'), the Cearense called themselves the 'new spiritual bakers' (*Os novos padeiros espirituais*). They wanted to demonstrate that the trend toward recognizing the cultures of Brazil's interior, begun by the Baianos in 1967, was not completed. What the Movimento Armorial had started in terms of uniting authentic folklore with classical music, the Cearenser continued with rock and jazz elements based upon Northeastern folklore. They, too, draw from folkloric folksingers, repentistas and literatura de cordel. Among the main figures working within this *música do padeiro*, or *xaxado intelectualizado*, were Belchior, Fagner and Ednardo. Ednardo regards the

Cearenses' music as being in conflict with the Baianos. He claims he discerns a controversy between *regionalismo* (his Northeastern origin) and *urbanismo* (the harsh realities of São Paulo) even in musical spheres. Thematically, his songs tend more toward social satire than protest.

Belchior recorded his first LP in 1974. Working in the purely rhythmical tradition of the Northeast and employing lyrical, concrete texts, he was unable to sell his records with any success. His second LP employed elements from rock with the same thematic content as the first (using lyrics by the Stones and Beatles), and it was a success. In 'Alucinação' he says, 'I am not interested in theory, in fantasy, not even in the color of my face; neither in things from the Orient nor in astral romances. My hallucination is putting up with everyday life. My delirium is experience with real things.' Belchior continues in this satiric vein in his 'Rapaz Latino Americano' ('A Latin American Boy'):

I'm just a Latin American lad
No money in the bank
No influential parents
I come from the countryside
But I still can't forget that song they play on the radio
Written by an old Bahian composer
Everything is divine, everything is marvelous
But I know everything is forbidden ...

... But don't worry, my friend,
About the horrors I'm telling you
For this is only a song.
Real life is something different.
'Live' is even worse.

Fagner differs from Belchior in his use of compositions from the Ceará region as well. One of his lyricists is Capinan, who has enjoyed a successful partnership with Edu Lobo for many years. Fagner's first LP is sold today at collector's prices.

Rockers and Paulistas

Gilberto Gil in his day could not resist its appeal. He said he felt better in the center of *iêiêiê Brasileiro* than in Salvador or Rio. São Paulo was, and still is, the center of Brazilian rock and all its variants in the shallow waters and torrential currents of MPB.

For a long time, just about the only thing one can hear reported about Roberto Carlos were his record sales. The quality of his music is seldom mentioned. A headline from the *Journal do Brasil*, November 22, 1981, reads: '1,600,000 copies of the new LP already sold even before delivery to the stores!' And, of course, this one is his 'best LP' 'Basta!' Such are the slippery methods which Paulistano Sidney Magal and other performers have used.

The 'Dry and the Wet' — a pun on a Brazilian expression for 'general store' — was an apt description of the Secos & Molhados. They turned up suddenly on São Paulo's music scene in 1973, only to drop out of sight completely a year later. Nevertheless, that year was an electrifying one. Selling a half million copies per LP, they achieved a market value that only the Beatles before them had been able to attain in Brazil. Their slogan was 'freedom' in every respect — freedom of musical expression, demolishing the barriers that had been arbitrarily erected between musical forms; freedom of movement on stage; freedom of dress, masks and gesture.

They combined elements from Brazilian musical traditions with rock, jazz and classical structures. Synthesizer and bamboo flute coexisted in easy harmony. They painted their faces with all the colors of the rainbow, with colored black-and-white rings around their eyes and dressed up in the most outrageous feathered costumes — all aspects of presentation we are accustomed to not only from punk, but also from modern ballet and opera performances.

The majority of their compositions were written by the group's founder and leader, João Ricardo. Texts were often taken from the works of such great Brazilian poets as Carlos Drummond de Andrade, Vinicius de Moraes or Manuel Bandeira. Ney Matogrosso's high, fine voice has come to stand for the characteristic vocal sound of Secos & Molhados. The group's early breakup resulted from internal squabblings with him. Ney Matogrosso became a celebrated soloist and continued performing in the most scurrilous feathered costumes imaginable, half-naked and androgynous in image. Critics called him 'Brazil's Alice Cooper'.

Secos & Molhados regrouped themselves in 1978 with a new lead singer to replace Ney Matogrosso. Success, however, remained out of reach.

The Queen of Brazilian Rock is Rita Lee, from São Paulo. During Gil's São Paulo period she was a member of Os Mutantes, which Gil accompanied for their first appearance. Rita left the group in 1973 to try her luck at a solo career, and formed her own band, Tutti Frutti. The record industry saw in Secos & Molhados' demise the opportunity to fill the gap with Rita. They struck gold. But her critics, and Rita herself, were well aware that this first LP 'Fruto Proibido', was no musical novelty. Her next LP was a true flop. Bad times were ahead for Rita. She got pregnant and was arrested for possession of drugs and jailed. These hard times found their reflection in her work. Once free, she turned to writing ironic, satirical songs. But upon meeting Gilberto Gil again in 1977 she found a new lease on life. The partnership (on the LP 'Refestança') revitalized her and helped her recognize that all her previous work was *uma coisa fria* ('a cold thing'). Critics confirmed her judgment that her next work had succeeded in 'Brazilianizing' the rock medium, offering a true alternative to the old carnival marchinhas ('Veja', 1983). 'Lança Perfume' (1983) was the name of her most successful show and LP. Of late she performs with her husband, guitarist Roberto Carvalho.

In the seventies the Freneticas, six girls from São Paulo, let loose a twister in the disco scene with their 'Música pra Pular' ('Music To Hop To').

Billy Bond, an Italian musician raised in Argentina, produced Ney Matogrosso's first LP shortly after Secos & Molhados's breakup. Years later he appeared with Tico Terpins and others, including Joelho de Porco, Brazil's first satirical punk band.

Other rock musicians and groups from São Paulo are Guilherme Arantes, Pholhas, Made in Brazil and 14-Bis. New rock bands began springing up like mushrooms in Rio and São Paulo in the mid-eighties. After the mid-eighties, many new rock bands came into existence. From Biquini Calvadão to Elas, they were on their way toward a Brazilian variety of modern rock music.

Rock Brasil

The MPB stars of the sixties generation (Chico, Bethania, Gal, Gil etc.,) were not automatically adopted by the following generation. Brazil's urban youth accepted Rita Lee and few others from the pioneer days of iêiêiê Brasileiro.

Punk, the music and the look, initiated a movement in Brazil that carried far more weight than the Beatles and Stones imitations of the previous period. Rock Brasil began in 1979 with Brazilian punk groups like Inocentes and the festival 'O Começo do Fim do Mundo' in São Paulo. The first Brazilian New Wave title to hit the charts was 'Perdidos na Selva', by Julia Barroso & Gang 90 (*and* As Absurdettes) from Rio, in 1981. In 1982, Blitz made its debut with an LP, the astronomical sales of which signalled to the Brazilian recording industry the potential of the new Rock Brasil. Even so, the instrumentalists from MPB and jazz had, with their *selos independentes* (independent labels) demonstrated to their new rock colleagues how records can be brought out even without an industry contract. These now appeared in great numbers. Those who didn't get recording contracts found ways to produce under their own direction and to distribute through countless independent firms.

International rock stars who seldom came to Brazil (because of currency, customs and technical problems) now, increasingly, aimed for it: Police (1982), Van Halen (1983), Kiss (1983), Kid Creole (1986) and more.

Festivals were organized and dedicated to the new rock music: MPB Shell by TV Globo, Punkfestival at PUC in São Paulo and 'Rock in Rio'. This festival, 'Rock in Rio', over ten days in 1985 (and again in 1991) presented the cream of Brazilian rock music, next to international stars; among others, Brazil's punk couple Pepeu Gomez and Baby Consuelo. Despite this there were complaints. The Brazilian artists protested to the organizers that the technicians had managed the light and sound for the native groups poorly, in contrast with the technical management for the foreign groups. The festival organizers countered that the Brazilian groups and their roadies were less experienced than their foreign guests. Even so, 'Rock in Rio', arranged by Roberto Medina for an audience of 355,000 was an event with far-reaching consequences for the further development of Brazilian rock music.

In 1988 there was a successor festival in Rio and São Paulo, likewise in January, that was called 'Hollywood Rock'.

Magazine publishers focussed on the new rock enthusiasm of Brazilian youths as well with publications such as *Roll* (1982–85) and *Bizz* (established 1985). Soon the first rock groups began to tour other countries. The Paralamas do Successo traveled to New York (1983) and Montreux (1987), Blitz to the USSR (1985), and Titãs to Montreux (1988).

Musically, Rock Brasil was as distant from MPB, especially in the initial years, as international rock music is. The mixing of Brazilian music with elements of jazz and rock had already been undertaken by the idols of the previous generation. The young Brazilian rock groups (the so-called 'third generation' of rock in Brazil) took the same road taken by European rock musicians in the late seventies, which led to the New Wave: rock music of all shades, but with Portuguese texts. This was relatively new, because in earlier years it had been fashionable to sing rock music in English.

The new development made it possible for many bands to go public before they were really ready. Many had very little experience, but they had ideas; they knew a few standard rhythms and phrases from the international rock scene — but everyone had something to say. It was often critical and witty, it sounded fresh and sometimes the lyrics were spontaneous: 'Sex and karate on my TV, they make me sick, I rang you up but a Chinese answered, he said in English that you don't like me any more' (Plebe Rude).

Critical, intelligent lyrics could be found before this in Brazilian, in the songs of Chico, Gonzaguinha, Geraldo Vandré, but the young people want none of the bossa nova or the tropicalism of their grand-fathers. They want their own idols. They don't have to fight the censors, they needn't torment themselves to invent metaphors. The message comes across spontaneously and directly.

Most of the members of Rock Brasil groups are the same age as their audience. Who cares about voice quality, when gestures, clothing, hair, and the hum of the PA matter more than musical criteria? Thus Rock Brasil can be omitted from a deeper evaluation within MPB; objectively the two have little in common.

The best-known bands from the eighties are Blitz, Legião Urbana, Paralamas do Successo, Inocentes, Olho Seco, Ultraje a rigor, Irã, Plebe Rude, Capital Inicial, Barão Vermelho, Os Titãs, Biquini Cavaldão, RPM, Replicantes, Engenheiros do Hawaii. Solo performers include Arnaldo Batista (previously with Mutantes), Lobão, Cazuza (previously Barão Vermelho), Lulu Santos, Ritchie ...

Rock and reggae are combined by the Paralamas and Central Africana more than by other groups from Bahia. Africa and the black population of Brazil are the recurring themes of these groups. The lyrics are political, speaking for the plight of the blacks one hundred years after the abolition of slavery, denouncing discrimination and disadvantage. In contrast to the texts of the Jamaican rasta-reggae musicians, however, they are not militantly anti-white. Instead they look for commonalities, seeking understanding without discriminating themselves.

The South

The number of young musicians who came from Porto Alegre, Santa Catarina, and other southern sites to seek their fortunes in the center of the MPB is negligible. However, the South has its traditions, too. Choirs, harmonica ensembles and música caipira flourish here. What certainly does not flourish is urban life. In the South you can find big, new, sterile cities fresh from the drawing board, with not a trace of a tradition that could produce even a samba or a frevo. Farmers and cattle herders live outside the cities. Cultural affinities with Argentina and Uruguay are strong.

In 1974 a student band called Almondegas began making headlines in Rio Grande do Sul. Its success stemmed from its original and lively mixture of gaucho music and big city tunes with elements from rock and MPB. The brothers Kleiton and Kledir, a popular vocal duo in Brazil today, were originally with the Almondegas. In the eighties young rock groups from the South have also become well known. The instrumental career of Gaitero Renato Borghetti has gone beyond Brazil's borders.

Panlatinoamericana

For many years the rigorous censorship of the Brazilian dictatorship isolated Brazil from its Latin American neighbors. The new political song movement of the sixties remained unknown to a larger public. Argentina, Uruguay, Chile and, later, Cuba witnessed the growth of new folkloric movements, the *nuevas canciones* and *nuevas trovas*. The murder of Victor Jara and many of his friends immediately after the military coup in Chile attests to the strength of this movement and to its ability to echo and express the people's experiences and yearnings under conditions of poverty and repression. The Brazilian censors suppressed practically everything and everybody seeking to enter the country that could have documented the fact that national (censored) song poets such as Chico Buarque and Luiz Gonzaga Jr. were actually part of a movement that had gripped the entire continent. While the best known Chilean groups of that time, like Inti Illimani or Quilapayun, went into European exile, the Brazilians stayed at home, to work for change from within. Their efforts were a model for the new generation of Chilean musicians (Canto Nuevo) who remained in their own country and renewed their commitment to the anti-Pinochet NO-vote.

It was not until the censorship was partly lifted in the aftermath of the *abertura* that records from the *nueva canción* movement, which had been banned for years, could appear in Brazil as well. And then, for the first time, Chico, Milton and others could openly demonstrate their sympathies with these songwriters whom they as yet knew only from festivals abroad. Mercedes Sosa came frequently to Brazil from Argentina, enjoyed great concert successes, and made recordings together with Milton Nascimento. Milton himself recorded songs by Violetta Parra and Pablo Milanes. Musicians from various Latin American countries living in Brazil banded together in 1980 to form *Raizes de América*. Their concerts aimed at communicating for the first time to a wider public the general consensus that existed among the continent's progressive artist community.

Chapter 8

The Instrumentalists

Revolt of the Instrumentalists

The revolt among Brazilian musicians succeeded on its second try. After decades of an unnoticed, underprivileged existence in the shadows of the MPB's great vocal stars, with many a timid protest but with nothing to show for them, Brazilian instrumentalists launched a counter offensive in the mid-seventies. In contrast to earlier times, Brazil experienced a flood of records that appeared on the market produced and distributed by independent cooperatives, which never tired of proudly proclaiming, '*Isto é mas um disco independente*': 'This one, too, is an independent record production.'

Instrumental musicians from MPB spoke of 'liberating' and 'realizing' themselves. The act of liberation was seen, first and foremost, as directed against the Brazilian music industry. Whether it is nationally or internationally constituted, the music industry ignores the instrumental music of the country and regards musicians as underemployed, and therefore inexpensive hired hands for the studio. In a few cases it was forced to open its eyes to the excellence of its own instrumentalists when they attained fame abroad. Baden Powell, Egberto Gismonti, Hermeto Pascoal, Sivuca and Sebastião Tapajós traveled this road back home. Other Brazilian artists, such as Airto, Dom Um Romão and Paulinho da Costa took the opportunity to work a stint in the United States, introducing there an exotic percussive element into their jazz and rock bands in hope of making a career in their own country later.

Meanwhile, musicians in Brazil remained practically without work. The bossa nova had radically reduced a music group's instrumentation, and it was not until the Bahian tropicalism of the sixties around Gilberto Gil and Caetano Veloso that electronic instruments appeared on the scene, chiefly in São Paulo. Gil is considered the mentor of Brazilian rock since he first performed before the mike at a song festival with an electric guitar. Even today jazz and rock musicians barely eke out a living. For as the established recording companies in Brazil never tire of repeating: 'you just can't sell sufficient number of records in Brazil without songs on them.'

Years ago the guitarist Macumbinha was found dead in his São Paulo apartment. The thirty-four-year-old musician, widely regarded as an up-and-coming talent with a great future, had taken his own life, as had his wife and children. The job situation in Brazil was a dismal one, offering him neither a future in which he could provide for his family nor a place where he could realize his musical ideals.

As early as 1977 the popular music journalist Nelson Motta published a manifesto in defence of instrumental musicians in the daily paper *O Globo*. It contained nineteen demands for an improvement of the situation, including:

> An end to the discrimination between musicians and singers. All are necessary for a record's success!
>
> An end to the humiliation of our own musicians vis-à-vis foreign musicians!

At the same time TV Globo took up the subject in a detailed report entitled 'Fantastico', broadcast on Sunday evening prime time. The program ended with an appeal from the show's producers for action by the Brazilian labor minister.

The abundance of new records appearing on the market each year hides the fact that it is almost always the same musicians who accompany the singers for every production. Black saxophonist Paulo Moura told me in an interview in October 1976: 'There is a group here which records in all the studios in Rio and these musicians can make good money. But they hardly have time to do anything else. At the same time, they're the best that we have. Others try to organize bands, but they never gain access to the studios. They can't record with their bands, and they also can't survive by accompanying singers in the studio, for instance. This characterizes our situation, and it works enormously to stiffle instrumental MPB.'

Paradoxically, '*Disco é Cultura*' ('Records are Culture') is written on every Brazilian record jacket cover. A musician has added ironically,

'One day we'll see "Music for those with money. Radio and television for the rest".'

Popular music education in Brazil is in a sorry state. Universities offer only classical training, although soloists from abroad are often engaged to play for Brazilian symphony orchestras. Despite the wealth of popular music present in the country, it has yet to find a place in the academy. There were, however, timid attempts to bring the two musical branches together. Conductor Julio Medaglia brought the Brazilian Symphony Orchestra together with musicians and singers from the Mangueira Samba School in Rio for a concert. Their colorful program ranged from Mozart to sambas do morro.

Until the end of the seventies Brazilian musicians were at a loss over how to deal with their critical situation. Musicians' self-help groups or initiatives were practically nonexistent. Instead of banding together to form cooperatives and fighting to improve their conditions, they only cursed and waited for things to get better. Theirs was an almost childlike naiveté kindled by their simple desire to make music. In fact, so much so that their understanding of reality became clouded. Was this all a problem of mentality? Certainly, in part. But it was also a result of the generally unsatisfactory situation of musical life in Brazil.

Is racism also a cause of the problem? Paulo Moura and several of his colleagues reject this as an explanation. But Moura admits that it was easier for him as a black to have a career as a musician, since such jobs are typical for blacks. He might have had his problems if he had wanted to be a doctor. However, one certainly cannot deny that white musicians frequently have better connections to producers than do blacks.

Maurício Einhorn's apartment on Praia do Leme has established itself as a gathering place for musicians, both with and without jobs. The harmonica player, now over fifty years old, is a prominent example of an extraordinary instrumentalist who is totally underrated in Brazil. He already has world-acclaimed compositions to his credit, such as 'Batida Diferente', written together with Durval Ferreira in the bossa nova era. Toots Thielemans, himself a famous harmonica player, values his friend Maurício as at least equal to himself. But in his long music career, Maurício had yet to be allowed to make his own records. As a soloist, on the other hand, he had already had parts on hundreds of discs. I first tried to help Maurício make his own record in Rio in 1977. Weeks of negotiations brought nothing but, 'We're sorry. The man is very good, world-class. But things are tight, and we can't afford to produce an instrumental recording with him in Brazil.' After hearing the crushing news, we were all sitting together at Maurício's, wondering what to do next. The problem seemed solved as a number of musicians declared spontaneously that they would do without a fixed salary and would help pitch in for the studio costs. But a problem still remained. Who would market the record? We finally decided to produce it ourselves, and we later released it through MPS in Germany and Clam in Brazil. I am convinced that Baden Powell, too, would have had to fight similar odds had not a German producer taken an interest in him in the sixties. Sebastião Tapajós, too, had to record fifteen albums abroad before anyone in Brazil took notice of him. The Brazilian Star Show columnist inquired publicly: 'How could it happen that we didn't notice this man ourselves?'

Paulo Moura told me in October 1976, 'Our greatest strength is our quality.' In view of this quote, the first edition of this book raised the demand that Brazilian instrumentalists should unite in common action. Marlos Nobre, classical composer and FUNARTE director at the time, said, 'Brazilian musicians must finally learn to realize just how good they are.'

By 1980 discontent among instrumentalists had created an explosive situation. Constant bickering and complaining transformed themselves into a new tendency toward self-help. Resistance was their answer. Olmir Stocker, pen-name 'Alemão' ('German'), one of the first guitarists to have his own album, says, 'Traveling abroad and accompanying Brazil's stars taught me many things. I heard many melodies, felt the vibrations of many a rhythm. Those which said something to me, however, were not those coming from the stage where I was accompanying the big stars, but rather those from my country and its citizens. So I began to compose, without censoring myself anymore. I finally began to be a Brazilian. I did my work as a free-lance artist ... and felt what a compromise it was to be a Brazilian musician. I understood that I could resist with music.' Resistance took the form of presenting music that the media and industry had already branded 'unpopular'. It was a sharp answer uttered by an increasingly conscious body of Brazilian artists who were protesting against what was normally held for 'popular', that is, disco music, youth-oriented films and drugs. Musicians are not alone in their aspirations. There are similar movements at present in film and literature.

Latin American popular music would be hard to imagine without the creative participation of instrumental musicians. Without them there would be no such thing as the Buenos Aires tango, the choro from Rio or the danzón and mambo, offshoots of the habanera. Urban musicians are to be credited with having popularized Latin American folkloric music forms born out of a cultural interaction process. The samba, tango and danzón all sounded in their early form like instrumental combinations of different musical forms. The Brazilian samba, for example, is unthinkable without Pixinguinha's brilliant innovations in counterpoint and arrangement.

Since colonial days, Latin American musicians have had to cede to their foreign colleagues control of the internationalization of their music. Buenos Aires, Rio and Havana have for centuries served as nothing but a supplier of 'exotic' raw material to North American and European dance orchestras that had a knack for mutilating them beyond recognition. Most Latin American pop music forms of a very lively character owe their existence primarily to the almost slave-like devotion the urban middle classes of the early nineteenth century showed for all cultural products and influences coming from Europe. Folkloric musical cross breeds of African, Amerindian and European origin, which underwent a change as a result of such European influences, were subjected once again to further modifications as Brazilian music became internationalized. Their original aesthetic was replaced by the aesthetic of a new, non-Latin American consumer.

Medusa, a progressive group from São Paulo, said: 'There exists a fundamental conflict in our culturally colonized country. Things are implanted from outside, and then consumed right away as if they were the real thing. Our group is a product of this conflict. The colonized can learn from the colonizer to a certain extent. But he can't stop using his own head. Our work is a kind of musical proposal without prejudice or barriers. Its objective intent is to achieve a musical fusion, but without breaking with our own tradition. The differing musical backgrounds, informational universes, vitality and personal experiences of each member of our group gives us the integration of form that we aspire toward.'

Internationalization means, inevitably, the inclusion of international musical developments. For Brazil, that means, above all, jazz and rock, which, for their part, are seen as vehicles for expression and not as content in themselves.

Most musicians find, however, that a free sound is only possible after they have discovered and realized their own musical freedom. They founded publishing houses, production companies, marketing offices and concert agencies. They still have to depend on the established music industry for many things. Only the music industry, for example, has at its disposal record-cutting machines and presses. Since Brazil's record industry has also been afflicted by lean years, such job orders are a welcome extra, besides relieving them of the duty of attending to instrumental musicians (since the musicians are well capable of doing this themselves). By European standards the number of copies that independent labels produce is small. It means a great deal to them just to sell a few thousand records. But it isn't the number that counts but rather, the steadily growing offering of alternatively produced records and their total sales is turning into a serious rival to the established record industry. It is significant that this is happening at a time when, for example, a firm like Ariola, which was established a few years back with a large initial capital and musicians' recruitment fees running in the millions, had to throw in the towel and see itself bought up by the giant Polygram Brazil.

Alternative record labels have tried their hand at all sorts of music, from Brazilian creations to western pop, from established forms and artists to fledglings on the scene. The suddenly newfound freedom has engendered a flowering of creative activity, with artists attempting to realize long-cherished musical visions and dreams. (One disadvantage of the new opening is the great amount of superfluous productions, and just plain junk that keeps on appearing on the market.)

From folklore to progressive jazz to rock, everything undergoes a period of testing and experimentation. A similar situation probably occurred in the last century as the emancipation of the slaves led many musicians to leave the plantations and make their way into the cities. There, for the first time, they could play undisturbed by plantation aristocracy and Church, thus utilizing their new-found space to create the earliest forms of Brazilian popular music.

The established record companies first reacted in 1984. The empire struck back! Polygram, for example, released a series of instrumental LPs under the motto 'Todos os Sons' ('All the Sounds') on the Barclay label (formerly Ariola). There was no sign of a boycott of the newly awakened musicians' initiatives, and certainly Polygram had no difficulties in engaging a number of outstanding musicians. After all, practically every musician had to contend with meager ticket sales, financial problems and quarrels among themselves. Polygram and other giant companies could offer them unlimited studio sessions, honoraria and advance licence payments, a professional marketing agency and the promotional apparatus that only a large firm has at its disposal. Only the future will tell to what extent all these possibilities will really be exploited to the fullest, or whether such productions will degenerate to prestige and tax write-off projects. The Barclay series, for example, soon stopped after the first few releases.

Changing companies was not unheard of. Boca Livre, (a vocal instrumental quartet from Rio), for example, produced and distributed two of its own LPs and achieved very respectable sales (around 100,000 copies). They moved to an established company, and their sales dwindled considerably.

The Musicians

Flute, guitar and percussion made up the original instrumentation of Brazil's urban popular music. Pixinguinha added the saxophone; other choro musicians introduced the cavaquinho and bandolim. MPB's traditional instrumentation was supplemented by jazz and North American dance music and later by rock and reggae. The last twenty years have seen those artists attain popularity outside Brazil who chose traditional Brazilian instruments, i.e. guitarists and percussionists.

Guitarists

Guitarist Laurindo Almeida was the first. He had already left for the United States in the forties. Later, many guitarists from the bossa nova milieu followed him, most importantly Luiz Bonfá. Baden Powell excited European audiences in the seventies, although he never could gain a following in the United States. He was followed by Sebastião Tapajós, a classically trained guitarist. In my opinion (and I can say this because I have worked with him for twelve years) Tapajós is the most underrated guitarist of our era. He plays with a technical brilliance and a maturity that few can match, but still he does not conform to musical trends, as Baden Powell does, quite successfully, with jazz.

Still relatively unknown outside Brazil is a young guitarist by the name of Rafael Rabello. Earlier he played the violão-7-cordas in Choro Conjuntos and in 1987 he presented his first solo album with works by Radamés Gnatalli. Paco de Lucia: 'Rafael seems to me to be one of the best instrumentalists I've heard in a long time. He is one of those guitarists who have overcome their dependence on technique and whose music goes straight to the heart; I admire that.' In fact Rabello has a vitality and a swing, along with incomparable virtuosity.

Nonato Luiz comes from the north of Brazil (Ceará), has written over 300 compositions for guitar and, in addition, is known as a soloist on Milton Nascimento's recordings.

Egberto Gismonti (born 1947 in Rio) also enjoyed a classical music education. His father was Arab, his mother Italian. He started his professional career in 1968, soon making his way to Europe to prosper from its lively, traditional music culture. He studied in Vienna and worked for a long time in France (with Marie Laforêt, among others). In addition to the European and North African influences he received from his family background, Gismonti's musical language embraces the situation of the Third World as well. Despite the many influences from western pop and jazz, it is above all Brazilian. Gismonti says, 'It includes a culture built by people existing upon the same economic, social and political basis as our country.' Gismonti is many-faceted. He composes, arranges, plays piano and keyboard, flute and guitar and sings. He is at home in many different contemporary musical styles. Like Airto, he not only plays the music of his countrymen, but also studies it. A ballet and music project among the Indians of the Xingú Amazon reservation, for example, provided him with material and ideas for the first LP by his Academia de Danças. This was also one of the first big-selling instrumental records in Brazil, a country generally hostile to such music. Gismonti's personal finances allow him the luxury of his own sound and rehearsal studios in Rio.

Gismonti has been producing for many years for the German ECM label. These recordings sound very different from recordings of identical pieces made in Brazil. Certainly playing together with European jazz musicians demands a different feeling and sensibility. But even more importantly, it demands of Gismonti that he do without certain fundamental Brazilian musical structures. Gismonti gave an example in a *Downbeat* interview. 'We think in two, jazz musicians in four.' In other words, the Afro-Brazilian traditions cause Brazilians to play and feel in 2/4 time, jazz musicians in 4/4. In practice, this means that Gismonti either has to play in European studios without rhythmic accompaniment, or he has to adapt himself to European musicians. This is especially noticeable in arrangements with Naná Vasconselos and in recordings with the trio including Ralph Towner (guitar) and Jan Gabarek (soprano sax). When one compares these recordings with those done of the same pieces in Brazil with Gismonti's Academia de Danças, then the compositional foundation on which the title was based becomes clear. One could risk a comparison with Argentinian tango music, which made a small comeback in Europe in 1983. Public interest was less keen on the likes of Sexteto Major's authentic tango than for Juan José Mossalini's jazz and rock-oriented Bandoneón titles. Mossalini and Gismonti would surely have been less successful had they not adapted to the European ear. Proof of this is the fact that Gismonti was hardly noticed before his ECM productions, even though he gave many concerts and had already released an LP. Mossalini, too, had been consigned to oblivion for many years in Paris.

Of late Gismonti has played in Europe with the entire Academia de Danças. He formulates the group's character as follows: 'The world of the Academia reveals and embraces the entire cosmos.'

Percussionists

Brazilian percussionists traveling abroad tend to dominate their surroundings. They are obsessed wherever they go with collecting every possible sort of object that could be used in some way to produce a beat or a sound. Brazil itself is a country whose Amerindian and African cultures provide an unbelievably large reservoir of such objects.

Wayne Shorter, a great admirer of Brazilian music, said, 'Brazilian percussionists have contributed toward developing a new musical vocabulary. There's lots that is new in this respect in Brazil, in contrast to what's going on in the U.S.'

Airto Moreira and Naná Vasconselos are two of these highly rated artists. And yet they are very different. Airto is more devoted to popular music, with an occasional excursion into large compositional works, as his mass (arranged by Gil Evans) demonstrates. Naná Vasconselos moves easily from authentic folklore to experimental music to *música erúdita*. He has worked with psychiatrists in Paris, where he attempted to employ percussion as a form of therapy. This coincides, in fact, with Naná's interpretation of his own music as reflecting a unity of body and instrument.

Naná was born in Recife in 1944. He began playing drums there in a local bar. After working together with João Gilberto for a while, he went to Rio in 1967 and developed an intensive partnership with Milton Nascimento. In 1968 he joined the Quarteto Livre, which Geraldo Vandré accompanied at various song festivals, as well as the Trio Bagaço (later Boca Livre) with Nelson Angelo and Mauricio Maestro. A year later he visited New York and established contacts in the international jazz scene (Don Cherry, Rolf Kühn, Jean-Luc Ponty, Oliver Nelson). He then went to France, which he set up as his home base, and from there worked throughout Europe for many years (with Joachim Kühn, Quarteto Iansã and others). His Orquestra de Vozes (Orchestra for Voices) became especially well known. Naná can also be heard on disc together with Egberto Gismonti.

Airto Moreira was born in 1941 in Itaiopolis in Santa Catarina. He enjoyed a classical education. At only thirteen he sang in a band called Jazz Estrela, later in a bar in Curitiba. His further travels took him to São Paulo (Guimarães and his group, today Uakti) as a singer and percussionist, the Sambalanço Trio (Cesar Camargo Mariano), to dancer Lennie Dale (later Dzi Croquettes), and in 1963 to Rio (Sambossa Trio, Quarteto Novo with Hermeto). In 1967 he accompanied Edu Lobo for the latter's successful song 'Ponteio' ('Festival'). Soon after afterwards, he met Flora Purim, who later became his wife.

Together they took off for the bright lights of Los Angeles. At first he did odd jobs while Flora worked in a restaurant called Lost and Found. Then Miles Davis offered him a place in his band. After that Airto played for two years with Chick Corea's Return to Forever before forming his own band, Fingers. He formed a new group with Gismonti, Raul de Souza, Ted Lô, Robertinho Silva, John Williams and David Amari. Airto once said in a *Jazz Podium* interview: 'Less rhythm and sound than feeling. I learned what freedom a musician can have when living in freedom. I am free to play percussion everywhere, not only in jazz. I'm not one of those idiots who just know a rhythm or an instrument. I listen to the music that I play.'

Several Brazilian percussionists got their start in the international music business thanks to Sergio Mendes. Dom Um Romão (born 1925) became a member of the Sergio Mendes Sextet in Rio in 1961 and later in Mendes's Bossa Rio. After playing in various bossa nova groups Dom Um went to the United States, toured with Stan Getz and Astrud Gilberto, returned to Mendes (Brasil '66) and in 1974 to Weather Report. Two years later, Norman Granz, the godfather of American jazz, helped him to release his first LP, called 'Hotmosphere', with Sivuca doing the musical direction. Paulinho da Costa was one of his successors with Mendes. He began in Rio's samba school milieu. He too, was able to release a debut LP, 'Agora', with Granz's Pablo label. Da Costa's musical style, tended toward a commercial variant of so-called 'fusion' music.

Percussionist Djalma Corrêa has made significant inroads. After years of playing on tour in an ensemble with Gil, Gal Costa and others in Montreux, France and Italy, 1982 was his breakthrough year. He got the opportunity to present his own group at the Berlin Jazz Days, side by side with Paulo Moura, the Brazilian Jazz All-Stars and the Arrigo Barnabé Project. Two years later he was called back to Berlin to take part in a percussion workshop, and directly thereafter Sebastião Tapajós presented him to European audiences during a four-week concert tour. Along with him on the tour was Pedro Sorongo Santos, without a doubt Brazil's most original percussionist.

Multi-instrumentalists

It was said simply by Hermeto Pascoal, of all people, whom I regard as the most Brazilian of all Brazilian musicians: 'There is no Brazilian music. But I am a Brazilian, and what I produce must be the result of my experiences and my fate. Music is everywhere in the air and can be heard by all who have an antenna for it.'

It seems only natural that Hermeto Pascoal (born 1936) should consider himself a musical cosmopolite. The feelings and motivations that fill his tone pictures have a natural quality that render them universal. By alternating the expressive character of his music between conventional folklore, abstract, impressionistic and even surrealisticly picturesque, he is able to elevate the listener to a higher plane, to nature and mystic, tangible and supernatural. There is only one religion in this world for Hermeto: 'Music, which holds our planet together.'

Hermeto comes from Lagoa de Canoa in the hinterland of Alagoas province in the northeast of Brazil. 'We don't have radios there. Only the sounds of the forest and the rain. The only musicians are the crickets.' Having grown up in such a close relationship with nature, Hermeto is himself a part of nature. And necessarily he subjects his musical activity to nature's laws. He makes structure out of presumed chaos, creativity from improvisation, and logic from apparent madness.

Hermeto hates routine. He has no patience with himself, and so is continually in a creative process. 'My blood boils, my head gets hot, and the music just comes.' At thirteen he was already aware that his calling was music. He learned how to play a variety of regional music instruments, playing them every chance he got. Not until he was thirty did he acquire his first musical theory. The Brazilian public first took notice of Hermeto Pascoal when he became popular as a member of the legendary Quarteto Novo in 1966. This quartet, to which Airto Moreira also belonged, exerted such a decisive influence upon Brazilian instrumental music in the sixties that its effects can still be felt today. The group combined the rich tradition of Northeastern musical folklore with the modern harmonic structures that had been introduced to Brazil through the bossa nova, and thereby established for itself a contemporary basis for extended improvisation.

Hermeto prefers most of all to play flutes and keyboard instruments of all varieties. His instrumentation also includes saxophone, violin, tuba, percussion and all sorts of sounds produced by the body or various objects.

In 1970 Airto Moreira invited Hermeto to the Unites States to record an album. Antônio Carlos Jobim, Duke Pearson and Flora Purim also sent him plane tickets. Hermeto's lack of English caused him problems. But as he says, the only thing that you have to know how to say in the United States is, 'Where's my money?'

While great success in the United States remained elusive, the praise he received abroad (at the Berlin Jazz Days and the Montreux Festival, for instance) increased the Brazilian public's interest in their countryman.

Today Hermeto Pascoal lives with his wife and six children in a three-room apartment outside Rio, a kind of father figure to modern popular artists. Too often he is styled, incorrectly, a jazz musician. As earthy as his improvisations may be, he still fills his music with the new material of his Brazilian homeland. Sambas, baiões, xotes and choros combine to form a colorful kaleidoscope of folklore and popular music — in a word, spontaneous music moving freely between styles. But then, suddenly, there is an about-face. Hermeto avoids at all costs being tagged with a stylistic label.

There is, however, no dearth of labels that have been designed for Hermeto's personality. They range from 'genius' to 'musical riot', 'ubiquitous maestro of madness', 'director of chaos', 'guerrilla fighter against routine' ...

No one has yet labeled him a cook, even though his kitchen and studio are right next to each other in his apartment. It's a wonder Hermeto has not yet torn down the bothersome wall dividing them.

Severino Dias de Oliveira, better known as Sivuca, was born in 1930 in Itabaiana, Pernambuco. He could pass for Hermeto's twin brother. But Sivuca is not happy with such a comparison. To be sure, he speaks of his Northeastern countryman with great respect — they even recorded a piece together once — but where the partnership began, it ended, too. Still, Sivuca is similar to Hermeto. He, too, senses his deep roots within the folk musical culture of his homeland. At a moment's notice he can turn up with his sanfona at a Northeastern fair and get the people dancing. Sivuca is a full-blooded musician. At nine he already had his first sanfona in hand; at nineteen he went to São Paulo; and at twenty-nine he visited Europe for the first time (with Os Brasileiros). He tinkled his way through Europe a second time as a member of Brasilia Ritmos (with Waldir Azevedo), and in 1964 came to the United States for the first time in Carmen Costa's band. From 1965 to 1969 he played as a guitarist for Miriam Makeba. In 1969 he directed Oscar Brown's musical *Joy* and then worked for Harry Belafonte for an additional five years.

Sivuca's return to Brazil went unnoticed. For six years the record companies found nothing better for him to do than 'clean door handles', as he told me bitterly. Living with his wife, Glorinha Gadelha, who sings with him and writes many of his lyrics, he had to tighten his belt and live modestly for a number of years. No one seemed interested in the fine art of arranging, which Sivuca had brought back with him from North America. Even today Brazilians have yet to give Sivuca the attention that is his due. It may have been resignation that led him to venture into new terrain, focusing his energies chiefly upon recording traditional Northeastern dance music (forrós, frevos …). In 1984 a meeting could finally be arranged with Rio's accordion master Chiquinho da Acordeon (Christian name: Romeu Seibel). The Brazilian record producers were fearful of having too much improvisation on an LP, a fear that produced unfavorable consequences for the choro and its documentation over many years. So, in this case, the two sanfoneiros were, unfortunately, only allowed to improvise with each other on one piece.

As a pianist with classical training Arrigo Barnabé turned relatively late to MPB (at the beginning of the seventies). His contribution to Brazil's current music scene has been all the more personal and original for that. His composition 'Diversões Eletrônicas' provoked a storm in 1979, but still came out on top at TV Cultura's first University Festival. That same year his 'Sabor de Veneno' was victorious at TV Tupi's Festival in São Paulo. Considering the era in which he made his pop career, it was almost inevitable that he would turn to Bahian tropicalism, which he regarded as a significant structural concept, although lacking in improvisational possibilities. Barnabé's song parts, on the other hand, are greatly influenced by contemporary classical music.

With Hermeto Pascoal, the 'omnipotent sorceror of musical madness', Barnabé shares a deep-seated aversion to musical routine. The latter, therefore, treats his audiences to the unexpected. But the more popular his songs become, the more the unexpected becomes expected, and thus reproducible. The tropicalism generation prior to Barnabé (i.e. Caetano Veloso and Gilberto Gil) saw a danger in the adherence to form and structure. They were wary that these elements might take on a life of their own, while the lyrical content of their songs would remain ignored. So their *som livre* employed a technique of continual alternation of musical style, both from song to song as well as within a song, thereby fully exploiting the possibilities of 'collage' composition available to them. Arrigo Barnabé followed in this tradition. He added to it by relocating the vocalist away from his position in front of the band, as was customary in tropicalism, back into the circle of instrumentalists. This principle is not a new one. We have only to think of Gunter Hampel and Jeanne Lee in jazz, or of the authentic samba (a far cry from the commercialized world of carnival), where voice and instrument have an equal say. For this reason Barnabé regards the sambistas Nelson Cavaquinho and Paulinho da Viola, in addition to Tom Jobim and Caetano Veloso, as the most important influences upon his work.

And like tropicalism's artists before him, Barnabé's texts drew inspiration from the concrete poetry movement (initiated by the de Campos brothers), although not in such a direct manner as Gil and Caetano. Barnabé's subject matter is everyday life and people. His song 'Orgasmo Total' is a satire on the marketing of sex:

> Don't be ridiculous.
> You, too, can be happy like your neighbor.
> Enough! Write today —
> Box 6969
> For your copy of
> *Orgasm For Everyone!*

According to Barnabé's own description, his compositions consist of periodically repeated modules. The variation of these modules determines the formal structure of his music.

The modules are frequently atonal (as in 'Clara Crocodile', 'Sabor de Veneno') or dodecaphonic ('Diversões Eletrônicas', 'Infortunio', 'Acapulco Drive-In').

Arrigo Barnabé builds compositional unity by transforming the modules, e.g. inversion and reversal, or an inversion of the reversal. For example, the first part of 'Diversões Eletrônicas' contains module A; the second part consists of an inversion of part one; and the third part consists of two transformations of the first part with dodecaphony.

The rhythm is variable. For example, in the first part of 'Acapulco Drive-In', we hear 4/4, 2/4 and 3/8, and in the second part 9/8 and 6/8. Not only is atonality the order of the day, but a number of different rhythms occur within a module. A new rhythmical structure has been created, as yet unheard of in Brazilian popular music.

Many songs employ snippets from comic strips, radio programs, newspapers and even classical music. 'Clara Crocodile' takes passages from Stockhausen's *Gesang der Jünglinge* and Schumann's *Florestan*.

At present, Arrigo Barnabé is, without a doubt, the most ambitious progressive musician active in MPB. In addition to prizes already mentioned in this chapter, he won two others in 1981, including the TV Globo Festival prize for best arrangement (for his song 'Londrina').

One of the most highly acclaimed Brazilian films, recipient of many prizes, is titled *Cidade Oculta*. It was a collaboration of the director Chico Botelho, the author Walter Rogério and the musician Arrigo Barnabé. *Cidade Oculta* is set in the sub-milieu of a large Brazilian city. Musicians, prostitutes, punks, street gangs and corrupt police figure in this story of a love affair, of dreams and reality, of coming-of-age and its obstacles. The movement of Rock Brasil accompanied this film in the same way that the 1984 film *Bete Balanço* by Lael Rodriguez was accompanied by

the music of Barão Vermelho. *Cidade Oculta* was Arrigo Barnabé's fifth
film score.

Instrumental Groups

Jazz and pop instrumental groups rarely remain long on the scene. No
musician can earn a living solely by playing in a single band. Within
Rock Brasil the conditions may be more favorable, for the time being,
but the commercial difficulties, especially for progressive, avant-garde
groups are so immense that it is nothing rare for a band to form for a
single recording session and then, through lack of public response, to
dissolve and try again with a new combination. Only the big names of
progressive instrumental music, for example, Hermeto Pascoal, Egberto Gismonti and Wagner Tiso, can survive with a regular group.
Most musicians, however, are dependent upon work in the backup
orchestras of MPB artists. There the opportunities for work and gaining
experience are excellent. Milton Nascimento and Edu Lobo are but two
who started in this way.

Azymuth was formed in 1971 with Alex Malheiros, Ivan Conte and
José Roberto Bertrami (in 1976 with Flora Purim and Airto who left in
1989). Its success has been greater abroad than in Brazil itself. Uakti,
from Minas Gerais, (Bento Meneses, Marco Antonio Guimarães, Décio
and Paulo) on the other hand has a hard time of it even in Brazil. The
musicians work with a battery of different, large panpipe-like plastic
tubes covered on their top sides with skin. They also play flutes,
marimba, guitar and percussion. Uakti's sound calls forth associations
with the music of tribal people from the Amazonian selva or the Balinese
gamelan orchestra. Bass and percussion are paired in the duo Jorge
Degas/Mercelo Salazar. Degas also works frequently in Berlin as a
bassist on studio sessions for various jazz musicians. Uakti have accompanied many of Milton Nascimento's productions and in 1987 Paul
Simon traveled to Brazil to discuss recording together. In the same year,
Uakti even played with a group of flamenco artists in Spain.

Many MPB artists claim to use the voice as an instrument. Very few
actually do so with any measure of consistency and without compromise. Eliete Negreiros, who works closely with Arrigo and Paulo Barnabé,
does, as does her colleague Tete Espindola from Tão Grosso. Tete
entitled her first album 'Birds in My Throat', and on it she performs a
lively mixture, ranging from traditional samba to folkloric song verse to

avant-garde operatic arias. Her motto goes, 'Freedom, as the birds know it, is like a light that cannot be rationally explained. But when I sing I feel this sensation, this light.'

Chapter 9

Brazilian Show Business

The possibilities for growth in the Brazilian music industry are set certain limits by the geographic, social, economic and political situation in the country.

— Brazil comprises almost half the entire South American continent. (With 3.3 million square miles it is nearly as big as the United States.) The South is densely populated, whereas the Amazon area is practically unsettled. Over half the population resides in cities, the rest in the thinly settled hinterland. The music industry's potential market includes, then, both urban metropoles (sometimes with over a million inhabitants) and large, sparsely settled rural areas. It was inevitable that economic factors would induce the music industry to concentrate its efforts upon such urban centers.

— Over 80 per cent of Brazil's 130 million inhabitants are poor and propertyless. Fifteen per cent at most, that is, 16 million people, are potential record buyers and concert-goers. This figure applies to all of Brazil; it is even less when calculated only for the cities. The ability of the media (television, radio, film, the press) to reach different regions of the country is uneven at best.

— The country's economic problems, characterized by strong inflationary tendencies, place the music industry's commodities beyond the means of most Brazilians.

— Political problems complicate matters even more.

— These conditions produce a situation in which the free flow of information, a major necessity for true communication, becomes practically impossible. This oppressive reality leads many consumers to flee into a world of banality and illusion.

Some Aspects of the Music Industry

The Brazilian music industry has developed, parallel to that of other western countries, primarily over the last sixty years. The new media forms of our century — mechanical Edison phonograph recordings (later, records), introduced in 1902, and the first radio broadcasts — lent substantial impetus to this development.

The musical information flooding into Brazil in the wake of the new media has left its mark. Foreign markets, techniques and organisational forms have all had an impact upon the Brazilian music industry.

The foreign music industry has had far better success in establishing parent firms in Brazil than Brazilian firms have had abroad. As a result, foreign firms have acquired great power and influence over Brazil's popular music.

The bossa nova movement, as well as developments in other cultural spheres parallel to it, was instrumental in strengthening the position of the Brazilian music industry at home. This was due, on the one hand, to the suddenly awakened interest in the bossa nova by the international public. This, in turn, gave a tremendous lift to the self-confidence of everyone involved in the business. On the other hand, the bossa nova's demise encouraged increased foreign intervention in the Brazilian market, which produced an answer in the form of the protest song and the tropicalism movement.

'Records are Culture'

According to statistics released by the national association for the German phonograph industry, by the end of the 1970s, 2.5 per cent of all records produced in the western world were sold in Brazil. By 1986 Brazil had increased to have the seventh highest sales figure for recordings — of all the countries in the world — 67.5 million, and of those, 70 per cent were produced in Brazil. And that was supposed to have been a bad year. President Sarney's freeze on Brazilian prices led to a buying frenzy that increased record industry sales figures in 1987 by

30 per cent, until a new 90-day price freeze put an abrupt stop to the increase.

In 1990 the restrictive economic policy of the new President Collor plunged the Brazilian music industry into a cash crisis. Production schedules were restricted and new releases were held to a minimum. Groups willing to record inexpensive cover versions of original songs did a brisk business. Also *música sertaneja* increased its sales.

If one considers that at least 40 per cent of all Brazilians receive a minimum monthly wage of about $27 US and that even this lost 30 per cent of its purchasing power in the same period, with inflation at over 300 per cent, then it becames clear that the Brazilian record market exists between huge extremes and that it fails to reach a large portion of the population. The first CD factory came to Brazil in 1984. Only 100,000 Brazilians, less than 0.1 per cent, owned a CD player in 1988.

Multinational firms control the largest share of the market. The market leaders are Polygram, EMI Odeon, BMG Ariola Brasil, WEA and CBS. National companies, such as Sigla, Som Livre and RGE concentrate on TV-merchandised compilations, soundtrack LPs and samba artists (especially those who perform the *pagode*, which is a form of samba popular in Rio).

Exclusively Brazilian firms like Disco Continental, RGE, and SOM (Copacabana) cater chiefly to the market for música caipira and música sertaneja, although they often act as scouts for new talent until the offers of the multis lure the artists away. In the independent scene, labels such as SDG (Som da Gente in São Paulo), Kuarup, Lira Paulistana, and Eldorado, among others, appear to have discovered in the early eighties a market need for productions of high artistic merit. VISOM in Rio was the first label to produce instrumental music digitally and release it on CD. Beside the multinationals, it has been the independents who have, in the late eighties, been able to gain a tentative foothold in the international market, while the large Brazilian firms have been unable to arouse international interest in their catalogues.

I am uninformed as to the ownership of the record company belonging to the Globo media concern, Som Livre and Sigla where United States participation is surmised. In 1987 Globo opened an American sister company to better serve the growing Latin market in North America.

It should be noted here that the North American term 'latin music' includes Brazil only tangentially, at least with respect to the music industry. Above all, the North Americans use 'latin music' to refer to the 'needs' of Caribbean and Central American immigrants.

Because the subsidiaries of the multinationals automatically have the opportunity to release the parent companies' recordings, the Brazilian firms have difficulty surviving without international pop stars. The subsidiaries, on the other had, are naturally limited to marketing the products of their parents in Brazil.

Nevertheless, the variety, quality and sales potential of the home scene lead all Brazilian record companies to court it intensively. When André Midani, undisputed principal of the Brazilian recording branch, left Phonogram in 1976 after having built it into a prosperous undertaking, and decided to take on the challenge of establishing a subsidiary for WEA Warner Brothers in Brazil, rumors were widespread that he might take along all the big names he had created. But nobody thought of the inevitable: WEA's American catalog was given top priority. Even in the first national catalog, which Midani brought out in 1977, two national LPs (by Tom Jobim and João Gilberto) were produced in American studios.

Years later the newly founded Ariola outdid all previous practices by offering tremendous recruitment payments. The worldwide slump that hit the recording industry reached Brazil at the beginning of the eighties. Ariola, a Bertelsmann firm in Brazil, was subsumed into the Polygram catalog, becoming the Barclay label. WEA, with its continual bad luck in Brazil, handed over its distribution department to EMI-Odeon. RCA swallowed Motown and was soon subsumed by the German media giant Bertelsman into BMG Ariola Brasil, which in its turn left Polygram. Discos Continental purchased TAPE-CAR, and Top Tape gave up. Globo bought RGE. In personal terms this meant, for example, that Chico Buarque changed once to Ariola (with a high salary offer) but finally landed again with Polygram, which had to pay these high premiums: *A voz do Dono é o Dono da voz* ('The voice of the Master is the Master of the voice.' — Chico Buarque).

A governmental decree stipulates that at least 50 per cent of the entire recorded repertoire must be of Brazilian national origin and character, and records are often released for regional sale at different times. No studies have been conducted to find out why more national products are sold on the average in São Paulo than in Rio. One guess would be that in São Paulo, with its large numbers of Japanese and Italians on the one hand, and a large industrial proletariat on the other, 'exotic' music takes precedence in the one group, 'national' music in the other. In Rio the middle-class cariocas might feel more attracted to an international sound since they have 'national' music in their own backyard.

There are also products released solely in Rio or solely in São Paulo.

Sales lists and similar charts released in other countries must, of course, be taken with caution. Dealer sales figures can be easily manipulated by figuring in unsold consignment stock and other tricks. Reliable figures are not available. Even radio and television stations rely upon such professional lists, dealer polls or listener magazines for their hit parades.

Since many broadcasting stations are in private hands and, moreover, are often operated as part of a single concern, along with a recording company and publishing house, manipulation and swindles run rampant.

I always used to wonder why young people preferred to purchase imported records, even when the same record was released on a Brazilian label. The reason is actually quite simple. Records manufactured in Brazil are of inferior quality, so that consumers with high-quality record players choose their albums accordingly. But Brazilian record producers cannot be blamed. The record-cutting machines, presses, studios and electronic equipment they require all stand on the list of goods hit by exorbitant tariffs. Dilapidated equipment, a lack of spare parts and a lack of capital hardly facilitate the manufacture of high-class products, despite the introduction of home-produced CDs for those who can afford the equipment to play them on.

These products are expensive for Brazilians. A Brazilian *salário minimo* would be enough to buy around twenty LPs in the United States; in Brazil, only ten. Record prices vary in different parts of the country.

H. Alvarenga

Minimum Wage

(Salário Minimo)

I'm exhausted from all the work
Living with the illusion that things will get better
Five children, a wife and mother-in-law to feed
750 cruzeiros, that's not enough
That's not enough, that's not enough, no, that's not enough.
Because of them I'm overworked
They run around dressed like Adam and Eve
They've gotten used to living poorly
But that's not good at all
This life which we lead.

Production costs are especially high in Brazil because the musicians take up the studios with rehearsals and recording sessions for months on end. And the fees that have to be paid for backup orchestras and guest performers (*convidados*) really hit hard.

Best-selling albums are almost always compilation albums (*The Best of ...*) or music tracks from so-called *tele-novelas*, closely followed by the newest productions from national singers of different stripes (from the sambista Agepé to progressive Milton Nascimento), and, of course, licensed editions of international products. Brazil's number-one bestselling records, however, belongs neither to MPB nor the international market. It is TV-Globo's Xuxa, presenter of the popular daily television show for children. Albums are frequently released later in Brazil than in other countries. In fact, they often reach the charts abroad long before the Brazilian recording companies get a clearance from customs for the master tapes.

Of late, a number of companies have become active in compiling anthologies. They have combed through their archives in order to present much valuable historical, documentary or purely musical material, often accompanied by outstanding explanatory notes. Several of these anthologies are products of partnerships with the Ministry of Education and Culture and FUNARTE, the state cultural organization.

A magazine publisher even took part. At weekly intervals *Editora Abril* distributed MPB anthologies in the seventies to numerous newspaper kiosks around the country. Each release was devoted to a single composer or singer and was furnished with excellent liner notes and texts.

Marcus Perreira from São Paulo was a pioneer in his field. Through his own small record label of the same name, he attempted to recapture and popularize authentic Brazilian folklore. His documentary series with music from Brazil's north, south and east — for which such luminaries as Nara Leão, the Quinteto Violado, Elis Regina and Carmen Costa offered their services, side by side with original recordings — is unprecedented among anthologies. Perreira's courageous releases of forgotten choro musicians and sambistas did not earn him enormous profits, but they accomplished something more important. They brought talented artists back into the public eye, helping them to a new start. A recent example of such a 'rediscovery' was Cartola, who was to make an important contribution to the samba canção and to MPB more generally.

Marcus Perreira was also one of the very few Brazilian producers represented each year at Midem in Cannes, although without success.

The policy employed by European record companies concentrates on introducing from Brazil solely the so-called compilation LPs having twelve or twenty-four popular titles. Imports are also negligible.

The situation is more favorable in France, Italy and Portugal. There, people's mentalities show greater affinities to Brazilian music, and

270 -- Música Brasileira

language barriers present less of a problem. For these reasons Brazilian artists can be found more frequently on tour in these southern European countries, and, accordingly, more original records are offered on the market also.

Finally, two concluding observations about the record business: *First*: Paulinho da Viola once said, 'Write a samba and someone will market it.' In fact, the record business was largely transformed into an industrial samba factory. The major part of the total offerings found in stores consisted of samba records by the most varied of performers. Singers popped up almost daily out of the inexhaustible reservoir provided by the samba schools. They would write a hit and then be 'industrially' processed further. The quality of text and music became a secondary consideration. Unfortunately, the stranglehold that the samba had on the music industry limited the capacity of producers to venture into other musical forms, such as instrumental music or progressive. At the same time, high record prices placed a limit on the customer's options. *Second*: Times have changed. Singers of international rock and Brazilian *iêiêiê* have a considerable share of the market. The companies do not make their biggest money with the samba anymore: foreign rock and pop, together with Rock Brasil now earn more. Many Brazilian composers and singers have even begun using English pseudonyms and sing in English.

Media Connections

The media in Brazil are overwhelmingly in private hands and controlled by giant companies.

There is also state radio and television programming, and they are, as one might expect, less attractive than privately owned broadcasting spiced up by advertising money.

The electronic media exert an enormous influence upon Brazilian show business. In a country with high illiteracy rates and poverty, television and radio especially are the chief vehicles for communicating cultural, political and commercial information. Moreover, the media serve as a substitute for theater, concerts and other cultural institutions (especially outside the urban centers, but also in the cities themselves) for which ticket prices are unaffordable for all but the privileged few. TV Globo, with its twenty-two stations and 25 million viewers, broadcasts (as do other stations) three or more soap operas (*tele-novelas*) daily. The music industry has its part to play here too. Each actor has his own melody played when he makes his appearance on stage. These melodies, as well as the soap opera's title theme are relased on an LP and sell like hotcakes at the top of the best-selling list. Sales of 600,000 to 1 million copies is average. TV Globo presents an especially interesting case. In addition to its television stations, the Globo empire owns a large daily newspaper, a radio station, a recording company, a music publishing house and a sound studio. In other words, the production of a tele-novela runs something like this: a composer from the TV Globo publishing house writes the music; the recording company releases it; the publicity office beats its own drum; and the radio station airs the record. In this way Brazil has joined the international scene. And as if that were not enough, an international edition with licensed pro-ductions is often made parallel to the sound track in order to make the most out of a novela's popularity. In 1983 the media giant Bloch founded a television station with grand designs (Rede Manchete) called *TV do ano 2000*. Right away, in its first months, it dedicated a series ('Bar Academia') to the leading singers and composers in MPB. For some years now MTV has also been showing its music videos in Brazil.

The media know full well how to use MPB to their advantage by broadcasting countless music shows or recorded tapes with Brazilian (and international) music. There are about forty-two AM radio stations in Brazil that broadcast music. The infamous Brazilian *jeitinho* ('in-fluence') is customary in the media world; payola paid to disc jockeys is called *jabaculê*. A scandal in 1981 brought this practice to the public's attention.

A law requires broadcasting stations to present a 50–50 ratio of national to international products. Most stations get around this by transmitting their national quota at the worst times of the day, leaving prime time free for foreign hits.

How can we account for the popularity gained through the media? The portable radio (*radio pilha*) has its part to play. The lower classes in particular listen to them day-in and day-out. Their programs accom-pany the housemaid doing her chores from morning until night, offering her an illusionary escape from a very harsh reality. Since programs and songs are repeated a number of times each day on the radio, melodies and text are easily memorized. People enjoy singing along. This is one reason why purely instrumental pieces seldom appear on the market. Melodies without lyrics are hard to remember. Radio pilhas prepare concertgoers too. It becomes easy to sing along to the best-known songs.

Television played an important role in the pop music festivals that arose at the end of the bossa nova era (TV Excelsior, TV Record, etc.). TV Globo began staging festivals once again at the end of the eighties.

José Itamar de Freitas developed a new form of Television entertainment in his popular weekly program *Fantástico*, sponsored by TV Globo. The show is a clever mixture of reports, features and news on a variety of subjects (including politics and economics) as well as music (both pop hits as well as quality stuff). What was true for the recording industry applies to the media as well. Commercial products (which also function as advertisements for the media) are combined with a cultivation of the MPB's noncommercial varieties.

The commercial character of the private stations enables them to pay very high salaries to singers (only to the most prominent, naturally). This ends up spoiling the artists, who are then shocked at the lower offers European stations (mostly government-owned) make to them.

A career in music is impossible in Brazil without the media. High prices mean that nobody becomes famous by selling records alone.

Newspapers and magazines devote much more space to the music scene than is the case, for example, in Europe. Educated, knowledgeable journalists such as Ana Maria Bahiana, Sergio Motta, Tarik de Souza and Ari Vasconsellos have their own regular columns in all daily newspapers. Here they report in detail and, one might say, lovingly on all aspects of the MPB. Their columns serve as an important source of advertising for the city concert scene.

The state television station TVE has done an excellent job of putting together an authentic documentation of MPB, concentrating on historical, regional and musical themes.

On the other hand, the state did exert a negative influence over the media. In addition to its former censoring practices, it had also moved to cancel programs (as it did with a performance of the Bolshoi Ballet) and suspend journalists.

Confusion over Copyright

Composers in Brazil generally consider their country's copyright laws to be a pro-forma regulation. For a long time there were seven licensing companies, while other countries usually had only one. In concrete terms this meant that a composer from one licensing company and a songwriter from another were not allowed to work together. Should they risk it, then they could not be sure of getting their percentage.

Paulo Cesar Pinheiro, poet and lyricist of many Baden Powell hits, said, 'In the United States I get at least 86 per cent of the royalties, in Brazil only 8 per cent.'

Where the rest of the money went to was not always clear. One thing was certain, however: the authors were unhappy. The government responded by merging the seven corporations into a single national entity. But not all authors trusted the new Escritorio Central de Arrecadação e Distribuição (ECAD), a kind of collection agency under the auspices of the Conselho Nacional do Direito Autoral (CNDA). So in 1975 a number of them founded Sombras (Sociedade Musical Brasileira). A spokesman explained (in *Veja*, May 11, 1977) that the new organ was necessary since the representatives of the older corporations were once again present in ECAD. They could not be trusted then, so why should they be trusted now? The new Sombras works in two groups. One attended to organizing its own shows (directed by Aldir Blanc), the other to the copyrights (Vitor Martins). Soon afterwards SICAM (Sociedade Independente de Compositores & Autores Musicais) and ASSIM (Associão de Intérpretes & Músicos) were founded.

Artists even demanded initially that the performance fees for concerts and shows be paid in advance. They finally settled with SERPRO (a state agency for data processing) for a commitment on the part of the concert producers to subsequently pay the 10 per cent royalties on all ticket proceeds. The old corporations still exist in part. The governmental supervisory board reduced their commissions from 50 per cent to a maximum 5 per cent of their members' revenues. When one of the country's most powerful corporations SBACEM, thereupon closed its offices in a number of cities and discharged twenty-two employees, it nevertheless continued to pay its directors their previous salaries, citing 'tradition and representational reasons'.

Bad experiences with copyright laws began for authors as American firms began to market the bossa nova. A contract did not always mean payment. So many a composer began demanding large advance sums from the publishing houses. This practice is common in the recording business, too, where singers are advanced large license payments. In both cases, however, singers and authors are dependent on the company for the advance. They have to hand over what the recording company or publishing house demands from them.

6:30 and 22

A concert style was established in Rio in 1976 that could serve as an example for other countries. The concerts, called *seis e meia* ('6:30'), are given each evening at 6:30 to accommodate the general public, which is just finishing work. A balanced program offered at affordable prices means there is something for everyone of all ages, tastes and income brackets. Paulo Albinho Pinheiro and Hermino de Bello Carvalho initiated the concert series at the Teatro João Caetano, also taken up later by the Museu de Arte Moderna.

The concert scenes in Rio and São Paulo differ from those in Europe in that so-called *temporadas* predominate; individual concerts have only taken place more frequently in the past few years. The term 'concert' does not apply anyway, since Brazilians call it *show*. 'Concerts' are *concertos* meaning classical music. Aloysio de Oliveira began his elaborate bossa nova shows in 1964. His artful use of lights, literary themes and stage sets helped to refine the genre immensely. This might be the reason that non-Brazilians have so many difficulties following and understanding these shows. A program consisting of one number after another on a bare stage, as so often occurs in Europe, is a rarity in Brazil. Audiences expect more than just the singing or playing of a piece. And after Elis Regina demonstrated that gesture, mimic, dance and other elements also belong to song, these shows have gotten even better.

Album sales as high as 600,000 per release are no guarantee of successful concerts. In 1975, at one of Martinho da Vila's temporadas on a Wednesday, I counted only about fifty in the audience, even though Martinho's records often reach the top of the charts.

But even with poor attendance, concert promoters are sometimes able to meet their costs since there are enough sponsors (i.e. advertising allowances) to go around, and since the costs of renting a hall and paying for advertising are manageable.

Outdoor poster advertising is unknown in Brazil. While single posters are hung up in record stores, the most important advertising is done through the newspapers (articles, announcements) and on television or radio (so-called *chamadas*, 'jingles').

The job of the concert promoter in Brazil is a nerve-racking one. Hours are spent each day in taxis in traffic-jammed streets, visiting the authorities, applying for copyrights, attending to media advertisements, organizing rehearsals, establishing contacts and more contacts ... It can happen that a program gets canceled shortly before showtime if the authorities are dissatisfied, or when they claim that the application forms were handed in late.

The Brazilian government has also taken an increasingly active role in putting on concerts. Acting through such agencies as FUNARTE and the National Institute of Music, it has especially committed itself to regions in which little or no previous concert activity had occurred.

Chapter 10

The State and Music

During the colonial period the authorities in Brazil officially recognized only that music which Iberian immigrants brought with them to the 'new world', that is, court and Church music. Independent 'Brazilian' developments that arose out of the interaction between different slave cultures and the free lower classes were regarded as a threat to the Portuguese crown, and were thus more likely to be suppressed than promoted. Only the planter and farming classes were relatively open toward accepting original African and Indian music and their mixed forms. Slave owners and the Church were also occasional benefactors. In 1807 the Portuguese court was forced to flee to its Brazilian colony. With the proclamation of a united kingdom in 1815 and a declaration of independence in 1822, literature, art and music profited greatly from the bohemian tendencies espoused by the new king. He encouraged the building of opera houses and theaters as well as the development of music, including such original folk music forms as the modinha and lundu. The musical life of the nation became even more open and vital with the proclamation of the republic in 1889, as many musically talented slaves left the coastal regions and headed for the cities. Here they contributed to the rapid development of urban folklore.

Various presidents succeeded the authoritarian regime headed by Getúlio Vargas (1930–54). Each was so busy coping with the political and economic plight of the country that active cultural work, especially in the spheres of popular music and folklore, could not be undertaken. The military regime which came to power in 1964 by way of a revolution was also the first to exert an influence over popular music. Before then, President Juscelino Kubitschek de Oliveira (1956–61) had already made a fundamental contribution to contemporary Brazilian architecture with the construction of Brasilia. The birth of the bossa nova and cinema novo also occurred during his term in office.

The new Brazilian constitution enacted in 1967 called for the setting up of a presidential democracy. A federal republic would comprise twenty-two states, a federal district (Brasilia), and four federal territories. The constitution, however, was annulled in 1968 through an ordinance (Institutional Ordinance Number V) that granted the president wide-ranging powers at the expense of parliament.

The relation between the state and music can be treated from many perspectives. Here I will emphasize two spheres that touch upon the world of popular music: the state's cultivation of popular music, and its control through censorship.

Cultivation of Music

I have already spoken in some detail about the role of the state within the music industry. In the summer of 1976 President Ernesto Geisel founded an important new organization to foster the arts and cultural life of the country. The Fundação Nacional de Arte, or FUNARTE as it is better known, had as one of its constituent organizations the National Institute of Music (INM, Instituto Nacional de Música), directed initially by the internationally acclaimed composer Marlos Nobre.* In April 1977, some months after the launch of FURNATE, I had the opportunity to conduct a lengthy interview with him, excerpts of which follow:

> *Author*: What is FUNARTE, what difficulties and tasks does it face, and how should they be solved?
>
> *Marlos Nobre:* FUNARTE was founded almost a year ago. Things began here in Rio in July 1976. It's a rather young institution founded as a follow-up to an earlier project intent on revitalizing art in Brazil. It was called 'Program for Artistic Action'. It was a program of revitalization which, we could say, attempted to survey the nature of the problem in Brazil. But it wasn't actually

---

*Marlos Nobre was dismissed from his post in 1979 as he was traveling abroad. He found out about his dismissal from the newspapers.

what we needed in the artistic sphere, and that is systematic, long-term work. Once FUNARTE had been established, a new organ arose by its side — the National Institute of Music. Here, for the first time, our music finally had a niche where it could withdraw and defend itself, a place where Brazilian musicians could come with their fears and problems, and where these could be examined and where solutions could be sought. We who have been seriously involved with Brazilian music, both classical and folk music, are well aware of a basic problem. The problem rests in our improvisational skills and creativity, which have been so admired and praised in the past, and in our ability to solve difficult problems at the last instant. This is, in reality, the famous Brazilian *jeitinho*. We create when we have to solve a particular problem, while the Europeans need a system to tackle the same thing. We have the ability to improvise solutions. I find that good. At the same time, we are aware that this is an emergency situation. A country like Brazil, which in cultural terms has become so important, cannot move forward as it should if it is not able to combine this ability with another dynamic — that of organization. I've always put it this way.

If we can manage to organize our creative spontaneity, then we will have made a concrete step toward revitalizing our cultural life in Brazil. At such a moment Brazil's culture has to energize the people's consciousness and lead them along a path toward an improved quality of life. I feel that this is a basic necessity for a culture; and this at a time when Brazil is attempting to fully exploit its economic opportunities, but also when major social problems are unfolding in the country. In practice, this is all very difficult for a European who has never lived here to understand. The government has attempted, for better or for worse, to solve these social problems; problems ultimately arising out of the great chasm existing between classes in Brazilian society. It has tried to initiate processes of social transformation by levying income taxes, land reform and a host of other projects. I would say that none of these projects can really be of any value until a cultural process begins to develop parallel to them, a cultural formation of popular consciousness. This is the major task for Latin American artists. The raising of consciousness. When the government approaches me at such a moment, if it approaches me as an artist, it does not automatically necessitate political compromise. I am an artistic creator working within the realm of what's possible for the general good, for culture. Not for an imposed culture, but for a culture advancing from the bottom to the top, and never from the top downward. When the government calls on me at such a time, I cannot say no. I accept such work under one condition, and that is that culture may not be imposed upon us. Instead, it must reflect the needs of the people. In this respect música popular has an important role to play. The people use música popular to express themselves. They literally announce their presence in the truest sense of the word. And when we support these activities of the people, then we have come closer to the roots of the problem that I just mentioned.

Author: Many people say they observe a developing chauvinism within Brazilian music. Is this true?

Marlos Nobre: That's ridiculous. Especially for a composer like myself who has not only national, but also international training. I believe in the interrelationship between cultures, from which each culture can only enrich itself. I have often maintained that culture is one thing, industry is something else. Of course, there exists an important culture industry. And we aren't naive. We know very well that folk art can't remain untouched by commercial and industrial influences. And that's not our goal, not at all. But there is a danger for all of Latin America, and for Brazil, too. The influence exerted by big industry, and especially by North American industry, represents a danger for the activities of the people. North American investments have tended to overwhelm us. So we have a situation in the recording industry, indeed, in the whole music industry, where 'foreign' is chiefly 'North American'.

It's also important to mention that we don't know European popular music at all. It never reaches us. It is an industrial product. As a vehicle for communication it is, to a certain extent, kept under control. And it is, to a certain extent, marketed with industrial support. This fundamentally limits an industrial musical product.

Nobre and his staff of fifteen were allotted about ten million cruzeiros (about $1 million) per year. Nobre had committed himself to a three-year stint at FUNARTE, during which time he intended to interrupt his compositional activities and devote himself entirely to the National Institute of Music. After that, another director would continue the work. Some of the chief duties of the post were promoting classical and folk music, staging concerts for youth, helping composers in their careers by commissioning compositions, founding a national music fund, releasing records and publications.

Concrete results have already been achieved. Working together with recording companies and the Ministry for Education, the National Institute of Music released a number of anthologies of recorded music (Pixinguinha, Lamartine Bobo, Almirante, etc.). In conjunction with a conference of MPB researchers (Encontro de Pesquisadores da MPB) choro concerts were held, lectures were given, and documentary films were shown. Each year the National Institute of Music stages instrumental concerts of classical and popular music throughout the country. They lay their main emphasis upon reaching rural regions that until now have lacked any cultural work. Projeito Pixinguinha, modeled after the *Seis e meia* concerts in Rio, has been running in Brazil's urban centers. Twelve artists performing twenty-five concerts per week in these cities over a period of ten weeks could reach about 600,000 people. Inexpensive ticket prices (ten cruzeiros, or about eighty cents) make the program even more attractive.

It remains to be seen whether FUNARTE's efforts to make the Brazilian public conscious of the quality and richness of its own folklore will be successful. Can it achieve results that raise popular consciousness and taste when confronted with the challenge presented by foreign imports? And can they achieve this without introducing protectionist measures? For, in the final analysis, import and export limits do more harm than good.

Censorship

On July 4, 1977, the censorship authorities canceled a concert by Chico Buarque, Milton Nascimento, Edu Lobo and others only hours before the scheduled start. Four thousand people were sent back home. Supposedly the concert program had not been handed in to the censorship board fourty-eight hours before, as required, and there were no censors available to make a visual check. After the passing of Institutional Ordinance number V in 1968, the censors clamped down hard. All publications, radio, television, films and music intended for performance required the prior issuance of a permit. With MPB this applied to all record releases, concerts, shows and publications.

Among the artists most plagued by the censors were Chico Buarque, Milton Nascimento ('Hoje o Dia de Reis' and other works), João Bosco and Aldir, Gilberto Gil and Zé Rodrix.

The formal musical freedom that Gil and Caetano had developed at the end of the sixties was restricted at the same time by thematic chains.

After that, thousands of song lyrics were censored or completely prohibited.

Even album covers were censored. (Caetano Veloso, for example, was not allowed to appear nude on the cover of his 'Joia' album with his wife and son.)

Chico Buarque is one of those authors whose songs suffered most under the censor's merciless pen for many years. His musical *Calabar* was not allowed to go on stage at all, plunging Chico himself into great financial distress. An album that should have been released as 'Chico Canta Calabar' came out mutilated as 'Chico Canta'. The cover, too, was censored, appearing in printless white. A list of Chico's censored songs, as well as those of many others, could go on for many pages.

Like Caetano Veloso, Gilberto Gil and other MPB artists, Chico tried years ago to escape the situation with a self-imposed exile in Italy. But like most of his colleagues, he returned to his native land.

In an interview given to the Brazilian weekly *Veja* in October 1976 Chico Buarque offered his thoughts on the question of censorship. Some excerpts follow:

'Censorship has to stop and never return. It mutilates what's characteristic of an epoch. These young people who are just beginning to play music, when all their first attempts — and there are certainly many, and many which we don't even know about — are banned, that produces in them a monstrous self-censorship. That's disastrous for all types of creative activity. Today we see a generation born in an age of censorship, for whom the censor's stamp is as familiar as their passport. For me, for a generation raised practically without censorship, it's shocking to have to hand your lyrics over to some official — and sometimes very personal lyrics, since all creativity is a kind of personal statement— who then examines them and decides whether or not they are fit to be published. For someone growing up today, everything is different. That's why so many people have turned to writing their lyrics in English. They get through easier. Today's young writer sees that he's been censored and thinks to himself, "Next time I'll make sure I do it right." He thinks that he has done something completely wrong.'

In another part of the interview Chico countered the misconception that frequent prohibitions increased record sales due to an added attractiveness the record might take on. The opposite was true, he said. Delays arising from the censorship board and outright bans only served to disconcert the record companies, resulting in a more expensive product and falling sales. Still, the censorship board's sudden about-face in allowing the release of Chico's song 'Calice' in 1979 helped it gain lots of radio play time.

Chico Buarque de Hollanda

In Spite of You
(Apesar de Você)

Tomorrow will be a new day

I
Today you're the one who gives the orders
You speak. Not another word!
No discussion, no!
My people
Are cautious with their words today
Their heads are hung low.
You see
You created this situation
You created it,
All this darkness
You created the sin
But forgot to create
Forgiveness
In spite of you
Tomorrow has to be a new day.

II
I'm asking you
Where will you hide
From the enormous euphoria?
How will you try to forbid it
When the rooster insists
Upon crowing.
New life is brewing
And we will be loving each other
Without stopping.
When that moment arrives
I will demand for my suffering
Interest and compound interest.
I swear to you!
So much repressed love
This samba echoing in the darkness.
You created sadness
Now,
Be so kind
And get rid of it
You are going to pay, and double,
For every tear I have shed

In my life.
In spite of you
Tomorrow has to be a new day.

III
I would pay any price
To see a garden in bloom
Which you couldn't bear seeing.
You will have to accept the fact
That one day the dawn will break
Without first having asked your permission.
I'll die laughing.
Because that day will come
Sooner than you think
In spite of you.

IV
You will have to see the day dawning
Ushered in by verses of poetry.
How will you be able to explain
The sky clearing
All at once and without punishment?
How will you strangle our people
When they sing
In front of you
In spite of you...
You're going to have a hard time of it,
etc.

Chico Buarque, like so many others, attempted to get his message across by hiding it between the lines. 'A square sun', for example, stands for prison and bondage.

Luiz Gonzaga Jr., son of the famous King of Baião, had great difficulties with the censors, too. In live performances he frequently departed from the edited version handed him and discussed it freely with his audience. I conducted an interview with him in October 1976:

> *Luiz Gonzaga Jr.:* The censors are always calling me. Everywhere I go they call me. They want to clarify things for me, or explain things, or just to talk with me.

> *Author:* What kinds of problems do you have with the censors?

> *L. G. Jr.:* I see it this way. I speak the truth that I am able to speak. The truth is mine, yours and ours. Truth hurts. A truth is the

truth. Another truth is not the truth. I don't know, but that's how I think. But with things like this which you have to live with in a country of the absurd, then you can only say, 'A problem is not a problem.' That's the basis. I must have about fifty or fifty-two compositions already banned. Chico Buarque has more. Sergio Ricardo, and several people here. For example, I am not allowed to appear on educational television in Rio. That's forbidden. I am not allowed to give shows in some parts of São Paulo. Forbidden. All these things are crazy. I am not preaching revolution; that's not my thing. It's something completely different to make a revolution. Still, I can't overlook the social problems. That's not my view alone, but of everybody who has a conscience and is alert.

Luiz Gonzaga Jr.

A Thrush Spoke of It

(O sabiá contou ...)

Look, my love
A thrush spoke of it
The blind saw it
The dumb repeated it
The deaf heard it
Only you have felt nothing
We live for love
We die for love
We kill for love
We exist for love
I sing for love
I cry, suffer and dance
I sweat but do not tire
It alleviates my pain
Because of love I follow
What I believe in
I do not negate myself and I say
This is the way I am
I go for love.

The truth is mine
The truth is yours
The truth is ours
Who does it belong to?
The truth is good
The truth hurts
It destroys and it builds

The truth is truth
The truth is valuable
Nowadays I ask
How much did the king pay
In order to possess her?
Lying aquarelles

Freedom is life
Freedom is death
Freedom is good fortune
Freedom is everything
Freedom is a thing
Good and inexpensive
Inexpensive things are rare
Rare things are expensive
What is expensive, my friend
Is never cheap
It is worth a great price
It is worth a typhoon
It is worth having in your hand.

In June 1977 *Veja* published another interview on the question of censorship in MPB, this time with Caetano Veloso. In it the co-founder of tropicalism talked about his exile in London and the events preceding it.

Veja: Do you think people who are working directly in politics are wasting their time?

Caetano: Society is an organization, and in it there is also politics. There's the city, the state and the country. There are people whose calling it is to direct it all, and to lead the discussion about the course of this organization. There are people who are very useful and suited to such a life. Somebody has to be a candidate for the presidency of the republic. Somebody has to fight for power.... There have been instances where the censors shortened parts of lyrics, or even entire texts. Although I'm not one of the composers most affected, I'll give you two illustrative examples relating to me. One is the song 'Negror dos Tempos' ('The Blackness of the Times') which I wrote for Maria Bethania's album 'Drama'. The censors weren't too happy about the line 'When I look at you with your cow eyes, you cow; with your big cow eyes, you big cow.' So they cut 'you cow' and 'you big cow,' which impaired the poetry of the song. We had to delete the line as we were mixing the recording, after it had already been completed. Another case was a frevo, one of the frevos I wrote for the carnival in Bahia, 'Deus e o Diabo' (God and the Devil). In this case I even drove all the way to Brasilia to speak with the director of the censorship board. I tried to explain why I wrote what I did. But, in the end, the piece was also shortened because of a line I sang at the end: 'Wonderful city, so full of magic, wonderful city, the pluck of my Brazil.' They deleted 'pluck' because they felt such a word didn't belong.*

Veja: Didn't all of this, your imprisonment as well as Gilberto Gil's in 1968, influence your work?

Caetano: We live through certain real experiences which offer us a new view of reality. I couldn't say I want to be like I was before my imprisonment. I just can't. I have been in prison. I was in England for two and a half years. When I returned, I was changed with new experiences and new musical tastes.

The Debate over Censorship

The number of prohibited plays reached four hundred in May 1975 when Plinio Marcos's play *Abajur Lilas* was struck down by the censor. As is so often the case, this intervention by the censors called forth the most varied responses. On the evening of May 15 all theater performances in São Paulo were quickly canceled as a sign of solidarity with Plinio Marcos. Instead, actors read a resolution reporting on their working conditions. When another play, *Roque Santeiro*, was banned, a group of twenty-three artists turned to President Ernesto Geisel with a manifesto of their own: 'The country lives caught in a deplorable contradiction. While society modernizes and is becoming de-nationalized, culture has become deformed and debased, thanks to an anachronistic, sacrosanct censorship.'

In a poll taken by the weekly magazine *Isto é*, (April 5, 1978), however, Brazilians gave answers to questions like these:

> *What do you think of the 1964 revolution?*
> In favor, 38 per cent were fully or in part; only 18 per cent were against (15 per cent were neutral, and 24 per cent had no opinion).
>
> *Are you for the abolishment of the censorship?* Only two per cent of those

---

* 'Pluck' has the double meaning of 'courage' and 'offal' — hence the censor's objection.

asked answered yes; nine per cent, on the other hand, were in favor of a reduction in living costs.

Seventeen per cent viewed the 1964 military coup as an act against communism.

A year later (March 21, 1979) *Veja* conducted a new poll as João Figueredo was entering office: 36 per cent expected the political situation to improve, as promised; 11 per cent expected it to get worse; 37 per cent thought no change would occur. In the same month Guilherme Figueredo, theater scholar and brother of the new president, spoke out in favor of an end to censorship.

Meanwhile the Geisel government was engaged in heated discussion of whether or not to centralize the decision-making authority over censorship. Until then decisions had been made at a regional level by local officials of the federal police. President Geisel had met with a group of artists and intellectuals and admitted that 'the problem of censorship must be solved' (from *Estado de São Paulo*, January 21, 1975). Talk began about the possibility of creating a federal censorship board (Conselho Superior da Censura), but meanwhile Brasilia continued its practice of confirming the censorship decisions made by regional boards. Rogério Nunes, then director of the censorship board in Brasilia, admitted (according to *Journal do Brasil* on March 14, 1976) that the number of censored music lyrics was extremely high, but that it would be impossible to determine the figure exactly, since the individual state departments of the federal police had jurisdiction over examining this form of artistic presentation. 'There are no tendencies toward loosening the censorship, but rather efforts to conduct the work in a critical and intelligent way,' said the director of this department of the federal police.

The same article continues: 'The "critical and intelligent" manner of censoring continues to threaten the creators of literary and artistic values, and widens the gulf between government and intellectuals. This serves to strengthen the tendency toward creating evasive art forms, since restrictive conditions prevent subject matter from treating the authors' and consumers' reality with the necessary thoroughness.'

The call for amnesty and the demand made upon President Figueredo to carry out his promise to pave the way back to democracy (*abertura*) resulted in a relaxation of censorship practices. Press censorship was officially abolished. MPB enjoyed greater freedoms, too, although it also became aware of its limits. The omnipotent censor's pen continued to make return visits in order to exercise its trade, often in an odd and inexplicable fashion.

Consequences

The consequences for the MPB have to be regarded from two vantage points. Chico Buarque had already addressed the first. Censorship restricts individual creativity and one's freedom to express an opinion. It represents a danger in that it forces the artist to conform, and thereby to lose his own personal style and character. Second, the large majority of the poor, the propertyless and the illiterate do not even participate in the public discussion of censorship. These social classes had no interest in intellectuals or critical lyrics since their sense of reality was undeveloped. So what are the consequences of censorship? On the one hand, many authors simply dispensed with critical lyrics altogether. As Gilberto Gil said, the consumers of his music came from strata of the population that knew about reality anyway, so it wasn't necessary to tell them about it again. On the other hand, there were a few authors (Chico, Gonzaga Jr.) who continued the struggle for freedom of expression in their lyrics. And finally, many simply escaped to a dream world of English lyrics and banal collections of words that they tried to pass off as poetry.

Gilberto Gil continued to show everybody that he was apolitical and uninformed. He told the local newspaper *Correio de Copacabana*:

> I come to Salvador, for example, to present Refavela with new musicians, new work and new musical forms. Then three reporters from Salvador's biggest newspapers came to me and began asking questions about politics. What did I think of the student movement, about the divorce law, the quarrel between MDB and ARENA, the withdrawal of Tito's mandate, Institutional Ordinance Number V, or President Geisel? Nobody is interested in knowing that I brought a new clarinet from the United States with me. It has a different sound. And a contrabass too. Or that Stevie Wonder sold 23 million records in the United States. That there are such things as punk, reggae and Black Rio, Cassiano, music from the interior, disco sound, or that João Gilberto has just released an extraordinary album in the United States. People ask me about economic statistics, who will be the next president, redemocratization, or whether the military will abdicate power to a civilian government.... How should I know? Personally, for instance, I find President Geisel a likable guy.

Gil's statements were the object of great controversy. People began wondering whether Gil had abandoned his critical view of the world once and for all.

Furthermore, a few months prior to this interview MPB musicians had a bitter pill to swallow as they found out that a well-known singer had been hired to gather information as a government spy in artists' circles. Colleagues and public distanced themselves from the singer, whose career suffered immeasurably for it.

Censorship also stood in blatant contradiction to the Brazilian folksinger tradition upon which the contemporary MPB was founded. For centuries repentistas have documented and commented upon their surroundings. Brazilian popular music itself is largely a product of the political, economic, social and cultural history of the country. Vinicius de Moraes: 'Samba has always been a music of protest for me, from its very beginnings until the present.'

In conclusion, let me quote some remarks by Chico Buarque: 'Art has to be left in peace. Only then can we begin to think about supporting and protecting it. First freedom, then protective laws and incentive clauses — the type of official support that really promotes the cause of the arts without suppressing it. So now is the time — it always was the time and always will be — for all to unite who are intent on defending Brazilian art in its indisputable power and force and in recognition of the necessity to be free to create.'

Chico Buarque de Hollanda / Francis Hime
My Dear Friend
(Meu Caro Amigo)

My dear friend, please forgive me
If I don't come to visit you
But since a messenger happened by
I'm sending you the latest news on this recording tape
People are playing football here
There's samba, choro and rock-'n'-roll
Sometimes it rains, sometimes the sun shines
But what I really wanted to tell you:
Things don't look good here
Quite bad, to get rid of this situation
And what we have to put up with on abuses and pig-headedness
We swallow it all, even without whiskey
Nobody can stop this march

My dear friend, I'm not trying to provoke you
I also don't want to rekindle your homesickness
But I can't keep myself from
Giving you the latest news
Here in this country people are playing football

There is samba, choro and rock-'n'-roll
There are days when it rains and others
When the sun shines
But what I really wanted to tell you:
Things don't look good here
You have to do somersaults
Just to earn your daily bread
And the irritations and filth you wallow in while doing it.
We've learned to smoke without cigarettes.
Nobody can stop this march

My dear friend, I even wanted to call you
But the telephone charges are no joking matter
I try my best to keep you abreast
About everything happening here.
People are playing football here
There's samba, choro and rock-'n'-roll
But what I really wanted to tell you:
Things don't look good here
Quite horrible, to have to swallow the whole business
And we do swallow it, every last crumb
And we make love without tenderness
Nobody can stop this march

My dear friend, I really wanted to write you
But the mailman has sand in his gears
If they'll let me, I'll tell you the latest news
In this recording
People are playing football in this country
There's samba, choro and rock-'n'-roll
There are days when it rains and days
When the sun shines
But what I really wanted to tell you:
Things don't look good here
Marieta sends you a kiss
A kiss for the family, for Cecilia and the children
Francis takes the opportunity to send his greetings too
To everyone
Adieu.

Glossary

Please note: Only idioms frequently referred to are listed here. No definitions are given for names if they are explained in the text, for which readers should consult the index.

Amerindian — used here in place of 'Indio'

auto — popular dramatic staging of religious themes

baile — dance, ball

balanço — swing rhythm

batucada — rhythm group/percussion play/festival

batuque — synonym for African dance

Bela Epoca — 1870–1920

bloco — social group/music, dance or parade group

BN — bossa nova

bossa nova — music genre beginning in 1956

caboclo — mulatto from northeast Brazil

canção — successor of the modinha, song type

cancioneiro — folksinger

cantador — travelling folksinger (with double-stringed guitar or viola)

canto — song

carioca — citizen of Rio

choro — urban, mostly instrumental musical form originating in 1870

chorão — musicians of the choro

Cidade Nova — poor & working-class neighborhood in Rio

conjunto — musical group

cordão — 'band', similar to bloco

dança — dança dramatica — ritual, religious, collective dance

desafio — competition (also embolada)

desfile — parade, presentation at carnaval

duplo — vocal duet

embolada — poetic musical form (Northeastern)

enredo — composition including music, dance, costume and decoration of a samba school for the desfile at carnival escola de samba — samba school (club)

folguedo — see dança dramatica

folia — song and dance group for religious (Catholic) occasions

forró — dance, dance performance (Northeastern)

guitarra — electric guitar

iêiêiê — Brazilian expression for rock music ('yeah yeah yeah' of the Beatles)

irmandade — brotherhood

lundu — song and dance, originating from Batuque (African)

marcha — Brazilian march form

Mineiro — person from Minas Gerais

moda — song form of Portuguese origin

modinha — lyrical song form (from moda)

Morro — mountains in Rio (also name of favelas, or slums and samba school)

movimento — movement (literary, musical, political)

MPB — Música Popular Brasileira

música caipira — music folklore of the back country

música clásica — classical music

música erúdita — 'learned' music, borderline region between classical and composed folk/popular music

música indigena — music of the original inhabitants

música sertaneja — folk-like music of the back country

Nordestino — person from Northeastern Brazil

parceiro — partner, colleague

poema — poem

ponto — improvised text/melody of African origin

quilombo — organization of refugee slaves during the colonial era

rainha — queen

rancho — club/parade group of the Bahians

rei — king

repentista — see cantador

roda — circle

salário minimo — legal minimum wage

samba — general synonym for Afro-Brazilian dances of the backcountry

sambista — samba musician, composer or singer of samba

Sertão — semi-arid desert in Northeastern Brazil

som — tone

syncretism — the combining of Christianity with African and Indian religions

tango Brasileiro — a polka/lundu influenced by the Cuban habanera

terno — small ensemble or group

terreiro — cult holy place (Afro-Brazilian)

toada — song form

toque — rhythmic definition of the basic beat, tempo

tropicalismo — Bahian musicians' movement (influenced by rock and jazz)

violão — guitar (six-stringed)

viola — country guitar (five or six double strings)

Zona Norte — Rio's northern zone, working-class neighborhood

Zona Sul — Rio's southern zone, beaches from Leme to Leblon

Samba Schools in Rio (a selection)

Date of Founding / Colors / Location

Unidos de Vila Isabel
1946 / Blue & White / Rua Barão de S. Francisco

Unidos de São Carlos
1955 / Red & White / Cidade nova, Rua Miguel de Frias

União da Ilha
1953 / Red & White / Ilha do Governador

Mangueira
1928 / Green & Pink / Rua Visconde de Niteroi

Salgueiro
1953 / Red & White / Tijuca

Beija-Flor
1948 / Blue & White / Nilopolis

Unidos da Tijuca
1931 / Peacock Blue & Gold / Rua São Miguel

Portela
1923 / Blue & White / Rua Arruda Camara

Mocidade Independente
1952 / Green & White / R. Coronel Tamarindo

Imperatriz Leopoldinense
1959 / Green, Gold & White / Rua Leite de Abreu / Muda

Império da Tijuca
1940 / Green & White

Império Serrano
1947 / Green & White

União de Jacarepagua
1956 / Green & White

Unidos da Ponte
1952 / Blue & White

Unidos de Lucas
1966 / Red & Gold

Lins Imperial
1963 / Green & Pink

Unidos de Bangú
1937 / Red & White

Académicos de Santa Cruz
1959 / Green & White

Império de Maranga
1957 / Blue & White

Unidos de Cabuçu
1945 / Blue & White

Arrango
1930/1937 / Blue & White

Em Cima da Hora
1959 / Blue & White

Caprichoses dos Pilares
1949 / Blue & White

Académicos da Cidade de Deus
1970 / Red, Green & White

Unidos de Manguinhos
1964 / Green, Gold & White

São Clemente
1955 / Yellow, Black & White

Unidos do Uraiti
1960 / Green & White

Tupy de Bras de Pina
1948–1955 / Blue & White

Paraiso de Tuiuty
1952 / Peacock Blue & Gold

Independentes de Cordovil
1946 / Blue, Gold & Yellow

Unidos do Jacarezinho
1966 / Pink & White

Académicos do Engenho da Rainha
1949 / Green, Pink & White

Unidos de Nilopolis
1952 / Green & White

Grande Rio
1971 (merger) / Blue, Red & White

Foliões de Botafogo
1950 / Red & White

Unidos de Padre Miguel
1957 / Red & White

União de Rocha Miranda
1960 / Blue & White

Império de Campo Grande
1949 / Blue & White

Unidos de Vila Santa Teresa
1956 / Blue & White

Unidos de Zona Sul
1972 / Blue, Gold & White

Académicos do Cachambá
1961 / Green & White

Unidos de Cosmos
1948 / Green & White

União de Vaz Lobo
1947 / Pink, Blue & White

As well as several hundred blocos and at least a dozen ranchos.

Bibliography

General

Almeida, Renato, *Historia da Música Brasileira*, Briuguiet & Comp., Rio, 1926

Andrade, Mario de, *Pequenha Historia da Música*, Martins, São Paulo, 1977

Aspectos da Música Brasileira, Martins/MEC, Brasilia, 1975

Ensaio sobre a Música Brasileira, Martins/MEC, Brasilia, 1972

Enciclopedia da Música Brasileira, 2 Bände, Art Editora São Paulo, 1977

Appleby, David, *The Music of Brazil*, University of Texas Press, Texas, 1983

Freyre, Gilberto, *O Brasileiro entre os outros Hispanos*, J. Olympia/MEC, Rio, 1975

Krich, John, *Why Is This Country Dancing?:* A One-Man Samba to the Beat, Simon & Schuster, New York, 1993

Lévi-Strauss, Claude, *Tristes Tropiques*, Plon, Paris, 1955

Mariz, Vasco, *A Canção Brasileira*, Civilização Bras./MEC, Brasilia, 1977

Figuras da Música Brasileira Contemporánea, Imprensa Portuguesa, Porto, 1948

Moraes, Filho Mello, *Cantares Brasileiros–Cancioneiro Fluminense*, Inst. do Livro, Rio, 1982

Ribeiro, Darcy, *Unterentwicklung und Zivilisation*, Suhrkamp, Frankfurt, 1980

Schreiner, Claus, *Música Latina – Musikfolklore zwischen Kuba und Feuerland*, Fischer, Frankfurt, 1982

Tinhorão, José Ramos, *Pequenha Historia da Música Popular*, Vozes, Petropolis, 1975

Os Sons que vem da Rua, Tinhorão, Rio, 1976

Música Popular, Vozes, Petropolis, 1975

Vasconcelos, Ari, *Raizes da MPB*, Martins/MEC, Brasilia, 1977

Panorama do MPB na Belle Epoque, Livros Santanna, Rio, 1977

Folklore

Almeida, Renato, 'Folclore', *Cadernos de Folclore* 3, MEC/FUNARTE, Rio, 1976

Azevedo, Téo, *Cultura Popular do Norte de Minas*, Top Livros, São Paulo, 1979

Bastide, Roger, *As Religiões africanas no Brasil*, Vol. 1 &. 2 Liv. Pioneira/ Univ. de São Paulo, São Paulo, 1971

Bastos, Rafael José de Meneze, *A Musicológica Kamayura*, Fund. Nacional de Indio, Brasilia, 1978

Brandão, Carlos Rodrigues, *O Divino, O Santo e A Senhora*, MEC/ FUNARTE, Rio, 1978

Cacciatore, Olga Gudolle, *Diccinario de Cultos Afro-Brasileiros*, Forense Universitaria, Rio, 1977

Cadernos de Folclore, Ministerio da Educação e Cultura, FUNARTE, Rio

Caméu, Helza, *Introdução ao Estudo da Música Indigena Brasileira*, Cons. Fed. de Cultura, Rio, 1977

Capoeira, Nestor, *O pequenho Manual do Jogador de Capoeira*, Ground, São Paulo, 1981

Carneiro, Edison, *Folguedos Tradicionais*, Conquista, Rio, 1974

Cascudo, Camara, *Dicionário de Folclore Brasileiro*, de Ouro, date of publication not available

Claudio, Afonso, *Trovas e Cantares Capixabas*, MEC/FUNARTE, Rio, 1980

da Costa Giradelli, Elsie, *Ternos de Angola*, MEC/FUNARTE, Rio, 1981

Dantas, Beatriz, G., 'Taieira', *Cadernos de Folclore* 4, MEC/FUNARTE, Rio, 1976

'Cheganca', *Cadernos de Folclore* 14, MEC/FUNARTE, Rio, 1976

Diegues Junior, M., 'Literatura de Cordel', *Cadernos de Folclore* 2, MEC/FUNARTE, Rio, 1975

Faber, Gustav, 'Brasilien', *Merian* 11/ 28, Hamburg

Fichte, Hubert, *Xangô*, Fischer, Frankfurt, 1976

Figge, Horst H., *Geisterkult, Besessenheit und Magie in der Umbanda Religion Brasiliens*, Alber, Freiburg/ München, 1973

Fonseca, Wilson, *Santarem Cantando*, published by author, Rio, 1974

Freyre, Gilberto, 'Aspectos da Influenca africana no Brasil', *Cultura* 23, Brasilia, 1976

Friedenthal, Albert, *Musik und Dichtung bei den Kreolen Amerikas*, Hans Schnippel, Berlin, 1913

Girardelli, Elsie da Costa, *Ternos de Congos*, MEC/FUNARTE, Rio, 1981

Gomes Neide Rodrigues et al, *Brasil, Música e Folklore*, Edart, São Paulo, 1982

Harrer, Heinrich, *Huka-Huka*, Ullstein, Frankfurt/Berlin/Wien, 1979

de Lery, Jean, *Histoire d'un voyage fait en la terre du Brésil*, date of publication not available

Khallyhabby, Tonyan, 'A Influenca africana na música brasileira', *Cultura* 23, Brasilia, 1976

de Lima, Rossini Tavares, *O Folclore do Litoral Norte de São Paulo*, MEC/ FUNARTE, Rio, 1981

Lira, Mariza, *Calendário Folclorico do Distrito Federal*, Secr. Educaçâo e Cultura, Rio, 1956

Moraes, Filho Mello, *Cantares Brasileiros*, SEEC-RJ, Rio, 1981

Mota, Leonardo, *Cantadores* Catedra/ MEC, Brasilia, 1976

Violeiros do Norte, Catedral/MEC, Brasilia, 1976

Münzel, Mark, *Medizinmannwesen und Geistervorstellungen bei den Kamayura (Alto Xingu) Brasilien,* Franz Steiner, Wiesbaden

Münzel, Mark/Lindig, Wolfgang, *Die Indianer,* dtv, München, 1978

Mukuna, Kazadi wa, *Contribuição Bantu na MPB,* Global, São Paulo, date of publication not available

Neves, Guilherme Santos, *Espirito Santo,* MEC/FUNARTE, Rio, 1978

Oderigo, Nestor Oritz, *Macumba,* Plus ultra, Buenos Aires, date of publication not available

de Oliveira, Valdemar, *Frevo Capoeira e Passo,* Pernambuco, Recife, 1971

Porto, Guilherme, *As Folias de Reis no Sul de Minas,* FUNARTE/INF, Rio, 1982

Ribeiro, Joaquim, *Folclore do açucar,* FUNARTE, Rio, 1977

Ribeiro, José, *Brasil no Folclore,* Aurora, Rio

Romero, Silvio, *Cantos Populares do Brasil,* José Olympio, Rio, 1954, 2 Bände

Rodrigues, Nina, *Os Africanos no Brasil,* Comp. Ed. Nacional, São Paulo, 1977

Shaffer, Kay, *O Berimbau de barriga e seus Toques,* MEC, Rio, 1977

Siqueiria, Baptista, *Ficcão e Musica,* Folha Carioca, Rio, 1980

Os Cariris do Nordeste, Catedra, Rio, 1978

Modinhas do Passado, 1979 Private Publication, Folha Carioca, Rio

Soares, Doralice, *Aspectos do Folclore Catarinense,* published by author, Rio, 1970

Staden, Hans, *Zwei Reisen nach Brasilien,* Traufetter & Fischer Nachf, Marburg/Lahn, 1970

Teixeira, José, A., *Folclore Goiano,* MEC, São Paulo, 1979

Vale, Flausino Rodrigues, *Elementos de Folclore Musical Brasileiro,* Comp. Editora Nacional, MEC, São Paulo, 1978

Various, *Vom Rio Grande Zum La Plata,* Erdmann, Tübingen, 1977

Villas Boas, Orlando e Claudio, *Xingu,* Zahar, Rio, 1976

MPB

de Abreu, Daisy Cury, 'Choro', article: source unknown

Ahangueira, James, *Corações Futuristas/ MPB,* Regra do Jogo, Lisbon, 1978

Alencar, Edigar de, *O Carnaval Carioca atraves da Música,* Francisco Alves, MEC, Rio, 1979

Nosso Sinhô do Samba, Civilaçâo Brasileria, Rio, 1968

Almirante, *No Tempo de Noel Rasa,* Fransciso Alves, Rio, 1977

de Andrade, Mario, *Modinhas Imperias,* Itatiaia, Belo Horizonte, 1980

Araujo, Ari, *As Escolas de Samba,* Vozes, Rio, 1978

Bahiana, Ana Maria, *Nada será como antes MPB nos anos 70,* Civilização Brasileira, Rio, 1980

Barbosa, Orestes, *Samba,* MEC/ FUNARTE, Rio, 1978

Borges, Beatriz, *Samba-Canção,* Codecri, Rio, 1982

Buarque, Chico/Guerra, Ruy, *Calabar*, Civilização Brasileira, Rio, 1978

Opera do Malandro, Liv. Cultural, São Paulo, 1978

Cabral, Sergio, *ABC*, Codecri, Rio, 1979

As Escolas de Samba, Fontana, Rio, 1974

Cabral, Sergio, *Pixinguinha*, MEC/ FUNARTE, Rio, 1978

de Campos, Augusto, *Balanço da Bossa e outras Bossas*, Perspectiva, São Paulo, 1974

Cardoso Junior, Abel, *Carmen Miranda*, published by author, São Paulo, 1978

Caymmi, Dorival, *Cancioneiro da Bahia*, Livraria Martins, date of publication not available

Efege, Jota, *Figuras e coisas da MPB*, Vols. 1 & 2, MEC/FUNARTE, Rio, 1980

Figuras e Coisas do Carnaval Carioca, MEC/FUNARTE, Rio, 1982

Filho, Claver, *Waldemar Henrique Ó Canto da Amazonia*, MEC/ FUNARTE, Rio, 1978

Galdas, Waldenyr, *Acorde na Aurora (M. Sertaneja)*, Comp. Ed. Nacional, São Paulo, 1977

Galvão, Walnice Nogueira, *Saco de Gatos*, Duas Cidades, São Paulo, 1976

Gil, Gilberto [Riserio, Antonio, ed.], *Gilberto Gil-Expresso 2222*, Corrupio, São Paulo, 1982

Goldwasser, Maria Julia, *O Palácio do Samba*, Zahar, Rio, 1975

Guimarães, Francisco (Vagalume), *Na Roda do Samba*, MEC/FUNARTE, Rio, 1978

de Hollanda, Chico Buarque, *A Banda (Noten + Texte)*, Francisco Alves, Rio, 1966

de Hollanda, Nestro, *Memorias do Café Nice*, Conquista, Guanabara, 1970

Leal, José de Souza/Barbosa, Artur Luiz, *João Pernanbuco*, MEC/ FUNARTE, Rio, 1982

Lira, Mariza, *Chiquinha Gonzaga*, MEC/FUNARTE, Rio, 1978

Martins, J. B., *Antropologia da Música Brasileira*, Obelisco, São Paulo, 1978

Da Matta, Roberto, *Carnavais, Malandros e Herois*, Zahar, Rio, 1979

De Mello, Jose Ed. Homen, *Música Popular Brasileira*, Univ. de São Paulo, São Paulo, 1976

de Moraes, Mario, *Recordações de Ary Barroso*, MEC/FUNARTE, Rio, 1979

de Moraes, Vinicius, *Pra viver un grande amor*, José Olympio, Rio, 1976

Morelli, Rita, C., *Industria Fonografica*, Unicamp, Campinas, 1991

Saravah, Gedichte und Lieder Vervuert, Frankfurt, 1982

Motta, Nelson, *Música Humana Música*, Salamandra, Rio, 1980

O som do pasquim, Div. Interviews, Codecri, Rio, 1976

Perreira, Marcus, *A Historia do Jogral*, Hucitec, São Paulo, 1976

Pinto, Alexandre Goncalves, *O Choro*, MEC/FUNARTE, Rio, 1978

Rodrigues, Francisco, *Fumando Espero*, published by author, Rio, 1980

Sá, Sinval, *O Sanfoneiro do Riacho da Brigida*, Thesaurus, Brasilia, 1978

Sant' Anna, Affonso Romano de, *Moderna Poesia Brasileira*, Vozes, Petropolis, 1978

da Silva, Marilia T. Barbosa/Santos, Lygia, *Paulo da Portela*, MEC/ FUNARTE, Rio, 1980 de Oliveira, Filho, *Silas de Oliveira*, MEC/FUNARTE, Rio, 1981

da Silva, Marilia T. Barboza, *Filho de Ogum Bexiguento*, FUNARTE, Rio, 1979

Souza, Tarik de/Andreato, Elifas, *Rostos e Gostos da MPB*, L & PM,

Porte Alegre, 1979

Tinhorão, José Ramos, *O Samba agora vai*, JCM, Rio, 1969

Valença, Suetonio Soares, *Tra-la-la*, MEC/FUNARTE, Rio, 1981

Vasconcellos, Gilberto, *Música Popular de olha na festa*, Graal, Rio, 1977

•SATIE•
Seen Through
His Letters

Ornella Volta

Translated by Michael Bullock

Introduced by John Cage

Much of the laconic wit, discipline and charm of Satie's music is to be found in the man himself, as demonstrated by his letters. Many of them published here for the first time in any language, these letters create a uniquely revealing portrait of Satie himself, his music and his time. Edited and annotated by an eminent Satie scholar, this volume includes correspondence with such major figures as Cocteau, Picasso, Picabia, Debussy, Ravel and Stravinsky. It is illustrated with 75 line drawings by Cocteau, Magritte, Picasso and other contemporaries, as well as drawings and musical scores by the composer himself.

Erik Satie (1866–1925) is acknowledged as an important influence in modern music. A notorious but amiable eccentric, he was the founder and sole member of a church in whose name he issued furious denunciations of the moral and aesthetic lapses of his contemporaries. He was also the urbane centre of a wide circle of friends and admirers. His compositions (which include *Parade* and *Three Pieces in the Form of a Pear*) remain hugely popular.

Ornella Volta has gathered the material to form a portrait of Satie and his contemporaries at a time when Parisian artistic life was teeming with originality. She is the Artistic Director of the Satie Foundation in Paris, and the foremost authority on his life and work.

Michael Bullock is a leading translator and well-known surrealist novelist. He lives in Canada.

'*Buddy Bolden began to get famous right after 1900 come in. He was the first to play the hard jazz and blues for dancing . . . Always looked good. When he bought a cornet he'd shine it up and make it glisten like a woman's leg.*'— Louis Jones 1909

Set in New Orleans at the turn of the century COMING THROUGH SLAUGHTER tells the enigmatic story of the legendary trumpet player Buddy Bolden, the first of the great trumpeters who some say was the true originator of jazz.

Bolden's career was short and remarkable and it is strange that for all his power we should know so little of his life. His music was never recorded. He was married and he had children. In the daytime he worked in a shaving parlour where he talked and drank and cut hair while the great block of ice in the window slowly melted and kept them cool. In the evenings he would play, music that had never been heard before; music that was his alone and which later would be taken up by King Oliver and Bunk Johnson and Louis Armstrong. Sometimes he would play his music with several bands in one evening, but wherever he played the people would follow, crazy to hear the man who could reach out into the air and set them all alight. At the height of his fame he vanished, only to re-appear two years later, playing even more brilliantly. Then, in 1907 he went mad in a parade. From that day on, until his death twenty-four years later, Buddy Bolden stayed in a mental home. He rarely spoke and showed no interest in music at all.

From these facts, from the recollections of his friends and lovers and from the tantalising gaps and silences that shaped Buddy Bolden's life, Michael Ondaatje creates a dazzling reincarnation of the great jazz man's spirit. For Bolden not only mirrors the first mad flush of the jazz age with its wildness, beauty and its cruelty, he also exemplifies the destructive and creative forces that abound in our world.

This novel won Michael Ondaatje the Books in Canada First Novel Award.

'One of the best, most imaginative books I have read in ages. Ondaatje is an innovative and brilliant writer.'   *Library Journal*

'We understand the slow ceremonial sense of time . . . we see the leaking colours of the houses and streets, and we feel the brilliant pressures of the music.'   *New Yorker*

COMING THROUGH SLAUGHTER

Michael Ondaatje

SAMUEL CHARTERS

THE ROOTS OF THE BLUES

'I went to Africa to find the roots of the blues'. It was with this intention that Samuel Charters, the blues and jazz expert and author of *The Legacy of the Blues*, journeyed through West Africa, trying to uncover the origins of a music which had a profound impact on the art, music, culture and politics of the West and in particular in the United States. What began as a genealogical study of how the blues was handed down from the African slaves to musicians of today via the slave ships, the farms and the urban ghetto became something much more complex.

In Africa, Samuel Charters discovered a music which was not just a part of the past but a very vital living part of African culture. This book details and analyzes the meeting between a Westerner and a thriving culture new to him. It reveals Charters' remarkable analytical talent in discussing African folk music and its relationship with American blues and demonstrates his power as a descriptive writer. It is a musical exploration and at the same time a travelogue of the Africa he uncovered: markets, villages, the heat and dust and the road. The author also draws on the accounts of earlier explorers. His extensive quotations of lyrics from songs and wonderful photographs of the musicians make this a unique contribution to our understanding of a culture and its music.

JELLY ROLL MORTON'S LAST NIGHT AT THE JUNGLE INN

an imaginary memoir
Samuel Charters

Whether or not he is the orginator of jazz and blues'—as he claimed when refuting Ripley's attribution of this title to WC Handy on a 'Believe It or Not' radio program in the late Thirties—Ferdinand 'Jelly Roll' Morton was certainly the jazz musician without a peer. Like the setting of this Imaginary Memoir, the Jungle Inn, itself always changing its name, Morton's life, as he recounted and constantly embellished it, was a swaggering 'work in progress'. No one to this day has been able to sift the fact from fiction. The author accurately catches the breezy tone of Morton's recorded narrative and expands throwaway biographical hints into a kind of Morton apocrypha which will be reveled in by all the master's afficionados.

MANUEL DE FALLA
On Music and Musicians

Translated by David Urman and J. M. Thomson

In the English-speaking world Manuel de Falla is known for his remarkable musical works that, although rooted in his own country, reach a universal audience. In this first translation of de Falla's writings one gains insight into the remarkable way he was able to seize on what was genuine in his own tradition and infuse it with new life.

Falla discusses the very basis of his own music in such subjects as the *cante jondo*, the primitive Andalusian song; the work of his contemporaries, such as Albeniz; and at the same time writes freshly on Debussy, Ravel and Wagner. His writing has lucidity and charm at its best and a somewhat obstinate tenacity at its worst. Here can be found all the nervous energy, the restlessness, the passionate involvement of a dedicated artist, moreover, blessed with an original mind. This book will add a new dimension to an appreciation of Falla as composer and musician.

'. . . a book that not only chronicles the resurgence of Spanish music over the past 100 years but also draws an attractive self-portrait of the author.' *Records and Recordings*

'De Falla's lucid writing style, rendered in a graceful translation, has the same sunny spontaneity and charm of his music.' *Publishers Weekly*

'The Spanish composer's writings on music . . . illustrate his distinctive ideas on musical theory and history and his enthusiastic and admiring opinions of his contemporaries.' *Booklist*

THE COMPOSER IN HOLLYWOOD

'The life and works of 11 of the great creators of film scores from 1930 to 1950 . . . should do a great deal to help the movie score gain acceptance as a legitimate form of composition. (Palmer) recreates the powerful spells that many of the famous scenes in movies from Hollywood's Golden Age exerted on audiences and shows how mood was achieved by the brilliant interweaving of music and drama.'

Publisher's Weekly

'In example after example, Mr Palmer illustrates entertainingly the use of orchestration, tonality, rhythm and humor, and how they enrich the films we call classic. . . His insights are valuable and provocative. Few technically attuned ears have closely examined the luxurious aural sheen of the Hollywood classics or considered the men who created it. . . Mr Palmer has now done this.' *Washington Times*

'(Palmer's) account of their methods of work fascinates, and his high regard for these old masters convinces . . . perceptive and persuasive.' Wilfred Mellers, *Musical Times*

'Palmer's story is about that strange transplanted *Mitteleuropa* called Hollywood. His book pierces me to the heart. I have had only one real ambition in life, and that was to be a film composer. . . How much sweat and tears go into it, Palmer's excellent book joyfully delineates.'

Anthony Burgess, *The Independent*

'Palmer is a fine, intelligent writer, who combines knowledge with enthusiasm and achieves the tricky feat of writing about music in a way that non-musicians can understand-

Classical Music

'For newcomers to the genre and confirmed devotees alike, this book will not fail to inform and entertain.' *Gramophone*

'*The Composer in Hollywood* is a milestone for the alert musician, the drama lover and the celluloid buff.'

Malcolm Williamson, *The Observer*